Wiley 11th Hour Guide for 2019 Level II CFA Exam

Thousands of candidates from more than 100 countries have relied on these Study Guides to pass the CFA® Exam. Covering every Learning Outcome Statement (LOS) on the exam, these review materials are an invaluable tool for anyone who wants a deep-dive review of all the concepts, formulas, and topics required to pass.

Wiley study materials are produced by expert CFA charterholders, CFA Institute members, and investment professionals from around the globe. For more information, contact us at info@efficientlearning.com.

Wiley 11th Hour Guide for 2019 Level II CFA Exam

WILEY

Contents

Portfolio Management

Foreword

Wiley 11th Hour Guide for 2019 Level II CFA Exam is a concise and easy-to-understand review book that is meant to supplement your review for the CFA Level II exam. It becomes extremely difficult to go through the entire curriculum in the last few weeks leading up to the exam, so we have condensed the material for you. You must remember, though, that this book is not meant to be a primary study tool for the exam. It is designed to help you review the material in an efficient and effective manner so that you can be confident on exam day.

About the Author

Wiley's Study Guides are written by a team of highly qualified CFA charterholders and leading CFA instructors from around the globe. Our team of CFA experts work collaboratively to produce the best study materials for CFA candidates available today.

Wiley's expert team of contributing authors and instructors is led by Content Director Basit Shajani, CFA. Basit founded online education start-up Élan Guides in 2009 to help address CFA candidates' need for better study materials. As lead writer, lecturer, and curriculum developer, Basit's unique ability to break down complex topics helped the company grow organically to be a leading global provider of CFA Exam prep materials. In January 2014, Élan Guides was acquired by John Wiley & Sons, Inc., where Basit continues his work as Director of CFA Content. Basit graduated magna cum laude from the Wharton School of Business at the University of Pennsylvania with majors in finance and legal studies. He went on to obtain his CFA charter in 2006, passing all three levels on the first attempt. Prior to Élan Guides, Basit ran his own private wealth management business. He is a past president of the Pakistani CFA Society.

There are many more expert CFA charterholders who contribute to the creation of Wiley materials. We are thankful for their invaluable expertise and diligent work. To learn more about Wiley's team of subject matter experts, please visit: www.efficientlearning.com/cfa/why-wiley/.

STUDY SESSION 1: ETHICAL AND PROFESSIONAL STANDARDS (1)

CODE OF ETHICS AND STANDARDS OF PROFESSIONAL CONDUCT; GUIDANCE FOR STANDARDS I–VII
Cross-Reference to CFA Institute Assigned Readings #1 & #2

All CFA Institute members and candidates enrolled in the CFA Program are required to comply with the Code of Ethics and the Standards of Professional Conduct (Code and Standards). The CFA Institute Bylaws and Rules of Procedure for Proceedings Related to Professional Conduct (Rules of Procedure) form the basic structure for enforcing the Code and Standards.

The Rules of Procedure are based on the following two principles:

1. Fair process.
2. Maintaining confidentiality of process.

The CFA Institute Board of Governors is responsible for implementing the Professional Conduct Program (PCP) through the Disciplinary Review Committee (DRC).

The CFA Institute Designated Officer, through the Professional Conduct staff, carries out professional conduct inquiries. Circumstances which can initiate an inquiry include:

- Information disclosed on the annual Professional Conduct Statement.
- Written complaints received by Professional Conduct staff.
- Questionable conduct as publicized by the media or any other source.
- A violation report submitted by a CFA examination proctor.

Once an inquiry is initiated, the Professional Conduct staff undertakes an investigation which can include:

- Requesting a written explanation.
- Interviewing related person(s).
- Collecting any supporting documents.

The information collected is reviewed by the Designated Officer, who may conclude that:

1. No disciplinary action is needed
2. A cautionary letter needs to be issued
3. Proceedings need to be continued.

If it is concluded that there has been a violation of the Code and Standards, the Designated Officer can propose a disciplinary sanction. The member or candidate has the right to accept or reject the decision. A rejection would require the matter to be referred to a hearing by a panel of CFA Institute members. Sanctions by CFA Institute may include condemnation by peers, consequences for current or future employment or suspension from the CFA program.

The adherence of investment professionals to ethical practices benefits all market participants.

- Clients are reassured that investment professionals they hire prioritize their interests.
- Investment professionals benefit from the more efficient and transparent operation of the market that integrity promotes.

Sound ethics is fundamental to capital markets and the investment profession as it increases investors' confidence in global financial markets. Ethics is also of paramount importance because of the interconnectedness of global financial markets, which gives rise to the issue of market sustainability. It is imperative that top management foster a strong culture of ethics not just among CFA charter holders and candidates but among all staff members who are involved directly or indirectly with client relations, the investment process, record keeping, and beyond.

However, new challenges continually arise for members and candidates in applying the Code and Standards. This is because ethical dilemmas are not unambiguously right or wrong and require a bit of judgment.

The CFA Institute Code of Ethics plays an integral role in maintaining the integrity of CFA Institute members and upholding professional excellence. All CFA Institute members and CFA candidates must abide by this code and are encouraged to notify their employers of any violations. Violations may result in disciplinary sanctions by CFA Institute, which may include revocation of membership, candidacy in the CFA program and the right to use the CFA designation.

The Code of Ethics requires all members and candidates to:

- Act with integrity, competence, diligence, respect, and in an ethical manner with the public, clients, prospective clients, employers, employees, colleagues in the investment profession, and other participants in the global capital markets.
- Place the integrity of the investment profession and the interests of clients above their own personal interests.
- Use reasonable care and exercise independent professional judgment when conducting investment analysis, making investment recommendations, taking investment actions, and engaging in other professional activities.
- Practice and encourage others to practice in a professional and ethical manner that will reflect credit on themselves and the profession.
- Promote the integrity of, and uphold the rules governing, capital markets.
- Maintain and improve their professional competence and strive to maintain and improve the competence of other investment professionals.

Standards of Professional Conduct:

I. **Professionalism**
    A. Knowledge of the Law
    B. Independence and Objectivity
    C. Misrepresentation
    D. Misconduct

II. **Integrity of Capital Markets**
    A. Material Nonpublic Information
    B. Market Manipulation

III. **Duties to Clients**
    A. Loyalty, Prudence and Care
    B. Fair Dealing
    C. Suitability
    D. Performance Presentation
    E. Preservation of Confidentiality

IV. **Duties to Employers**
    A. Loyalty
    B. Additional Compensation Arrangements
    C. Responsibilities of Supervisors

V. **Investment Analysis, Recommendations and Actions**
    A. Diligence and Reasonable Basis
    B. Communication with Clients and Prospective Clients
    C. Record Retention

VI. **Conflicts of Interest**
    A. Disclosure of Conflicts
    B. Priority of Transactions
    C. Referral Fees

VII. **Responsibilities as a CFA Institute Member or CFA Candidate**
    A. Conduct as Participants in CFA Institute Programs
    B. Reference to CFA Institute, the CFA Designation, and the CFA Program

The best way to prepare for Ethics is to thoroughly read the Standards themselves, along with related guidance and examples.

TRADE ALLOCATION: FAIR DEALING AND DISCLOSURE
Cross-Reference to CFA Institute Assigned Reading #4

The CFA Institute Standards of Professional Conduct require members to not only disclose trade allocation procedures fully, to adopt such trade allocation procedures that treat clients in an equitable manner. This means that members should adhere to allocation procedures that ensure that investment opportunities are allocated to all clients in an appropriate and fair manner.

To ensure that adequate trade allocation practices are followed, the CFA Institute Standards of Practice Handbook suggests that members and their firms should:

- Obtain advance indications of client's interest for new issues.
- Allocate new shares by client rather than by portfolio manager.
- Adopt a pro rata or similar objective method or formula for allocating trades.
- Treat clients fairly in terms of both trade execution order and price.
- Execute orders timely and efficiently.
- Keep accurate records of trades and client accounts.
- Periodically review all accounts to ensure that all clients are being treated fairly.

CHANGING INVESTMENT OBJECTIVES
Cross-Reference to CFA Institute Assigned Reading #5

When managing pooled investment funds, it is extremely important for portfolio managers to adhere to the investment strategy stated in the fund's prospectus. This enables investors:

- To judge the appropriateness and suitability of the fund for themselves; and
- Protects them from style drift and exposure to investment strategies, asset classes, and risks other than those explicitly stated.

A material deviation from the fund's stated objectives, if not approved by shareholders, is a violation of Standard III (C.2) – Suitability, and Standard V (B.1) – Communication with Clients and Prospective Clients

In order to abide by the CFA Institute Standards, portfolio managers should take the following steps:

- Determine the client's financial situation, investment experience, and investment objectives. This information should be updated at least annually.
- Adequately disclose to clients the basic format and general principles of the investment processes by which securities are selected and portfolios are constructed.
- Conduct regular internal checks to ensure that portfolio characteristics meet the account's investment mandate, or the stated investment strategy in the case of pooled funds.
- Notify clients and investors of any potential changes in the investment objectives or strategies of the managed portfolios, including the impact of the change on the portfolio, and secure documented authorization of the change in strategy from the client.

STUDY SESSION 3: QUANTITATIVE METHODS

FINTECH IN INVESTMENT MANAGEMENT
Cross-Reference to CFA Institute Assigned Reading #6

Fintech refers to the use of technology-based innovations that are changing the way financial services and products are being designed and delivered to clientele.

Big Data refers to the massive amounts of data produced by financial markets, businesses, governments, individuals and sensor networks.

- Structured data can be stored in database tables.
- Unstructured data cannot be stored in tables.
- Semi-structured data can have both characteristics.

Artificial Intelligence (AI) is designed to perform cognitive or decision-making tasks in a comparable or superior manner to human intelligence.

Machine learning (ML) consists of computer programs that use algorithms to learn how to complete tasks over time so that greater experience translates into better performance.

Analysts must ensure that they select appropriate input data and appropriate data analysis techniques. They must always be wary of overfitting data (which occurs when the program learns inputs and targeted outputs too precisely) and underfitting data (which occurs when a program is too simplistic, precluding the ML program from identifying relationships and patterns when training with a dataset). Finally, they must be wary of their programs becoming "black box" approaches, which can create results that are inexplicable or hard to understand.

Types of Machine Learning

Supervised learning involves labeling or identifying inputs and outputs to the algorithm so that it can be trained to identify relationships for labeled data and work with other data sets.

Unsupervised learning does not involve giving programs labeled data, but instead requires algorithms to describe the data and its structure on its own.

Deep learning (or deep learning nets) is a technique that uses neural networks to perform multistage, nonlinear processing to identify patterns and relationships in data through a supervised or unsupervised approach.

Data Science

Data science is an interdisciplinary field that uses advances in computer science (including machine learning), statistics, and other disciplines for the purpose of extracting information from Big Data (or data in general). Data processing methods include data capture, curation, storage, search, and transfer.

Data visualization refers to how the data will be formatted, displayed, and summarized in graphical form. Traditional structured data can be visualized using tables, charts, and trends, while non-traditional unstructured data require new techniques of data visualization. Some of these newer techniques that can be applied to textual data include tag clouds and mind maps.

Common programming languages used in data science include Python, R, Java, C/C++, and Excel VBA. Common databases include SQL, SQLite, and NoSQL.

Fintech Applications in Investment Management

- Text analytics is the use of programs to retrieve and analyze information from unrelated sources to conduct predictive analysis and find indicators of future performance.
- Natural language processing (NLP) is the analysis and interpretation of language using artificial intelligence, including translation, speech recognition, and text mining.
- Robo-advisory services aim to provide cost-effective and easily accessible investment solutions through the Internet without the interaction of human financial advisers.
- Risk analysis applications include stress-testing financial institutions, identifying adverse near-term market trends, detecting declining corporate earnings, analyzing real-time trading patterns, portfolio scenario analysis and back-testing, and assessing alternative data quality.
- Algorithmic trading involves computerized buying and selling based on prespecified rules and guidelines for lowering costs, improving execution speed, and providing anonymity for investment managers.
- High-frequency trading (HFT) is a form of algorithmic trading that uses real-time, granular market data to execute trades in fractions of a second through ultra-high-speed networks when certain conditions are met.

Distributed Ledger Technology

Distributed ledger technology (DLT) is a new form of financial recordkeeping that allows entities to share database information through networks. A DLT network consists of a digital ledger and a consensus mechanism that involves networked computers (or nodes) validating transactions and agreeing on updates to create unchangeable records that are easily accessible to participants on a near-real-time basis. To provide security for networks and database integrity, DLTs use cryptography (or algorithms) to encrypt data so that it is unusable to any unauthorized parties.

Blockchains are digital ledgers where information is sequentially recorded in "blocks" that are "chained" together using cryptography. This means transactions are grouped together into blocks that are linked to previous blocks through a secure link (or "hash").

- In permissioned networks, members might have restrictions on their activities and level of access to the ledger, such as adding transactions, viewing transactions, and seeing limited details of transactions.
- In a permissionless (or open) DLT network, all users can see every blockchain transaction and have the ability to perform all network functions.

Potential applications of DLT to investment management include cryptocurrencies, tokenization, post-trade clearing and settlement, and compliance.

Challenges to the Adoption of DLT by the Investment Industry

- Lack of DLT network standardization.
- Not be financially competitive with existing solutions.
- Substantial storage and power requirements.
- Accidental trades can only be undone by submitting offsetting trades (due to immutability of transactions).
- Regulatory approaches typically differ by jurisdiction.

CORRELATION AND REGRESSION
Cross-Reference to CFA Institute Assigned Reading #7

Scatter Plots

A scatter plot is a graph that illustrates the relationship between observations of two data series in two dimensions.

Correlation Analysis

The correlation coefficient measures the direction and extent of the linear relationship between two variables. It lies between −1 and +1.

- A positive correlation coefficient implies that the two variables generally move in the same direction.
- A negative correlation coefficient implies that the two variables generally move in opposite directions.
- A correlation coefficient of zero indicates that there is no linear relationship between the two variables. In this case, the value of one variable tells us nothing about the value of the other.
- If all the points on a scatter plot illustrating the relationship between two variables lie along an upward-sloping straight line, the correlation between the two variables would be +1 regardless of the slope of the line.
- If all the points on a scatter plot illustrating the relationship between two variables lie along a downward-sloping straight line, the correlation between the two variables would be −1 regardless of the slope of the line.

The correlation coefficient is easier to interpret than sample covariance because it is a simple number, while covariance is expressed in units squared.

Calculating and Interpreting the Correlation Coefficient

In order to calculate the correlation coefficient, we first need to calculate covariance. Covariance is a similar concept to variance. The difference lies in the fact that variance measures how a random variable varies with itself, while covariance measures how a random variable varies with another random variable.

Properties of Covariance

- Covariance is symmetric i.e., Cov(X, Y) = Cov(Y, X).
- The covariance of X with itself, Cov(X,X) equals the variance of X, Var(X).

Interpreting the Covariance

- Basically, covariance measures the nature of the relationship between two variables.
- When the covariance between two variables is *negative*, it means that they tend to move in opposite directions.
- When the covariance between two variables is *positive*, it means that they tend to move in the same direction.
- The covariance between two variables equals zero if they are not related.

$$\text{Sample covariance} = \text{Cov}(X, Y) = \sum_{i=1}^{n} (X_i - \bar{X})(Y_i - \bar{Y}) / (n - 1)$$

n = sample size
X_i = ith observation of Variable X
$\bar{X}$ = mean observation of Variable X
Y_i = ith observation of Variable Y
$\bar{Y}$ = mean observation of Variable Y

The numerical value of sample covariance is not very meaningful as it is presented in terms of units squared. Covariance is standardized by dividing it by the product of the standard deviations of the two variables. This standardized measure is known as the sample correlation coefficient (denoted by r) and is easy to interpret as it always lies between -1 and $+1$, and has no unit of measurement attached.

$$\text{Sample correlation coefficient} = r = \frac{\text{Cov}(X, Y)}{s_X s_Y}$$

$$\text{Sample variance} = s_X^2 = \sum_{i=1}^{n} (X_i - \bar{X})^2 / (n - 1)$$

$$\text{Sample standard deviation} = s_X = \sqrt{s_X^2}$$

Computed correlation coefficients are only valid if the means and variances of X and Y, as well as the covariance of X and Y, are finite and constant.

Limitations of Correlation Analysis

- It is important to remember that the correlation is a measure of linear association. Two variables can have a very strong non-linear relation and still have low correlation.
- Correlation may be an unreliable measure when there are outliers in the data. Analysts must evaluate whether outliers should be included in the data when calculating and interpreting correlation.
- Correlation does not imply causation.
- Correlations may be spurious, in that they may highlight relationships that are misleading. The term "spurious correlation" is used to refer to relationships where:
  - Correlation reflects chance relationships in a data set.
  - Correlation is induced by a calculation that mixes two variables with a third.
  - Correlation arises from both the variables being directly related to a third variable.

Uses of Correlation Analysis

- Investment analysis.
- Identifying appropriate benchmarks in the evaluation of portfolio manager performance.
- Identifying appropriate avenues for effective diversification of investment portfolios.
- Evaluating the appropriateness of using other measures (e.g., net income) as proxies for cash flow in financial statement analysis.
- Analysis of large data sets (or big data).

Testing the Significance of the Correlation Coefficient

To test whether the correlation between two variables is significantly different from zero:

$$H_0: \rho = 0$$
$$H_a: \rho \neq 0$$

$$\text{Test-stat} = t = \frac{r\sqrt{n-2}}{\sqrt{1-r^2}}$$

n = Number of observations
r = Sample correlation
$n - 2$ = Degrees of freedom

The value of sample correlation (r) required to reject the null hypothesis decreases as sample size (n) increases:

- As n increases, the degrees of freedom also increase, which results in the absolute critical value (t_{crit}) for the test falling.
- The absolute value of the numerator (in calculating the test statistic) increases with higher values of n, which results in higher t-values.

Note:

- All other factors constant, a false null hypothesis ($H_0: \rho = 0$) is more likely to be rejected as we increase the sample size.
- The smaller the size of the sample, the greater the value of sample correlation required to reject the null hypothesis of zero correlation.
- When the relation between two variables is very strong, a false null hypothesis ($H_0: \rho = 0$) may be rejected with a relatively small sample size.
- With large sample sizes, even relatively small correlation coefficients can be significantly different from zero.

Linear Regression with One Independent Variable

Linear regression is used to make predictions about a dependent variable (Y) using an independent variable (X), to test hypotheses regarding the relation between the two variables and to evaluate the strength of this relationship. The regression computes the line of best fit that minimizes the sum of the regression residuals (the sum of the squared vertical distances between actual observations of the random variable and predicted values of the variable based on the regression equation).

> Regression equation $= Y_i = b_0 + b_1 X_i + \varepsilon_i, i = 1,\ldots, n$
>
> b_1 and b_0 are the regression coefficients
> $b_1 =$ Slope coefficient
> $b_0 =$ Intercept
> $\varepsilon =$ The error term that represents the variation in the dependent variable that is not explained by the independent variable.

Classic Normal Linear Regression Assumptions

1. The relationship between the dependent (Y) and the independent variable (X) is linear in the parameters, b_1 and b_0.
2. The independent variable, X, is not random.
3. The expected value of the error term is zero: $E(\varepsilon) = 0$
4. The variance of the error term is constant for all observations $(E(\varepsilon_i^2) = \sigma\varepsilon^2, i = 1,\ldots, n)$. This is known as the homoskedasticity assumption.
5. The error term is uncorrelated across observations.
6. The error term is normally distributed.

An unbiased forecast is one where the expected value of the forecast error equals zero.

The Standard Error of Estimate

The standard error of estimate (SEE) is used to measure how well a regression model captures the relationship between the two variables. It indicates how well the regression line "fits" the sample data and is used to determine how certain we can be about a particular prediction of the dependent variable (Y_i) based on a regression equation. The SEE basically measures the standard deviation of the residual term (ε_i) in the regression. The smaller the standard deviation of the residual term (the smaller the standard error of estimate), the more accurate the predictions based on the model.

$$SEE = \left(\frac{\sum_{i=1}^{n}(Y_i - \hat{b}_0 - \hat{b}_1 X_i)^2}{n-2} \right)^{1/2} = \left(\frac{\sum_{i=1}^{n}(\hat{\varepsilon}_i)^2}{n-2} \right)^{1/2}$$

The Coefficient of Determination

The coefficient of determination (R^2) tells us how well the independent variable explains the variation in the dependent variable. It measures the fraction of the total variation in the dependent variable that is explained by the independent variable.

Calculating the Coefficient of Determination

1. $R^2 = r^2$

   The coefficient of determination equals the correlation coefficient squared. This calculation only works in linear regression i.e., when there is only one independent variable.

2.
$$R^2 = \frac{\text{Explained variation}}{\text{Total variation}} = \frac{\text{Total variation} - \text{Unexplained variation}}{\text{Total variation}}$$
$$= 1 - \frac{\text{Unexplained variation}}{\text{Total variation}}$$

Hypothesis Tests on Regression Parameters

$$\text{Test statistic} = t = \frac{\hat{b}_1 - b_1}{s_{\hat{b}_1}}$$

The critical t-value (t_{crit} or t_c) is determined with $n - 2$ degrees of freedom.

In testing whether the regression coefficient equals a particular hypothesized value, the null hypothesis is rejected when the absolute value of the test statistic is greater than t_{crit}.

Confidence Intervals for Regression Parameters

$$\hat{b}_1 \pm t_c s_{\hat{b}_1}$$

- If the hypothesized value of the parameter (b_1) lies within the interval (which is based on the observed value of the parameter, $\hat{b}_1$), we fail to reject the null hypothesis.
- If the hypothesized value of the parameter (b_1) lies outside the interval (which is based on the observed value of the parameter, $\hat{b}_1$), we can reject the null hypothesis.

Confidence Intervals versus Hypothesis Tests

- In a confidence interval, we aim to determine whether the **hypothesized value of the population parameter** lies **within** a computed interval (where the interval is based around, or centered on the **estimated parameter value from sample data**) with a particular degree of **confidence $(1 - \alpha)$**. The confidence interval represents the "fail-to-reject-the-null region."
- In a hypothesis test, we examine whether the **estimate of the parameter** lies in the rejection region or **outside** an interval (where the interval is based around, or centered on the **hypothesized value of the population parameter**), at a particular level of **significance (α)**.

Important Notes

- Choosing a lower level of significance increases the absolute value of t_{crit} resulting in a wider confidence interval and a lower likelihood of rejecting the null hypothesis.
- Increasing the significance level increases the probability of a Type I error, but decreases the probability of a Type II error.
- The p-value is the lowest level of significance at which the null hypothesis can be rejected for a null hypothesis, that the true population parameter equals zero.
- The smaller the standard error of an estimated parameter, the stronger the results of the regression and the narrower the resulting confidence intervals.

Analysis of Variance in a Regression with One Independent Variable

Analysis of variance (ANOVA) is used to evaluate the usefulness of the independent variable in explaining the variation in the dependent variable.

The F-statistic is used to test whether the slope coefficient in the regression equals zero ($H_0: b_1 = 0$ versus $H_a: b_1 \neq 0$). It equals the ratio of the average regression sum of squares to the average sum of the squared errors.

$$F = \frac{MSR}{MSE} = \frac{RSS/k}{SSE/(n-k-1)}$$

Degrees of freedom (numerator) = $k = 1$
Degrees of freedom (denominator) = $n - k - 1 = n - 2$

The *F*-test is a one-tailed test. The null hypothesis is rejected if the *F*-stat is greater than F_{crit}. Rejection of the null hypothesis means that the independent variable significantly explains the variation in the dependent variable.

- If the independent variable does not explain much of the variation in the dependent variable, the *F*-stat will be relatively small.
- If the independent variable does a good job of explaining much of the variation in the dependent variable, the *F*-stat will be relatively high.
- For regression analysis with only one independent variable, the *F*-test duplicates the *t*-test. In such a regression, the *F*-stat (F) equals the *t*-stat (t_{b1}) squared.

ANOVA Table for Simple Linear Regression ($k = 1$)

Source of Variation	Degrees of Freedom	Sum of Squares	Mean Sum of Squares
Regression (explained)	1	RSS	$MSR = \dfrac{RSS}{k} = \dfrac{RSS}{1} = RSS$
Error (unexplained)	$n - 2$	SSE	$MSE = \dfrac{SSE}{n - 2}$
Total	$n - 1$	**SST**	

Components of Total Variation

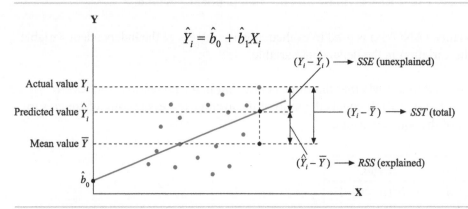

- SST measures the total variation in the dependent variable.

$$SST = \sum_{i=1}^{n}(Y_i - \bar{Y})^2 \rightarrow \text{Total variation}$$

- RSS measures the variation in the dependent variable that is explained by the independent variable.

$$RSS = \sum_{i=1}^{n}(\hat{Y}_i - \bar{Y})^2 \rightarrow \text{Explained variation}$$

- SSE measures the variation in the dependent variable that is not explained by the independent variable.

$$SSE = \sum_{i=1}^{n}(Y_i - \hat{Y}_i)^2 \rightarrow \text{Unexplained variation}$$

Prediction Intervals

There are two sources of uncertainty when we use a regression model to make a prediction regarding the value of the dependent variable.

- The uncertainty inherent in the error term, ε.
- The uncertainty in the estimated parameters, b_0 and b_1.

$$\text{Estimated variance of the prediction error} = s_f^2 = s^2\left[1 + \frac{1}{n} + \frac{(X - \bar{X})^2}{(n-1)s_x^2}\right]$$

- Once the variance of the prediction error has been computed, the $(1 - \alpha)\%$ prediction interval around the predicted value is estimated as:

$$\hat{Y}_1 \pm t_c s_f$$

Limitations of Regression Analysis

- Regression relations can change over time.
- Public knowledge of regression relationships may negate their usefulness going forward.
- If the assumptions of regression analysis do not hold, the predictions based on the model will not be valid.

MULTIPLE REGRESSION AND ISSUES IN REGRESSION ANALYSIS
Cross-Reference to CFA Institute Assigned Reading #8

Multiple Linear Regression

Multiple linear regression allows us to determine the effects of more than one independent variable on a particular dependent variable. The multiple regression equation is given as:

$$Y_i = b_0 + b_1 X_{1i} + b_2 X_{2i} + \ldots + b_k X_{ki} + \varepsilon_i, i = 1,2\ldots,n$$

where:
$\quad\quad Y_i$ = the ith observation of the dependent variable Y
$\quad\quad X_{ji}$ = the ith observation of the independent variable X_j, $j = 1,2,\ldots, k$
$\quad\quad b_0$ = the intercept of the equation
$b_1,\ldots, b_k$ = the slope coefficients for each of the independent variables
$\quad\quad \varepsilon_i$ = the error term
$\quad\quad n$ = the number of observations

- In multiple regression, a slope coefficient measures the impact on the dependent variable of a one unit change in the independent variable holding all other independent variables constant. This is why slope coefficients of multiple regressions are also known as partial slope coefficients.
- The intercept and the slope coefficients are all known as regression coefficients. Therefore, there are k slope coefficients in a regression model and $k + 1$ regression coefficients.
- The residual term, ε_i, equals the difference between the actual value of $Y(Y_i)$ and the predicted value of $Y(\hat{Y}_i)$.

$$\hat{\varepsilon}_i = Y_i - \hat{Y}_i = Y_i - (\hat{b}_0 + \hat{b}_1 X_{1i} + \hat{b}_2 X_{2i} + \ldots + \hat{b}_k X_{ki})$$

Confidence Intervals

$$\hat{b}_j \pm (t_c \times s_{\hat{b}_j})$$

estimated regression coefficient $\pm$ (critical t-value)(coefficient standard error)

- The critical t-value is a two-tailed value computed based on the significance level (1 − confidence level) and $n - (k + 1)$ degrees of freedom.
- A t-test with a null hypothesis of "equal to zero" at a significance level of α and a confidence interval with a $(1 - \alpha)$ level of confidence will always give the same result.

Predicting the Dependent Variable

- Obtain estimates for $\hat{b}_0, \hat{b}_1, \hat{b}_2, \dots, \hat{b}_k$ of regression parameters $b_0, b_1, b_2, \dots, b_k$.
- Determine the assumed values for independent variables $\hat{X}_1, \hat{X}_2, \dots, \hat{X}_k$.
- Compute the value of the dependent variable, $\hat{Y}_1$ using the equation

$$\hat{Y}_i = \hat{b}_0 + \hat{b}_1\hat{X}_{1i} + \hat{b}_2\hat{X}_{2i} + \dots + \hat{b}_k\hat{X}_{ki}$$

All the independent variables in the regression equation (regardless of whether or not their estimated slope coefficients are significantly different from 0), must be used in predicting the value of the dependent variable.

Assumptions of the Multiple Linear Regression Model

- The relationship between the dependent variable and the independent variables is linear.
- The independent variables are not random and no linear relationship exists between two or more independent variables.
- The expected value of the error term is zero.
- The variance of the error term is the same for all observations.
- The error term is uncorrelated across observations.
- The error term is normally distributed.

Hypothesis Tests on Regression Coefficients

The test statistic for each regression coefficient is calculated as:

$$t\text{-stat} = \frac{\text{Estimated regression coefficient} - \text{Hypothesized value of regression coefficient}}{\text{Standard error of regression coefficient}}$$

$$t = \frac{\hat{b}_j - b_j}{s_{\hat{b}_j}} = \frac{\text{Estimated regression coefficient} - \text{Hypothesized value}}{\text{Coefficient standard error of } b_j}$$

Degrees of freedom $= n - (k + 1)$

P-Values

- The p-value for each regression coefficient is the lowest level of significance at which we can reject the null hypothesis that the population value of the coefficient is zero, in a two-sided test.
- The lower the p-value, the weaker the case for the null hypothesis.

Results from Regression with Two Independent Variables

	Coefficient	Standard Error	t-Statistic
Intercept	b_0	$s_{\hat{b}_0}$	$b_0/s_{\hat{b}_0}$
First independent variable X_i	b_1	$s_{\hat{b}_1}$	$b_1/s_{\hat{b}_1}$
Second independent variable X_i	b_2	$s_{\hat{b}_2}$	$b_2/s_{\hat{b}_2}$

Residual standard error	SEE
Multiple R-squared	R^2
Observations	n

ANOVA

Source of Variation	Degrees of Freedom	Sum of Squares	Mean Sum of Squares	F	Significance
Regression	k	RSS	MSR = RSS/k	MSR/MSE	p-value
Residual	$n - (k + 1)$	SSE	MSE = SSE /$n - (k + 1)$		
Total	$n - 1$	**SST**			

Testing Whether All Population Regression Coefficients Equal Zero

Analysis of variance (ANOVA) provides the required information to test whether all the slope coefficients in a regression simultaneously equal zero. The F-test is used to conduct the following hypothesis test:

H_0: $b_1 = b_2 = \ldots = b_k = 0$

H_a: At least one slope coefficient does not equal zero

Information required to perform the F-test

- Number of observations (n).
- Total number of regression coefficients ($k + 1$).
- Sum of squared errors on residuals (SSE or total unexplained variation).
- Regression sum of squares (RSS or total explained variation).

$$F = \frac{\dfrac{RSS}{k}}{\dfrac{SSE}{[n-(k+1)]}} = \frac{\text{Mean regression sum of squares}}{\text{Mean squared error}} = \frac{MSR}{MSE}$$

- Degrees of freedom (numerator) = k
- Degrees of freedom (denominator) = $n - (k + 1)$

If the regression model does a good job in explaining the variation in the dependent variable, the F-stat will be relatively large.

Decision rule: **Reject null hypothesis if F-stat > F_{crit}.** Note that we use a one-tailed F-test.

Adjusted R^2

The coefficient of determination can be increased by adding independent variables that explain even a slight amount of the variation in the dependent variable to the regression equation. Adjusted R^2 does not automatically increase when another variable is added to the regression as it is adjusted for degrees of freedom.

$$\text{Adjusted } R^2 = \bar{R}^2 = 1 - \left(\frac{n-1}{n-k-1} \right)(1 - R^2)$$

- If k is greater than or equal to 1, R^2 is greater than adjusted R^2.
- If a new independent variable (k) is added, adjusted R^2 can decrease if adding the variable only results in a small increase in R^2.
- Adjusted R^2 can be negative while R^2 cannot.

Regression Equation

- Shows the relationship between the dependent variable and the independent variables.
- Can be used to predict the value of the dependent variable, given specific values for the independent variables.
- The significance of the individual regression coefficients is evaluated using t-tests or p-values.
- The t-stat for each regression coefficient is calculated by dividing the value of the coefficient by its standard error.

ANOVA Table

- Lists the regression sum of squares (RSS), sum of squared errors (SSE) and total sum of squares (SST) along with associated degrees of freedom.
- Also includes calculated values for mean regression sum of squares (MSR) and mean squared error (MSE).
- The F-stat can be calculated by dividing MSR by MSE. The F-test is used to test whether at least one of the slope coefficients on the independent variables in the regression is significantly different from 0.
- R^2 (and adjusted R^2) can be calculated from the data in the ANOVA table by dividing RSS by SST. R^2 is used to determine the goodness of fit of the regression equation to the data.
- The standard error of estimate (SEE) can also be computed from the information in the ANOVA table. $\text{SEE} = \sqrt{\text{MSE}}$

Dummy Variables

Using Dummy Variables in a Regression

Dummy variables in regression models help analysts determine whether a particular qualitative variable explains the variation in the model's dependent variable to a significant extent.

- A dummy variable must be binary in nature i.e., it may take on a value of either 0 or 1.
- If the model aims to distinguish between n categories, it must employ n-1 dummy variables. The category that is omitted is used as a reference point for the other categories.
- The intercept term in the regression indicates the average value of the dependent variable for the omitted category.
- The slope coefficient of each dummy variable estimates the difference (compared to the omitted category) a particular dummy variable makes to the dependent variable.
- If we use n dummy variables (instead of n-1) we would be violating the regression assumption of no linear relationship between the independent variables.

Violations of Regression Assumptions

Heteroskedasticity

Heteroskedasticity occurs when the variance of the error term in the regression is not constant across observations.

Effects of Heteroskedasticity

- Heteroskedasticity does not affect the consistency of estimators of regression parameters.
- However, it can lead to mistakes in inferences made from parameter estimates.
  - The F-test for the overall significance of the regression becomes unreliable as the MSE becomes a biased estimator of the true population variance.
  - The t-tests for the significance of each regression coefficient become unreliable as the estimates of the standard errors of regression coefficients become biased.
    - Typically, in regressions with financial data, standard errors of regression coefficients are underestimated and t-stats are inflated due to heteroskedasticity. Therefore, ignoring heteroskedasticity results in significant relationships being found when none actually exist. (Null hypotheses are rejected too often).
    - Sometimes however, heteroskedasticity leads to standard errors that are too large, which makes t-stats too small.

Types of Heteroskedasticity

- Unconditional heteroskedasticity occurs when the heteroskedasticity of the variance in the error term is not related to the independent variables in the regression. Unconditional heteroskedasticity does not create major problems for regression analysis.
- Conditional heteroskedasticity occurs when the heteroskedasticity in the error variance is correlated with the independent variables in the regression. While conditional heteroskedasticity does create problems for statistical inference, it can be easily identified and corrected.

Testing for Heteroskedasticity—The Breusch-Pagan (BP) Test

The BP test requires a regression of **the squared residuals from the original estimated regression equation** (in which the dependent variable is regressed on the independent variables) on the independent variables in the regression.

- If conditional heteroskedasticity does not exist, the independent variables will not explain much of the variation in the squared residuals from the original regression.
- If conditional heteroskedasticity is present, the independent variables will explain the variation in the squared residuals to a significant extent.

The test statistic for the BP test is a Chi-squared (χ^2) random variable, that is calculated as:

$$\chi^2 = nR^2 \text{ with } k \text{ degrees of freedom}$$

n = Number of observations
R^2 = Coefficient of determination of the **second regression** (the regression when the squared residuals of the original regression are regressed on the independent variables).
k = Number of independent variables

H_0: The original regression's squared error term is uncorrelated with the independent variables.
H_a: The original regression's squared error term is correlated with the independent variables.

Note: The BP test is a one-tailed Chi-squared test because conditional heteroskedasticity is only a problem if it is too large.

Correcting Heteroskedasticity

There are two ways of correction for conditional heteroskedasticity in linear regression models:

- Use robust standard errors (White-corrected standard errors or heteroskedasticity-consistent standard errors) to recalculate the t-statistics for the original regression coefficients based on corrected-for-heteroskedasticity standard errors.
- Use generalized least squares, where the original regression equation is modified to eliminate heteroskedasticity.

Serial Correlation

Serial correlation (autocorrelation) occurs when regression errors are correlated across observations. It typically arises in time series regressions.

- Positive serial correlation occurs when a positive (negative) error for one observation increases the chances of a positive (negative) error for another.
- Negative serial correlation occurs when a positive (negative) error for one observation increases the chances of a negative (positive) error for another.

Effects of Serial Correlation

Positive (negative) serial correlation:

- Does not affect the consistency of the estimated regression coefficients.
- Causes the F-stat (which is used to test the overall significance of the regression) to be inflated (deflated) because MSE will tend to underestimate (overestimate) the population error variance.
- Causes the standard errors for the regression coefficients to be underestimated (overestimated), which results in larger (smaller) t-values. Consequently, analysts may reject (fail to reject) null hypotheses incorrectly, make Type I errors (Type II errors) and attach (fail to attach) significance to relationships that are in fact not significant (significant).

Testing for Serial Correlation—The Durbin-Watson (DW) Test

The DW test-statistic is approximated as:

$DW \approx 2(1 - r)$; where r is the sample correlation between squared residuals from one period and those from the previous period.

- The DW-stat can range from 0 (when serial correlation equals +1) to 4 (when serial correlation equals −1).
- If the regression has no serial correlation, the DW stat equals 2.
- If the regression residuals are positively serially correlated, the DW stat will be less than 2.
- If the regression residuals are negatively serially correlated, the DW stat will be greater than 2.
- For a given sample, the critical DW value (d*) is not known with certainty. We only know that it lies between two values $(d_l$ and $d_u)$. The figure (on next page) depicts the lower and upper values for d* as they relate to the results of the DW test.

Value of Durbin-Watson Statistic

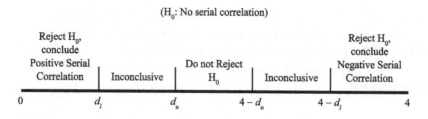

Decision rules for Durbin-Watson tests:

When testing for positive serial correlation:

- Reject H_0 of no positive serial correlation if the DW stat is lower than d_1. Conclude that there is positive serial correlation.
- The test is inconclusive if the DW stat lies between d_1 and d_u
- Fail to reject H_0 of no positive serial correlation when DW stat is greater than d_u.

When testing for negative serial correlation:

- Reject H_0 of no negative serial correlation if the DW stat is higher than $4 - d_1$. Conclude that there is negative serial correlation.
- The test is inconclusive if the DW stat lies between $4 - d_u$ and $4 - d_1$.
- Fail to reject H_0 of no negative serial correlation when DW stat is less than $4 - d_u$.

Correcting Serial Correlation

There are two ways to correct for serial correlation in the regression residuals:

- Adjust the coefficient standard errors to account for serial correlation using Hansen's method (which incidentally also corrects for heteroskedasticity). The regression coefficients remain the same but the standard errors change. After correcting for positive serial correlation, the robust standard errors are larger than they were originally. Note that the DW stat still remains the same.
- Modify the regression equation to eliminate the serial correlation.

Multicollinearity

Multicollinearity occurs when two or more independent variables (or combinations of independent variables) in a regression model are highly (but not perfectly) correlated with each other.

Effects of Multicollinearity

- Multicollinearity does not affect the consistency of OLS estimates and regression coefficients, but makes them inaccurate and unreliable.
- It becomes difficult to isolate the impact of each independent variable on the dependent variable.
- The standard errors for the regression coefficients are inflated, which results in t-stats becoming too small and less powerful (in terms of their ability to reject null hypotheses).

Detecting Multicollinearity

- High pair-wise correlations between the independent variables do not necessarily indicate that multicollinearity exists.
- A high R^2 and a significant F-stat (both of which indicate that the regression model overall does a good job of explaining the dependent variable) coupled with insignificant t-stats of slope coefficients (which indicate that the independent variables individually do not significantly explain the variation in the dependent variable) provide the classic case of multicollinearity.
  - The low t-stats on the slope coefficients increase the chances of Type II errors: failure to reject the null hypothesis when it is false.
- Multicollinearity may be present even when we do not observe insignificant t-stats and a highly significant F-stat for the regression model.

Correcting for Multicollinearity

Analysts may correct for multicollinearity by excluding one or more of the independent variables from the regression model. Stepwise regression is a technique that systematically removes variables from the regression until multicollinearity is eliminated.

Problems in Linear Regression and Their Solutions

Problem	Effect	Solution
Heteroskedasticity	Incorrect standard errors	Use robust standard errors (corrected for conditional heteroskedasticity)
Serial correlation	Incorrect standard errors (additional problems if a lagged value of the dependent variable is used as an independent variable)	Use robust standard errors (corrected for serial correlation)
Multicollinearity	High R^2 and low t-statistics	Remove one or more independent variables; often no solution based in theory

Model Specification

Principles of Model Specification

- The model should be backed by solid economic reasoning.
- The functional form for the variables in the regression should be in line with the nature of the variables.
- Each variable in the model should be relevant, making the model "parsimonious."
- The model should be tested for violations of regression assumptions.
- The model should be found useful out of sample.

Model Specification Errors

1. Misspecified functional form
   - One or more important variables may have been omitted from the regression. This error would result in estimates of the regression coefficients and their standard errors being biased and inconsistent.
   - One or more of the variables may need to be transformed before estimating the regression. For example, if the relationship between the variables becomes linear when one of the variables is presented as a proportional change in the variable, the misspecification may be corrected by using the natural logarithm of the variable.
   - The model may pool data from different sources that should not have been pooled.

2. Time-series misspecification results from the kinds of independent variables included in the regression. It causes a violation of the regression assumption that the expected value of the error term equals zero. Time series misspecification can result from:

- Including lagged dependent variables as independent variables to regressions with serially correlated errors. The lagged dependent variable (which serves as an independent variable in the regression) will be correlated with the error term, violating the assumption that independent variables are uncorrelated with the error term. Estimates of regression coefficients will be biased and inconsistent.
- Including an independent variable that is a function of a dependent variable in the regression. In such a case, the particular independent variable would be correlated with the error term.
- Independent variables are measured with error. Once again the independent variable would be correlated with the error term.
- Nonstationarity occurs when a variable's properties (e.g., mean and variance) are not constant over time.

Qualitative Dependent Variables

When trying to predict a qualitative outcome, probit and logit models are generally used.

- The probit model is based on the normal distribution. It estimates the probability that a qualitative condition is fulfilled given the value of the independent variable.
- The logit model is similar except that it is based on the logistic distribution.
- Discriminant analysis yields a linear function (similar to a regression equation) that is used to create an overall score on the basis of which an observation can be classified qualitatively.

QM

Steps in Assessing a Multiple Regression Model

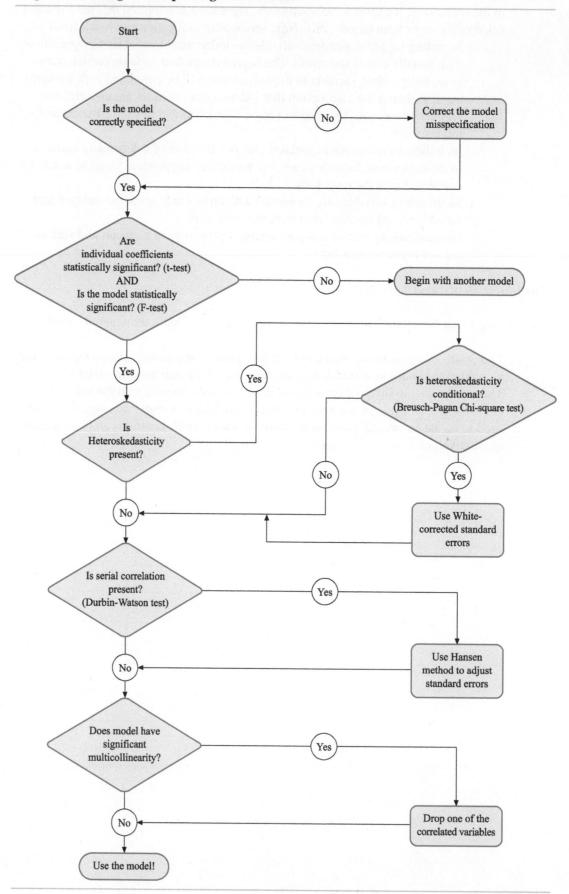

MAJOR FOCUSES OF DATA ANALYTICS

- **Measuring correlations:** To understanding the contemporaneous relationship between variables.
- **Making predictions:** To determine whether one or more variables can help forecast the value of a particular variable of interest.
- **Making causal inferences:** To determine whether a change in an independent variable **causes** a change in the dependent variable.
- **Classifying data:** To sort observations into **distinct categories**. When the dependent variable is **categorical** (not continuous), the econometric model is referred to as a classifier.
- **Sorting data into clusters:** To sort observations into **groups** (**clusters**) such that observations in the same cluster are more similar to each other than they are to observations in other clusters.
- **Reducing the dimension of data:** To reduce the number of independent variables while preserving the information contained in the data.

Machine learning (ML) lies within the broader field of artificial intelligence (AI). Basically, ML looks to program computers to improve performance in specified tasks with experience.

TYPES OF MACHINE LEARNING

Supervised learning is machine learning that makes use of labeled training data.

If the Y variable is continuous, then the task is one of regression. For example:

- **Penalized regression.** The greater the number of variables included, the larger the penalty. There is a tradeoff between the increase in explanatory power that a variable brings to the model versus the penalty for including it in the model.

If the Y variable is categorical or ordinal (then it is a classification problem). For example:

- **Classification and Regression Trees (CART).** Can be applied to predict either a **categorical** target variable (producing a **classification** tree) or a **continuous** outcome (producing a **regression** tree). The model also produces a complete decision tree, which is very useful for interpreting how any observation is classified.
- **Random Forests.** Collection of classification trees based on a random selection of features (instead of just one, as is the case for CARTs). Random forests tend to mitigate the risk of overfitting on the training data. Further, they also reduce the ratio of noise to signal because errors cancel out across the collection of classification trees.
- **Neural networks.** Can be applied to a variety of tasks characterized by nonlinearities and interactions among variables. DLNs have been shown to be useful in general for pattern recognition problems.

> Neural networks are commonly used for supervised learning but are also important in reinforcement learning, which can be unsupervised.

Unsupervised learning is machine learning that does not make use of labeled training data.

- **Clustering Algorithms.** Group observations solely on the basis of information found in the data. They uncover potentially interesting structures in data without leading the analysis with labeled data or any applicable theory. Further, it can be applied very quickly to very large datasets.
- **Dimension Reduction.** Reduces the set of features to a manageable size while retaining much of the variation (information) in the data as possible. Dimension reduction methods are applied not only to numerical data but also often to textual data and visual data (e.g., in face recognition), which may be in irregular formats. Principal component analysis (PCA) is a commonly used method of dimension reduction.

STEPS IN MODEL TRAINING

1. Specify the ML technique/algorithm.
2. Specify the associated hyperparameters (values chosen before training begins); these may include the number of training cycles.
   - More cycles might result in overfitting the model on in-sample data, resulting in poor out-of-sample predictive performance.
3. Divide data into a training sample and a validation sample.
   - A training sample involving correctly labeled targets, which will be used to train or fit the algorithm, and
   - A validation sample, which is used to evaluate how well the model that is fit to the training sample works out of sample.
     - Note that training and validation are often accomplished in a repeated process of randomly splitting the dataset into training and validation samples. In such a process, a data point might be used for training purposes in one split and for validation purposes in another split.
     - This process, known as cross-validation, is intended to control for bias in training data.
     - Intuitively, the bigger the dataset, the less cross-validation is needed.
4. Evaluate learning with performance measure P, using the validation sample, and adjust ("tune") the hyperparameters.
5. Repeat the training cycle the specified number of times or until the required performance level (e.g., level of accuracy) is obtained.

TIME-SERIES ANALYSIS
Cross-Reference to CFA Institute Assigned Reading #9

TREND MODELS

A **linear trend model** is one in which the dependent variable changes by a constant amount in each period.

$$y_t = b_0 + b_1 t + \varepsilon_t, \quad t = 1, 2, \ldots, T$$

y_t = the value of the time series at time t (value of the dependent variable)
b_0 = the y-intercept term
b_1 = the slope coefficient/ trend coefficient
t = time, the independent or explanatory variable
ε_t = a random-error term

- Ordinary least squares (OLS) regression is used to estimate the regression coefficients (b_0 and b_1) and the resulting regression equation is used to predict the value of the time series (y_t) for any period (t).
- A linear trend model is very similar to a simple linear regression model. In a linear trend model, the independent variable is the time period.
- In a linear trend model, the value of the dependent variable changes by b_1 (the trend coefficient) in each successive time period (as t increases by 1 unit) irrespective of the level of the series in the previous period.

Log-linear trend models work well in modelling time series that have exponential growth. Exponential growth is growth at a constant rate ($e^{b1} - 1$) with continuous compounding.

$$\ln y_t = b_0 + b_1 t + \varepsilon_t, t = 1, 2, \ldots, T$$

Linear Trend Models versus Log-Linear Trend Models

- A linear trend model predicts that $\mathbf{y_t}$ will grow by a **constant amount** (b_1) each period. For example, if b_1 equals 0.1%, y_t will grow by 0.1% in each period.
- A log-linear trend model predicts that **ln y_t** will grow by a constant amount (b_1) in each period. This means that y_t itself will witness a **constant growth rate** of $e^{b1} - 1$ in each period. For example, if b_1 equals 1% then the predicted growth rate of y_t in each period equals $e^{0.01} - 1 = 0.01005$ or 1.005%.

Also, in a linear trend model the predicted value of y_t is $b_0 + b_1 t$, but in a log-linear trend model the predicted value of y_t is $e^{b0} + {}^{b}{}_1{}^t$ because $e^{\ln y}t = y_t$.

Testing for Correlated Errors in Trend Models

Linear and log-linear trend models must be tested to ensure that the regression error term is not correlated across time periods (observations). This is done by performing the Durban-Watson test, which determines whether the errors are serially correlated.

QM

AUTOREGRESSIVE (AR) TIME SERIES MODELS

An autoregressive (AR) model is a time series that is regressed on its own past values. Past values of the dependent variable itself are used to predict its current value.

First-order AR model:

$$x_t = b_0 + b_1 x_{t-1} + \varepsilon_t$$

pth-order AR model:

$$x_t = b_0 + b_1 x_{t-1} + b_2 x_{t-2} + \ldots + b_p x_{t-p} + \varepsilon_t$$

In order to draw valid statistical conclusions, an AR model must be:

- Covariance stationary, which means that:
  - The expected value of the time series is constant and finite in all periods. The time series has defined mean-reverting level.
  - The variance of observations in the time series is constant and finite in all periods.
  - The covariance of the time series with itself for a fixed number of periods in the past or future is constant and finite in all periods.
- Specified such that the error terms do not exhibit serial correlation.
- Specified such that the error terms are homoskedastic.

Detecting Serially Correlated Errors in an AR Model

The Durbin-Watson test cannot be used to test for serial correlation in an AR model. Therefore, we determine whether the residuals of the time series model are serially correlated by testing whether the autocorrelations of the error terms (error autocorrelations or residual autocorrelations) are significantly different from 0.

- If any of the error autocorrelations are significantly different from 0, the errors are serially correlated and the model is not specified correctly.
- If all the error autocorrelations are not significantly different from 0, the errors are not serially correlated and the model is specified correctly.

Steps in performing the hypothesis test

- First estimate the autoregressive model starting with a first-order AR model
- Calculate the autocorrelation of the model's residuals

- Test whether the autocorrelations are significant

    - $\text{t-stat} = \dfrac{\text{Estimated residual autocorrelation}}{\text{Standard error of the autocorrelation}}$

        - Standard error $= 1/\sqrt{T}$
        - T = Number of observations
        - $T - 2$ = Degrees of freedom

Mean Reversion

A time series shows mean reversion if it tends to fall when it lies above its mean and tends to rise when it lies below its mean.

$$\text{Mean reverting level} = x_t = \frac{b_0}{1 - b_1}$$

All covariance stationary time series have a finite mean-reverting level. An AR(1) time series will have a finite mean-reverting level, as long as the absolute level of the lag coefficient (b_1) is less than one.

The chain rule of forecasting is used to make multi-period forecasts. The next period's value (which is predicted by the forecast equation) is used as an input to the equation to determine the value of two periods ahead. Multi-period forecasts are more uncertain than single period forecasts.

Comparing Forecast Model Performance

The smaller the variance of the forecast error from a model, the more accurate the model and the smaller the standard error of the time series regression.

- In-sample forecasts are made using observations from the data used to estimate the model. For time series analysis, in-sample forecasts use data from within the test period.
- Out-of-sample forecasts are made using data from outside the test period. These forecasts are used to evaluate how well the estimated model holds up outside the period used to develop the model.

The out-of-sample forecasting performance of forecasting models is evaluated by comparing their root mean squared error (RMSE), which is the square root of the average squared error.

- The smaller the RMSE, the more accurate the model as a forecasting tool.

Instability of Regression Coefficients

In determining which model to choose, the stability of the regression coefficients must also be considered.

- Using longer time periods brings greater statistical reliability, but there is a greater chance that underlying fundamentals may have changed over the longer time period. Judgment and experience play an important role in determining how to model a time series.

Random Walks

A random walk is a time series in which the value of the series in one period equals the value of the series in the previous period plus an unpredictable random error.

$$x_t = x_{t-1} + \varepsilon_t, E(\varepsilon_t) = 0, E(\varepsilon_t^2) = \sigma^2, E(\varepsilon_t\varepsilon_s) = 0 \text{ if } t \neq s$$

- The error term has a constant variance and is uncorrelated with the error term in previous periods.
- The model is a special case of the AR(1) model with $b_0 = 0$ and $b_1 = 1$
- The expected value of the error term equals 0.
- The best forecast of x is x_{t-1} in every period after $t - 1$

Regression methods cannot be used to estimate an AR(1) model on a time series that is a random walk as it is not covariance stationary because:

- A random walk has an undefined mean reverting level.
- The variance of a random walk has no upper bound.

Since standard regression analysis cannot be used on a time series that is a random walk, first differencing is applied to the time series to convert the data into a covariance stationary time series. This transformation subtracts the value of the time series in the prior period from its current value.

First Difference of Random Walk

$$y_t = x_t - x_{t-1} + \varepsilon_t, E(\varepsilon_t) = 0, E(\varepsilon_t^2) = \sigma^2, E(\varepsilon_t\varepsilon_s) = 0 \text{ for } t \neq s$$

The first-differenced variable (y_t) is covariance stationary:

- It has a mean reverting level of 0.
- Its variance is constant and finite in every period.

Therefore, y_t can be modeled using linear regression. However, since b_0 and b_1 both equal zero, the model is of no use in making forecasts.

Random Walk with a Drift

A random walk with a drift increases or decreases by a constant amount in each period. It has a b_0 that does not equal zero (unlike a random walk).

$$x_t = b_0 + x_{t-1} + \varepsilon_t, E(\varepsilon_t) = 0$$

A random walk with a drift also has an undefined mean reversion level as b_1 equals 1. Consequently, the AR model cannot be used to analyze the time series so we must first differentiate it.

$$y_t = x_t - x_{t-1}, y_t = b_0 + \varepsilon_t, b_0 \neq 0$$

Testing for Nonstationarity

If the slope coefficient of an AR(1) model equals 1, the time series is said to have a unit root. In this case, the time series is a random walk and is not covariance stationary. There are two ways to determine whether a time series is covariance stationary:

Examine the Autocorrelations in the AR Model

A time series that is covariance stationary will typically have:

- Time series autocorrelations that are not significantly different from zero at all lags; or
- Time series autocorrelations that decline towards zero as the number of lags increases.

The Dickey-Fuller Test

This test transfers the AR(1) model into the following form:

$$x_t - x_{t-1} = b_0 + (b_1 - 1)x_{t-1} + \varepsilon_t$$

or

$$x_t - x_{t-1} = b_0 + g_1 x_{t-1} + \varepsilon_t, E(\varepsilon_t) = 0$$

Note:

- The dependent variable is the first difference of the time series.
- If there is a unit root in the AR(1) model ($b_1 = 1$), g_1 will equal 0.
- The independent variable is the first lag of the time series.

H_0: $g_1 = 0$ (the time series has a unit root and is nonstationary)
H_a: $g_1 < 0$ (the time series does not have a unit root and is stationary)

To conduct the test, the t-statistic is calculated in the conventional manner but modified critical values are used. These critical values are larger in absolute value than conventional critical values.

Moving Averages

n-period moving average

$$\frac{x_t + x_{t-1} + \ldots + x_{t-(n-1)}}{n}$$

Plotting the moving average of a series allows us to zero in on long-term trends and to remove the effects of seasonal fluctuations (or noise) in the data.

A simple moving average gives an equal weight to all periods. It always lags large movements in the actual data. Consequently, moving averages are not very effective in predicting the future.

MOVING AVERAGE TIME SERIES MODELS

MA(1) model:

$$x_t = \varepsilon_t + \theta\varepsilon_{t-1}, \mathrm{E}(\varepsilon_t) = 0, \mathrm{E}(\varepsilon_t^2) = \sigma^2, \mathrm{E}(\varepsilon_t\varepsilon_s) = 0 \; for \, t \neq s$$

Note:

- Different weights are placed on the two terms (1 on ε_t and θ on ε_{t-1}) in the MA(1) model unlike the simple moving-average model.

MA(q) model:

$$x_t = \varepsilon_t + \theta_1\varepsilon_{t-1} + \ldots \theta_q\varepsilon_{t-q}, \mathrm{E}(\varepsilon_t) = 0, \mathrm{E}(\varepsilon_t^2) = \sigma^2, \mathrm{E}(\varepsilon_t\varepsilon_s) = 0 \; for \, t \neq s$$

If a MA(q) model fits the time series, the first q autocorrelations will be significantly different from 0, while all correlations beyond that will equal 0.

Determining whether a time series fits an autoregressive or moving-average model:

- For autoregressive time series, the autocorrelations typically start out large and then decline gradually.
- For MA(q) time series, the autocorrelations suddenly drop to zero after the first q autocorrelations.

Seasonality in Time Series Models

Seasonality in a time series may give the appearance that autoregressive time series models cannot be used to perform analysis on the data – the seasonal autocorrelation of the error term would be significantly different from 0. This problem can be solved by introducing a seasonal lag in the model.

Typically, the value of the time series one year before the current period is introduced in the autoregressive model to try to capture the effect of seasonality in the time series. In the case of quarterly data, the fourth autocorrelation of the error term would be significantly different from zero. The modified model may then be presented as:

$$x_t = b_0 + b_1 x_{t-1} + b_2 x_{t-4} + \varepsilon_t$$

If, after introduction of the seasonal lag, none of the autocorrelations are significantly different from zero, the updated model may be used to make forecasts.

Autoregressive Moving-Average Models (ARMA Models)

An ARMA model combines autoregressive lags of the dependent variable and moving-average errors in order to provide better forecasts than simple AR models.

ARMA (p, q):

$$lx_t = b_0 + b_1 x_{t-1} + \ldots + b_p x_{t-p} + \varepsilon_t + \theta_1 \varepsilon_{t-1} + \ldots + \theta_q \varepsilon_{t-q}$$
$$E(\varepsilon_t) = 0, E(\varepsilon_t^2) = \sigma^2, E(\varepsilon_t \varepsilon_s) = 0 \; for\, t \neq s$$

The model has p autoregressive terms and q moving-average terms.

Limitations of ARMA Models

- The parameters of the model can be very unstable.
- There are no set criteria for determining p and q.
- Even after a model is selected, it may not do a good job of forecasting.

Autoregressive Conditional Heteroskedasticity Models (ARCH Models)

Heteroskedasticity occurs when the variance of the error term varies with the independent variable. If heteroskedasticity is present, one or more of the lagged variables in the model may appear statistically significant when they are actually not.

For time series models, ARCH models are used to determine whether the variance of the error in one period depends on the variance of the error in previous periods. The squared residuals from a particular time series model (the model may be an AR, MA or ARMA model) are regressed on a constant and one lag of the squared residuals. The regression equation takes the following form:

$$\hat{\varepsilon}_t^2 = a_0 + a_1 \hat{\varepsilon}_{t-1}^2 + u_t$$

If a_1 is statistically different from 0, the time series is ARCH(1) and the error in period $t + 1$ can be predicted using the formula:

$$\hat{\sigma}_{t+1}^2 = \hat{a}_0 + \hat{a}_1 \hat{\varepsilon}_t^2$$

If ARCH errors are found to exist in the model, generalized least squares may be used to correct for heteroskedasticity and to correctly estimate the standard errors of the parameters in the time-series model.

Regression with More than One Time Series

To determine whether we can use linear regression to model more than one time series we must determine whether either of, or both the series contain a unit root. If a series contains a unit root, it is not covariance stationary and any results of regression analysis would not be valid.

The Dickey-Fuller test is used to determine whether the independent variable and the dependent variable have a unit root.

- If neither of the time series has a unit root, linear regression can be used to test the relationships between the two time series.
- If either of them has a unit root, linear regression cannot be used as results may be spurious.
- If both of them have unit roots, we must determine whether the time series are cointegrated.
  - If they are not cointegrated, linear regression cannot be used.
  - If they are cointegrated, the regression coefficients and standard errors will be consistent and they can be used to conduct hypothesis tests.

Two time series are cointegrated, if a long-term economic relationship exists between them such that they do not diverge from each other significantly in the long run.

Testing for Cointegration

If the time series used to construct a regression model both have a unit root:

1. Estimate the regression:

$$y_t = b_0 + b_1 x_t + \varepsilon_t$$

2. Test whether the error term (ε_t) has a unit root using the Dickey-Fuller test but with Engle-Granger critical values.
3. H_0: Error term has a unit root versus H_a: Error term does not have a unit root.
4. If we fail to reject the null hypothesis, we conclude that the error term in the regression is not covariance stationary, the time series are not cointegrated and the regression relation is spurious.
5. If we reject the null hypothesis, we conclude that the error term does not have a unit root, it is covariance stationary and therefore the results of the linear regression can be used to test hypotheses about the variables.

Suggested steps in time-series forecasting

The following is a step-by-step guide to build a model to predict a time series.

1. Understand the investment problem you have and make an initial choice of model. One alternative is a regression model that predicts the future behavior of a variable based on hypothesized casual relationships with other variables. Another is a time-series model that attempts to predict the future behavior of a variable based on the past behavior of the same variable.

2. If you have decided to use a time-series model, compile the time series and plot it to see whether it looks covariance stationary. The plot might show important deviations from covariance stationarity, including the following:
   - A linear trend;
   - An exponential trend;
   - Seasonality; or
   - A significant shift in the time series during the sample period (for example, a change in mean or variance).

3. If you find no significant seasonality or shift in the time series, then perhaps either a linear trend or an exponential trend will be sufficient to model the time series. In that case, take the following steps:
   - Determine whether a linear or exponential trend seems most reasonable (usually by plotting the series);
   - Estimate the trend;
   - Compute the residual;
   - Use the Durbin-Watson statistic to determine whether the residuals have significant serial correlation. If you find no significant serial correlation in the residuals, then the trend model is sufficient to capture the dynamics of the time series and you can use that model for forecasting.

4. If you find significant serial correlation in the residuals from the trend model, use a more complex model, such as an autoregressive model. First, however, reexamine whether the time series is covariance stationary. Following is a list of violations of stationarity, along with potential methods to adjust the time series to make it covariance stationary:
   - If the time series has a linear trend, first-difference the time series.
   - If the time series has an exponential trend, take the natural log of the time series and then first-difference it.
   - If the time series shifts significantly during the sample period, estimate different time series models before and after the shift.
   - If the time series has significant seasonality, include seasonal lags (discussed in step 7).

5. After you have successfully transformed a raw time series into a covariance-stationary time series, you can usually model the transformed series with a short auto regression*. To decide which autoregressive model to use, take the following steps:
   - Estimate an AR (1) model.
   - Test to see whether the residuals from this model have significant serial correlation.
   - If you find no significant serial correlation in the residuals, you can use the AR (1) model to forecast.

6. If you find significant serial correlation in the residuals, use the AR (2) model and test for significant serial correlation of the residuals of the AR (2) model.
   - If you find no significant serial correlation, use the AR (2) model.
   - If you find significant serial correlation of the residuals, keep increasing the order of the AR model until the residual serial correlation is no longer significant.

7. Your next move is to check for seasonality. You can use one of two approaches:
   - ○ Graph the data and check for regular seasonal patterns.
   - ○ Examine the data to see whether the seasonal autocorrelations of the residuals from an AR model are significant (for example, the fourth autocorrelation for quarterly data) and whether the autocorrelations before and after the seasonal autocorrelations are significant. To correct for seasonality, add seasonal lags to your AR model. For example, if you are using quarterly data, you might add the fourth lag of a time series as an additional variable in an AR (1) or an AR (2) model.

8. Next, test whether the residuals have autoregressive conditional heteroskedasticity. To test for ARCH (1), for example, do the following:
   - ○ Regress the squared residual from your time-series model on a lagged value of the squared residual.
   - ○ Test whether the coefficient on the squared lagged residual differs significantly from 0.
   - ○ If the coefficient on the squared lagged residual does not differ significantly from 0, the residuals do not display ARCH and you can rely on the standard errors from your time-series estimates.
   - ○ If the coefficient on the squared lagged residuals does differ significantly from 0, use generalized least squares or other methods to correct for ARCH.

9. Finally, you may also want to perform tests of the model's out-of-sample forecasting performance to see how the model's out-of-sample performance compares to its in-sample performance.

Using these steps in sequence, you can be reasonably sure that your model is correctly specified.

EXCERPT FROM "PROBABILITIC APPROACHES: SCENARIO ANALYSIS, DECISION TREES AND SIMULATIONS"
Cross-Reference to CFA Institute Assigned Reading #10

- Scenario analysis and decision trees are used to evaluate the impact of **discrete** risk.
- Simulations are used to evaluate the impact of **continuous** risk.

SIMULATIONS

Steps in Simulation

1. Determine probabilistic variables
   - Simulations place no constraint on the number of input variables that can be incorporated into the analysis.
   - Input variables may or may not be predictable. Probability distributions are defined for each variable that is allowed to vary in the simulation.
2. Define probability distributions for these variables
   - Generally speaking, there are three ways in which we can go about defining probability distributions:
     - Historical data:
     - Historical data can be used to develop probability distributions for variables that have a long history and reliable data over that history.
     - Note that in this approach, the implicit assumption is that the market has not undergone any structural shifts that might make historical data unreliable as an indicator of the future distribution of the variable.
   - Cross sectional data:
     - This approach uses differences in a specific variable across existing investments that are similar to the investment being analyzed as observations of the variable.
   - Statistical distribution and parameters:
     - This approach involves choosing a statistical distribution that best captures the variability in the input variable and estimating the parameters for that distribution.
     - While computer software offer a wide variety of distributions to choose from, picking the right distribution and specifying the parameters for the distribution remains difficult because:
     - Practically speaking, only a few inputs that are commonly required in the analysis conform to the assumptions made by statistical distributions.
     - Once the distribution has been selected, the parameters still need to be estimated.
3. Check for correlation across variables
   - Correlations can be estimated by looking at historical data.
   - If it is found that there is strong (positive or negative) correlation between input variables, one can:
     - Retain the variable that has a more significant impact on value in the analysis, and discard the other.
     - Build the correlation explicitly into the simulation.

4. Run the simulation
   ○ For each individual simulation/iteration, one outcome is drawn for each input variable (from its distribution) and the value of the output variable is computed.
   ○ This process is repeated several times. Note that the marginal contribution of each individual simulation drops off as the number of simulations increases.
   ○ The number of individual simulations run depends on:
     ▪ Number of probabilistic inputs.
     ▪ Characteristics of probability distributions.
     ▪ Range of outcomes.

Advantages of Using Simulations in Decision Making

- Offers insights to improve input estimation.
- Yields a distribution for expected value rather than a point estimate.

One should not conclude (1) that simulations yield better estimates of expected value than conventional risk-adjusted value models, or (2) that by providing estimates of expected value and the distribution in that value, simulations lead to better decisions.

Simulations with Constraints

- Book value constraints.
  - Regulatory capital restrictions.
  - Negative book value for equity.
- Earnings and cash flow constraints.
- Market value constraints.

Issues in Using Simulations in Risk Assessment

- Garbage in, garbage out.
- Real data may not fit distributions.
- Non-stationary distributions.
- Changing correlation across inputs.

Risk-Adjusted Value and Simulations

Generally speaking, cash flows outcomes obtained from simulations are expected cash flows that are **not** risk adjusted. Therefore, they should be discounted at a **risk-adjusted** rate.

There is however, one exception. This exception occurs when we use the standard deviation of the output variable (obtained from the results of a simulation) as a measure of risk and use this measure to make decisions. If we were to use a risk-adjusted discount rate in this case, we would be double counting risk.

COMPARING THE APPROACHES

Selective versus Full Risk Analysis

- In **scenario analysis**, we generally consider what we believe to be the most likely scenarios, and ignore all other scenarios.
  - Therefore, the sum of the probabilities of the scenarios considered can be less than one.
- With **decision trees** and **simulations**, we attempt to consider **all** possible outcomes.
  - Therefore, the sum of the probabilities of outcomes in decision trees and simulations equals one.

When we employ decisions trees or simulations, we can compute expected values across all outcomes, using the probabilities as weights.

Type of Risk

- **Scenario analysis** and **decision trees** are generally more suitable for discrete risks.
  - Decision trees are more useful in modeling **sequential** risks, where risks are considered in phases.
  - Scenario analysis is more useful when risks occur **concurrently**.
- **Simulations** are better suited for **continuous** risks.

Correlation across Risks

- If the various risks inherent in an investment are correlated, **simulations** are more appropriate because they allow for these correlations to be explicitly modeled into the analysis.
- In **scenario analysis**, these correlations can only be incorporated into the analysis to the extent that we can subjectively create scenarios that account for them.
- Correlated risks are difficult to model in **decision trees**.

Also note that the quality of information also affects the approach chosen:

> **Simulations** work best when there is substantial historical and cross sectional data available so that probability distributions and parameters can be assessed.
> **Decision trees** work best when risks can be assessed using past data or population characteristics so that estimates of probabilities of outcomes at each node can be made.
> **Scenario analysis** works best for new and unpredictable risk, even though it offers a rather subjective way of dealing with risk.

Complement or Replacement for Risk-Adjusted Value

- **Decision trees** and **simulations** can be used as either complements to or substitutes for risk-adjusted value.
- **Scenario analysis** however, can only serve as a complement to risk-adjusted value as it does not look at the entire spectrum of possible outcomes.

When using these approaches as *complements* to risk-adjusted value, bear in mind that:

- All three approaches use expected, not risk-adjusted cash flows and therefore, a risk-adjusted discount rate should be used, not the risk-free rate.
- In assessing risk however, it should not be double counted. If expected cash flows from risky investments are discounted as a risk-adjusted rate, then we should not simply reject them if the variation in possible outcomes is high.

When using simulations and decision trees as *substitutes* for risk-adjusted valuation, bear in mind that:

- Cash flows should be discounted at a risk-free rate.
- The standard deviation of outcomes obtained from the analysis should be used as the measure of risk in the investment.
- Comparing two assets with the same expected value (obtained with risk-free rates used as discount rates) from a simulation, we should pick the one with the lower variability in simulated values.
- However, in making such a decision we are ignoring the fact that the two assets may contain different levels of non-systematic risk, which can be diversified away.

Study Session 4: Economics

EC

CURRENCY EXCHANGE RATES: UNDERSTANDING EQUILIBRIUM VALUE
Cross-Reference to CFA Institute Assigned Reading #11

Spot Exchange Rates

Spot exchange rates (S) are quotes for transactions that call for **immediate delivery**.

When working with bid-ask quotes, to determine whether the bid or the offer rate in the exchange rate quote should be used in a particular transaction:

- First identify the base currency of the exchange rate quote; and then
- Determine whether the client is buying or selling the base currency.

Given bid and ask prices for a particular currency, the bid and ask prices for the other currency in the exchange rate quote can be determined as follows:

- The *b/a* ask price is the reciprocal of the *a/b* bid price.
- The *b/a* bid price is the reciprocal of the *a/b* ask price.

Currency Cross Rates

A **cross rate** is an exchange rate between two currencies that is derived from each currency's relationship with a third currency.

Cross Rate Calculations with Bid-Ask Spreads

Step 1: Bring the bid-ask quotes for the exchange rates into a format such that the common (or third) currency cancels out if we multiply the exchange rates.
Step 2: Multiply the exchange rates in a manner that maximizes the resulting bid-ask spread. The bid-ask spread is maximized when the bid is minimized and ask is maximized.

Foreign Exchange Spreads

The bid-ask spread that a dealer provides to clients is typically wider than the bid-ask spread observed in the interbank market.

Factors Affecting the Size of the Bid-Ask Spread

The size of the bid-ask spread in the interbank market: The more liquid the interbank market, the narrower the bid-ask spread. Liquidity depends on:

- The currency pair involved
- The time of day
- Market volatility

The size of the transaction: Generally speaking, the larger the transaction, the wider the spread that a dealer will quote to the client.

The relationship between the dealer and the client: Dealers may quote narrower bid-ask spreads to preferred clients based on prospective or ongoing business relationships.

Arbitrage Constraints on Spot Exchange Rate Quotes

The bid-ask quotes provided by a dealer in the interbank market must adhere to two arbitrage constraints:

1. The bid quoted by a dealer in the interbank market cannot be higher than the current interbank offer, and the ask offered by a dealer cannot be lower than the current interbank bid.
2. The cross rate bid quoted by a dealer cannot be higher than the implied cross rate ask available in the interbank market, and the cross rate ask quoted by a dealer cannot be lower than the implied cross rate bid available in the interbank market.

Forward Exchange Rates

Forward exchange rates (F) are quotes for transactions that are contracted (agreed upon) today, but settled at a pre-specified date in the **future** (settlement occurs after a period longer than the two days for spot transactions). Forward exchange rates (just like spot exchange rates) are also quoted in terms of bid and ask prices.

Forward exchange rates are calculated in a manner that ensures that traders are not able to earn arbitrage profits (a condition known as **covered interest rate parity**).

$$F_{FC/DC} = S_{FC/DC} \times \frac{(1+i_{FC})}{(1+i_{DC})}$$

$$F_{PC/BC} = S_{PC/BC} \times \frac{(1+i_{PC})}{(1+i_{BC})}$$

Currencies Trading at a Forward Premium/Discount

- If the forward exchange rate is *higher* than the spot exchange rate, the **base currency** is trading at a **forward premium**. At the same time, the price currency would be trading at a **forward discount**.
- The forward discount/premium equals the difference between the forward exchange rate and the spot exchange rate.

$$F_{FC/DC} - S_{FC/DC} = S_{FC/DC}\left(\frac{(i_{FC}-i_{DC})\times \text{Actual}/360}{1+(i_{DC}\times \text{Actual}/360)}\right)$$

$$F_{PC/BC} - S_{PC/BC} = S_{PC/BC}\left(\frac{(i_{PC}-i_{BC})\times \text{Actual}/360}{1+(i_{BC}\times \text{Actual}/360)}\right)$$

In professional FX markets, forward exchange rates are quoted in terms of points (pips), which simply represent the difference between the forward rate and the spot rate (forward premium or discount). These points (pips) are scaled so that they can be related to the last digit in the spot quote (usually the fourth decimal place).

Factors Affecting the Bid-Ask Spread in Forward Exchange Rate Quotes

In addition to the factors that affect spreads in the spot market, spreads in the forward market are influenced by the term of maturity of the contract. Generally speaking, spreads tend to widen with longer terms. This is due to:

- Lower liquidity of longer term contracts.
- Greater credit risk in longer term contracts.
- Greater interest rate risk in forward contracts. Forward rates are based on interest rate differentials. Longer maturities result in greater duration or higher sensitivity to changes in interest rates.

Steps Involved in Marking-to-Market a Position on a Currency Forward

- Create an equal offsetting forward position to the initial forward position.
  - Make sure that the settlement dates and the notional amounts of both the contracts are the same.
- Determine the all-in forward rate for the offsetting forward contract.
  - If the base currency in the exchange rate quote should be sold (purchased) in the offsetting contract, use the bid (ask) side of the quote.
- Calculate the profit/loss on the net position as of the settlement date.
  - If the currency that the investor was long on in the initial forward contract has appreciated (depreciated), there will be a profit (loss).
  - If the currency that the investor was short on in the initial forward contract has appreciated (depreciated), there will be a loss (profit).
- Calculate the present value (as of the date of initiation of the offsetting contract) of the profit/loss.
  - Remember to use the appropriate LIBOR rate and to unannualize it (if necessary).

INTERNATIONAL PARITY RELATIONS

Covered Interest Rate Parity

Covered interest rate parity describes a no-arbitrage condition where the **covered** or **currency-hedged** interest rate differential between two currencies equals zero. What this means is that there is a no-arbitrage relationship among risk-free interest rates and spot and forward exchange rates.

$$\text{Covered interest rate parity: } F_{PC/BC} = S_{PC/BC} \times \frac{1 + (i_{PC} \times \text{Actual}/360)}{1 + (i_{BC} \times \text{Actual}/360)}$$

The forward premium (discount) on the base currency can be expressed as a percentage as:

$$\text{Forward premium (discount) as a \%} = \frac{F_{PC/BC} - S_{PC/BC}}{S_{PC/BC}}$$

The forward premium (discount) on the base currency can be estimated as:

$$\text{Forward premium (discount) as a \%} \approx F_{PC/BC} - S_{PC/BC} \approx i_{PC} - i_{BC}$$

- If the risk-free rate on one currency is *greater* than the risk-free rate on another currency, the currency with the higher risk-free rate will trade at a forward *discount* relative to the other currency, such that the benefit of the higher interest rate will be offset by a decline in the value of the currency.

Generally speaking, covered interest rate differentials tend to be close to zero under normal market conditions, which indicates that covered interest parity tends to hold.

Uncovered Interest Rate Parity

Uncovered interest rate parity states that the **expected return** on an **uncovered** or **unhedged** foreign currency investment should equal the return on a comparable domestic currency investment.

$$(1 + i_{DC}) = \frac{(1 + i_{FC}) \times S_{FC/DC}}{S^e_{FC/DC}}$$

The above equality can be used to derive the formula for the expected future spot exchange rate:

$$S^e_{FC/DC} = S_{FC/DC} \times \frac{(1 + i_{FC})}{(1 + i_{DC})}$$

The expected percentage change in the spot exchange rate can be calculated as:

$$\text{Expected \% change in spot exchange rate} = \%\Delta S^e_{PC/BC} = \frac{S^e_{PC/BC} - S_{PC/BC}}{S_{PC/BC}}$$

The expected percentage change in the spot exchange rate can be estimated as:

$$\text{Expected \% change in spot exchange rate} \approx \%\Delta S^e_{PC/BC} \approx i_{PC} - i_{BC}$$

Covered versus Uncovered Interest Rate Parity

- In **covered interest rate parity**, we consider the **hedged** (against all currency risk) return on the foreign risk-free rate.
    - The investor locks in the **forward exchange rate** today so she is not exposed to currency risk.
    - If covered interest rate parity holds, the **forward premium/discount** offsets the yield differential.
- In **uncovered interest rate parity**, we consider the **unhedged** (against currency risk) return on the foreign risk-free rate.
    - The investor leaves his foreign exchange position uncovered (unhedged) and expects to convert foreign currency holdings back into her domestic currency at the **expected future spot rate**.
    - If uncovered interest rate parity holds, the **expected appreciation/ depreciation** of the currency offsets the yield differential.

Important:

- Note that under uncovered interest rate parity, the direction of the predicted change in spot rates is counterintuitive. All other factors constant, an increase in interest rates would be expected to lead to an appreciation of the currency, but uncovered interest rate parity implies that the opposite would be the case.
- Uncovered interest rate parity asserts that the **expected return** on the unhedged foreign investment is the same as the return on the domestic investment. However, the **distribution of possible return outcomes** is different. Due to the uncertainty associated with the future spot exchange rate, uncovered interest rate parity is often violated as investors (who are generally not risk-neutral) demand a risk premium for accepting the exchange rate risk inherent in leaving their positions unhedged (uncovered). As a result, future spot exchange rates typically do not equal the forward exchange rate. Forward rates (that are based purely on interest rate differentials to preclude covered interest arbitrage) are therefore, poor (or biased) predictors of future spot exchange rates.

Empirical evidence suggests that:

- Uncovered interest rate parity does not hold over the short and medium terms, but works better over the long-term. Over the short and medium terms, interest rate differentials do not explain changes in exchange rates, so forward rates (that are computed based on interest rate differentials) tend to be poor predictors of future exchange rates.
- Current spot exchange rates are also not good predictors of future spot exchange rates because of the high volatility in exchange rate movements. This suggests that exchange rates do not follow a random walk.

Forward Rate Parity

If both covered and uncovered interest rate parity hold, the forward premium/discount will equal the expected change in the spot exchange rate (they both will approximately equal the interest rate differential). As a result, the forward rate with also equal the expected spot exchange rate. This condition, where the forward rate equals the expected spot rate is known as **forward rate parity.**

$$F_{PC/BC} - S_{PC/BC} = S_{PC/BC}^e - S_{PC/BC} \simeq i_{PC} - i_{BC} \rightarrow F_{PC/BC} = S_{PC/BC}^e$$

In this condition, the forward rate is an **unbiased** forecast of the future spot exchange rate.

Purchasing Power Parity (PPP)

Purchasing power parity (PPP) is based on the **law of one price**, which states that identical goods should trade at exactly the same price across countries when valued in terms of a common currency.

According to the law of one price, a relative increase (decrease) in prices in one country will result in depreciation (appreciation) of its currency so exchange rate-adjusted prices are constant across countries.

Absolute Purchasing Power Parity (Absolute PPP)

Absolute PPP states that the broad or general price level (GPL) in a country should equal the currency-adjusted general price level in the other country:

$$\text{Absolute PPP: } GPL_{FC} = GPL_{DC} \times S_{FC/DC}$$
$$\text{Absolute PPP: } GPL_{PC} = GPL_{BC} \times S_{PC/BC}$$

Note that absolute PPP assumes that all goods are tradable and that prices indices (used to determine the GPL) in both countries include the same goods and services with identical weights.

$$\text{Absolute PPP: } S_{FC/DC} = GPL_{FC} / GPL_{DC}$$
$$\text{Absolute PPP: } S_{PC/BC} = GPL_{PC} / GPL_{BC}$$

Absolute PPP asserts that the equilibrium exchange rate between two countries is determined by the ratio of their respective national price levels. However, since (1) product-mixes and consumption baskets differ across countries and (2) there are transaction costs involved in international trade as well as trade restrictions, generally speaking, absolute PPP does not hold.

Relative Purchasing Power Parity (Relative PPP)

Instead of assuming that there are no transaction costs and other trade impediments (as is the case with absolute PPP), relative PPP merely assumes that these are constant over time. Relative PPP claims that **changes** in exchange rates are linked to relative **changes** in national price levels, even if the relation between exchange rate *levels* and price *levels* does not hold.

$$\text{Relative PPP: } E(S_{FC/DC}^{T}) = S_{FC/DC}^{0} \left(\frac{1 + \pi_{FC}}{1 + \pi_{DC}} \right)^{T}$$

According to relative PPP, changes in the spot exchange rate can be approximated as:

$$\text{Relative PPP: } \%\Delta S_{FC/DC} \approx \pi_{FC} - \pi_{DC}$$
$$\text{Relative PPP: } \%\Delta S_{PC/BC} \approx \pi_{PC} - \pi_{BC}$$

Relative PPP suggests that the percentage change in spot exchange rate ($\%\Delta S_{FC/DC}$) will be entirely determined by the difference between foreign and domestic inflation. In order to keep relative purchase power constant across countries, currencies of countries with higher (lower) rates of inflation should see their currencies depreciate (appreciate).

Ex Ante Version of PPP

The ex ante version of the PPP is based on relative PPP. While relative PPP asserts that *actual* changes in the exchange rate are driven by *actual* relative changes in inflation, ex ante PPP asserts that *expected* changes in spot exchange rates are entirely driven by *expected* differences in national inflation rates.

$$\text{Ex ante PPP: } \%\Delta S_{FC/DC}^{e} \approx \pi_{FC}^{e} - \pi_{DC}^{e}$$
$$\text{Ex ante PPP: } \%\Delta S_{PC/BC}^{e} \approx \pi_{PC}^{e} - \pi_{BC}^{e}$$

According to ex ante PPP, countries that are expected to see persistently high (low) inflation rates should expect to see their currencies depreciate (appreciate) over time.

The Fisher Effect

The **Fisher effect** asserts that the nominal interest rate (i) in a country equals the sum of the real interest rate in that country (r) and the expected inflation rate (π^e).

$$\text{Fisher Effect: } i = r + \pi^e$$

Real Interest Rate Parity and the International Fisher Effect

- **Real interest rate parity** asserts that real interest rates will converge to the same level across different countries. It assumes that both (1) uncovered interest rate parity and (2) ex ante PPP hold.
- The **international Fisher effect** asserts that if the real yield spread equals zero in all markets, the foreign-domestic nominal yield spread will be determined by the foreign-domestic expected inflation rate differential.

$$\text{International Fisher effect: } (i_{FC} - i_{DC}) = (\pi^e_{FC} - \pi^e_{DC})$$

The Carry Trade

An **FX carry trade** involves taking long positions in high-yield currencies and short positions in low-yield currencies (also known as **funding currencies**).

Studies have shown that carry trades have earned positive excess returns in most (normal) market conditions. During periods of low turbulence, investors do not see much potential for sudden, substantial, adverse exchange rate movements and are relatively confident of earning excess returns through the strategy. However, in relatively turbulent times (during which asset price and/or FX volatility rise significantly) realized returns on long high-yield currency positions have declined dramatically, and funding costs have risen significantly as well.

Returns of carry trades have not followed the normal distribution; instead the returns distribution has been more peaked with fatter tails that are negatively skewed.

- The peaked distribution around the mean indicates that carry trades typically earn small gains (more frequently that would be expected were the returns normally distributed, which is good).
- The negative skew and fat tails indicate that carry trades have resulted in (1) larger losses and (2) more frequent than implied by a normal distribution. This relatively high probability of a large loss is referred to as **crash risk**.

The primary reason for crash risk is that the carry trade is essentially a leveraged trade.

The Impact of Balance of Payments Flows

Balance of payments (BOP) accounts are an accounting record of all monetary transactions between a country and the rest of the world.

Current Account Imbalances and the Determination of Exchange Rates

Generally speaking, persistent current account deficits lead to depreciation of the domestic currency. The following mechanisms explain this relationship:

- The flow supply/demand channel
- The portfolio balance channel
- The debt sustainability channel

Capital Flows and the Determination of Exchange Rates

With greater financial integration of the world's capital markets and increased capital mobility, capital flows are now the dominant force in influencing exchange rates, interest rates and asset price bubbles.

MONETARY AND FISCAL POLICIES

THE MUNDELL-FLEMING MODEL

The Mundell-Fleming model assumes that there is enough of an output gap in the economy to allow changes in output without having a significant impact on price levels and inflation.

Expansionary Monetary Policy

With flexible exchange rates, expansionary monetary policy will lead to depreciation of the domestic currency as low interest rates cause a flight of capital to higher-yielding markets. Over time, the depreciation of the currency will also increase net exports and reinforce the aggregate demand impact (on investment and consumption spending) of expansionary monetary policy.

With fixed exchange rates, since there will be downward pressure on the currency due to the capital flight triggered by the low interest rates, the monetary authority will have to buy its own currency (using its foreign exchange reserves) in the FX market to keep the exchange rate at the desired (fixed) level. As a result, the monetary base will shrink and domestic credit will dry up, offsetting the desired expansionary affect of the monetary stance.

Expansionary Fiscal Policy

With flexible exchange rates, expansionary fiscal policy will lead to appreciation of the domestic currency as high interest rates stimulate capital inflows.

With fixed exchange rates, since there will be upward pressure on the currency due to the capital inflows triggered by the high interest rates, the monetary authority will have to sell its own currency in the FX market to maintain the exchange rate at the desired (fixed) level. The resulting expansion of domestic money supply will reinforce the aggregate demand impact of expansionary fiscal policy.

Impact of Capital Mobility

With high capital mobility:

- A restrictive (expansionary) monetary policy under floating exchange rates will result in appreciation (depreciation) of the domestic currency.
- A restrictive (expansionary) fiscal policy under floating exchange rates will result in depreciation (appreciation) of the domestic currency.
- If monetary and fiscal policies are both restrictive or both expansionary, the overall impact on the exchange rate will be unclear.

With low capital mobility, the impact of monetary and fiscal policy on the exchange rate comes more from trade flows rather than capital flows. Therefore, with low capital mobility:

- A restrictive (expansionary) monetary policy will lower (increase) aggregate demand, resulting in an increase (decrease) in net exports. This will cause the domestic currency to appreciate (depreciate).
- A restrictive (expansionary) fiscal policy will lower (increase) aggregate demand, resulting in an increase (decrease) in net exports. This will cause the domestic currency to appreciate (depreciate).
- If monetary and fiscal stances are not the same (i.e., one is restrictive while the other is expansionary) the overall impact on the exchange rate will be unclear.

MONETARY MODELS OF EXCHANGE RATE DETERMINATION

Monetary models of exchange rate determination assume that output is fixed and monetary policy's primary impact on exchange rates is through the price level and inflation.

The Monetary Approach with Flexible Prices

This approach is based on the quantity theory of money. If purchasing power parity holds, then the increase (decrease) in domestic price levels relative to foreign price levels that results from a relative increase (decrease) in domestic money supply will lead to a proportional decline (increase) in the value of the domestic currency.

The major shortcoming of the monetary approach is that it assumes that PPP always holds.

The Dornbusch Overshooting Model

The Dornbusch overshooting model assumes that prices are relatively inflexible in the short run, but are completely flexible in the long run. As a result the model predicts that:

- In the long run, since prices are completely flexible, an increase in domestic money supply will lead to a proportional increase in domestic prices and result in a depreciation of the domestic currency.
- In the short run, since prices are relatively inflexible, an increase in nominal money supply translates into an increase in real money supply. As real money supply increases, real interest rates fall, resulting in capital outflows and a substantial depreciation of the domestic currency in nominal and real terms. In fact, the domestic

EC

currency would overshoot its long run level, and actually fall to a level lower than predicted by PPP. Eventually, over the long run, as domestic prices and domestic interest rates rise, the nominal exchange rate will recover and approach the level predicted by the conventional monetary approach (in line with PPP) and the real exchange rate will converge towards its long run equilibrium level.

Fiscal Policy and the Determination of Exchange Rates

The **portfolio balance approach** focuses on the long-term exchange rate implications of sustained fiscal imbalances. It asserts that if a particular economy has persistent budget deficits, its persistent demand for financing would eventually lead to (1) investors demanding a higher risk premium to invest in its bonds and (2) domestic currency depreciation.

If the market believes that debt levels are unsustainable, the government may feel pressured into taking one of the following courses of action:

- Monetize the debt
- Reverse the fiscal stance

EXCHANGE RATE MANAGEMENT: INTERVENTION AND CONTROLS

Surges in capital flows can arise due to "pull" and "push" factors.

Pull factors represent a favorable set of developments in the **domestic economy** that attract capital from foreign countries. On the other hand, push factors represent a favorable set of factors in **foreign economies** that drive capital flows abroad.

Objectives of Central Bank Intervention and Capital Controls

Given the possible negative consequences that their economies would have to bear if there were an abrupt reversal of capital inflows, emerging market policy makers can resort to intervention in the FX market and/or capital controls to achieve the following objectives:

- Sell their currencies in the foreign exchange market to prevent them from appreciating too strongly in the wake of surges in capital inflows.
- Limit excessive capital inflows.
- Enable the monetary authority to pursue independent monetary policy without having to worry about the repercussions of changes in policy rates on capital flows (and the exchange rate).

In the past, capital controls were frowned upon as a policy tool for curbing undesired surges in capital inflows because it was believed that (1) such controls tended to generate distortions in global trade and finance, and eventually market participants would find ways to circumvent the controls, and (2) capital controls imposed by one country could deflect capital flows to other countries, which could complicate monetary and exchange rate policies in those economies. However, emerging market policy makers have learned from (painful) experiences that capital controls may be needed to prevent exchange rates from overshooting, asset bubbles from forming, and future financial conditions from deteriorating.

Evidence on the Effectiveness of Central Bank Intervention

- In the case of **developed countries**, studies have shown that the effect of central bank intervention in the FX market on the level and path of their exchange rates is insignificant.
- In the case of **emerging market currencies**, studies have shown that the effect of central bank intervention in the FX market is relatively more significant but still mixed overall.
  - Intervention has reduced the volatility of EM exchange rates.
  - Intervention has had limited (but more than in the case of developed countries) influence on the level and path taken by exchanges rates.

Potential Early Warning Signs of a Currency Crisis

1. Prior to a currency crisis, the capital markets have been liberalized to allow the free flow of capital.
2. There are large inflows of foreign capital (relative to GDP) in the period leading up to a crisis, with short-term funding denominated in a foreign currency being particularly problematic.
3. Currency crises are often preceded by (and often coincide with) banking crises.
4. Countries with fixed or partially fixed exchange rates are more susceptible to currency crises than countries with floating exchange rates.
5. Foreign exchange reserves tend to decline drastically in the lead-up to a crisis.
6. In the period leading up to a crisis, the currency has risen substantially relative to its historical mean.
7. There is some deterioration in the terms of trade in the lead-up to a crisis.
8. Broad money growth in nominal and real terms rises sharply in the two-year period leading up to a crisis.
9. Inflation tends to be relatively high in the pre-crisis period relative to tranquil periods.

EC

ECONOMIC GROWTH AND THE INVESTMENT DECISION
Cross-Reference to CFA Institute Assigned Reading #12

Preconditions from Economic Growth

- Savings and investment
- Financial markets and intermediaries
- Political stability, rule of law, and property rights
- Education and health care systems
- Tax and regulatory systems
- Free trade and unrestricted capital flows

Why Potential GDP Matters to Investors?

One of the primary factors that influence equity market performance is the anticipated growth in aggregate corporate earnings. Growth in potential GDP matters to investors because it places a limit on how fast the economy (and therefore, aggregate corporate earnings) can grow.

Over the short term, growth in stock market prices is a function of (1) the percentage change in GDP, (2) the percentage change in the share of earnings in GDP, and (3) the percentage change in the market price-earnings multiple. However, over the long-term, stock market performance is primarily driven by the growth rate of GDP.

Aside from its impact on equity values, growth in potential GDP is also relevant for fixed income investors through its influence on nominal and real interest rates.

The Cobb-Douglas Production Function

$$Y = AK^aL^{1-a}$$

The Cobb-Douglas production function exhibits the following two important properties:

- Constant returns to scale: This means that if quantities of all inputs are increased by the same percentage, then output would also increase by that same percentage.
- Diminishing marginal productivity of factor inputs: This implies that if we keep on increasing quantities of one of these inputs while holding quantities of the other input constant, the additional output produced will keep declining.

Capital Deepening versus Technological Progress

Growth in output per worker can come from two sources:

Capital deepening: Capital deepening refers to an increase in the capital-labor ratio and is reflected in a movement along the same per-capita production function. The increase in output per worker from increasing the capital-labor ratio becomes relatively insignificant once the capital-labor ratio reaches a relatively high level. This is because the marginal product of capital declines as more capital is added to fixed quantities of labor.

Technological progress: While capital deepening results in a movement along the same per-capita production function, improvements in TFP cause the entire production function to shift upwards. Improvements in technology enable the economy to produce a higher output per worker for a given level of capital per worker. Technological progress can therefore result in a permanent increase in output per worker despite the diminishing marginal productivity of capital.

Developed markets typically have high capital-labor ratios, while developing countries typically have low capital-labor ratios. Therefore:

- Developed countries have relatively little to gain from capital deepening and must rely on technological progress for growth in potential GDP.
- Developing countries on the other hand, have the potential to grow from both capital deepening and technological progress.

Growth Accounting

Solow's growth accounting equation is used to analyze the performance of economies. It is basically the production function written in the form of growth rates:

$$\Delta Y/Y = \Delta A/A + \alpha \Delta K/K + (1-\alpha)\Delta L/L$$

Uses of the Growth Accounting Equation

- Estimating the contribution of technological progress to economic growth.
- Empirically measure the sources of growth in an economy.
- Measure potential GDP.

Note that potential GDP may also be measured using the **labor productivity growth accounting equation**, which models potential GDP as a function of (1) labor input quantities and (2) labor productivity.

Growth rate in potential GDP = Long-term growth rate of labor force
+ Long-term growth rate in labor productivity

Natural Resources

- Renewable resources are those that are replenished, such as forests.
- Non-renewable resources are those that are limited in supply and are depleted once they are consumed, such as oil and coal.

Ownership and *production* of natural resources are not necessary for an economy to grow; it is more important for a country to be able to *access* natural resources (e.g., via trade).

Note that the presence of natural resources may sometimes even restrain economic growth, resulting in a "resource curse."

Labor Supply

The potential quantity of labor input in the economy is measured in terms of the total number of hours available for work, which can be estimated as:

> Total number of hours available for work = Labor force × Average hours worked per worker

The **labor force** is defined as the working age population (16–64 years old) that is either (1) employed or (2) available for work, but not working (unemployed).

Factors Affecting Labor Supply

- Population growth
- Labor force participation
- Net migration
- Average hours worked

Labor Quality: Human Capital

Human capital refers to the accumulated knowledge and skills that workers acquire from education, training, and life experience. Better-educated and more skilled workers are generally more productive and more adaptable to changes in technology and to other shifts in market demand and supply.

Capital: ICT and Non-ICT

Capital spending can be separated into two categories:

- **ICT investment** is a measure of the impact of the information technology (IT) sector on economic growth. Growth in the IT sector has led to **network externalities** (i.e., it has enabled people to interconnect and work more productively), which has led to increasing TFP and economic growth.
- **Non-ICT investment** results in capital deepening, and therefore has more of a temporary impact on economic growth.

Generally speaking, there is a high positive correlation between investment in physical capital and GDP growth.

- In the short run, this can be explained by capital deepening.
- Over the long run, this can be explained by a relatively higher portion of capital spending being allocated to ICT investment (which results in improving TFP).

Technology

Improvements in technology result in an upward shift in the production function, and allow economies to overcome limits on growth imposed by diminishing marginal returns to capital. Technological change may be brought about through investment in human capital, and/or new machinery, equipment, and software (especially ICT goods).

- Developed countries tend to spend a higher percentage of GDP on R&D as they primarily rely on innovation and the development of new products and production methods for growth.
- Developing countries tend to spend less on R&D as they (1) can acquire new technology through imitation, and (2) can foster economic growth in the short run through capital deepening.

Public Infrastructure

Investment in public infrastructure such as roads, bridges, municipal water, and dams improves the productivity of private investment.

THEORIES OF GROWTH

Classical Model (Malthusian Model)

This model asserts that growth in real GDP per capita is **temporary**. GDP per capita only grows until it rises above the subsistence level. Once it rises above the subsistence level, real GDP per capita falls due to a population explosion.

This theory predicts that standards of living remain constant over time even with technological progress as there is no growth in per capita output. In the long run, new technologies result in a larger population, but not a richer population.

Neoclassical Model (Solow's Model)

This model is based on the Cobb-Douglas production function. Both labor and capital are variable factors of production and both suffer from diminishing marginal productivity. The neoclassical model seeks to find the economy's equilibrium position, which it asserts occurs when the economy grows at the steady state rate of growth. In this state:

- The output-capital (Y/K) ratio is constant. This ratio is denoted by ψ and calculated as:

$$\frac{Y}{K} = \left(\frac{1}{s}\right)\left[\left(\frac{q}{(1-\alpha)}\right) + \delta + n\right] \equiv \psi$$

- Capital per worker (k = K/L), and output per worker (y = Y/L) grow at the same rate, which is given by:
  - Growth rate in k and y: $\theta/(1-\alpha)$
- Growth is total output (Y) equals the sum of (1) the growth rate in output per worker, $\theta/(1-\alpha)$, and (2) growth in labor supply, n.
  - Growth rate in output (Y) = $\theta/(1-\alpha) + n$
  - $n = \Delta L/L$ = Growth in labor supply
- The marginal product of capital is also constant, and equals the real interest rate:
  - $MP_K = \alpha Y/K = r$

Important takeaways:

- Even though the capital-labor ratio (k = K/L) is increasing [at the rate $\theta/(1-\alpha)$] in the steady state, which indicates that capital deepening is occurring in the economy, the marginal product of capital remains constant (at $MP_K = \alpha Y/K = r$). This can be explained by growth in TFP offsetting the impact of diminishing marginal returns to capital.
- Further, capital deepening has no effect on the growth rate of the economy in the steady state. The economy continues to grow at a constant rate of $\theta/(1-\alpha) + n$.

Impact of Changes in Different Variables on the Steady State

Saving rate (s): An increase in the saving rate increases the *levels* of k and y in the new steady state, but it has no impact on the *growth rates* of k and y. They continue to grow at their steady state rates of growth $\theta/(1-\alpha)$ while total output (Y) continues to grow at $\theta/(1-\alpha)+n$.

Labor force growth (n): An increase in labor force growth results in a lower capital-labor ratio and a lower output per worker at the new steady state. There is no impact on the *growth rates* of k and y. They continue to grow at their steady state rates of growth $\theta/(1-\alpha)$, while total output (Y) continues to grow at $\theta/(1-\alpha)+n$.

Depreciation rate (d): An increase in depreciation has the same impact as an increase in labor force growth. The new steady state equilibrium has a lower capital-labor ratio and lower output per worker. There is no impact on the *growth rates* of k and y. They continue to grow at their steady state rates of growth $\theta/(1-\alpha)$, while total output (Y) continues to grow at $\theta/(1-\alpha)+n$.

Growth in TFP (q): An increase in the growth rate of TFP results in a decline in the capital-labor ratio and output per worker. However, output per worker and capital per worker will grow faster going forward.

To summarize:

- Changes in (1) the savings rate, (2) labor force growth rate and/or (3) depreciation rate impact the level of output per worker but do not have a long-term impact on the growth rate of output per worker.
- Only a change in TFP has a permanent impact on the growth rate of output per worker.

ENDOGENOUS GROWTH THEORY

Endogenous growth theory focuses on explaining technological progress (which has proven to be the primary determinant of economic growth in the long run) as opposed to neoclassical growth theory (which treats technological progress as an exogenous variable).

Endogenous theory broadens the definition of capital to include human and knowledge capital and R&D. Investment in physical capital increases output, while investment in R&D results in ideas. The theory asserts that not only do these ideas have a positive impact on the company that comes up with them, but that they have positive externalities and spillover effects as they can be copied by competitors as well. Overall, R&D results in increasing returns to scale across the entire economy as companies benefit from the private spending of their competitors. Therefore, the economy does not reach a steady growth rate (as predicted by the neoclassical model). Instead, saving and investment can generate self-sustaining growth at a permanently higher rate as the positive externalities associated with R&D prevent diminishing marginal returns to capital from setting in. The production function in the endogenous growth model is an upward-sloping straight line given by:

$$y_e = f(k_e) = ck_e$$

Output per worker (y_e) is proportional to the stock of capital per worker (k_e), while c is the constant marginal product of capital.

Takeaways from Endogenous Growth Theory

- Since there are no diminishing marginal returns to capital from the perspective of the economy as a whole, an increase in the savings rate would permanently increase the rate of economic growth.
- Since R&D entails positive externalities, there may be a market failure in the sense that there would be underproduction of R&D from the societal perspective. Therefore, there may be a strong case for government intervention to increase investment in capital in the economy.
- Due to the constant (or sometimes even increasing) returns associated with investment in knowledge capital and R&D, developed countries can continue to grow faster than developing countries. As a result, there is no reason for incomes to converge over time (as predicted by the neoclassical model).

The Convergence Debate

Convergence means that countries with low per capita incomes should grow at a faster rate than countries with high per capita incomes, such that over time, per capital income differences will be eliminated.

- Absolute convergence means that regardless of their particular characteristics, output per capita in developing countries will eventually reach the level of developed countries.
- Conditional convergence means that convergence in output per capita is dependent (or conditional) upon countries having the same savings rates, population growth rates and production functions.

Studies have shown that some of the poorer countries are in fact diverging rather than converging towards the income levels of developed countries. This phenomenon is explained by **club convergence**. Countries with similar structural characteristics (e.g., production technologies, preferences, government policies, etc.) form a club. Within the club, countries with the lowest per capita incomes grow at the fastest rates, while countries outside the club fall further behind. Note that membership of the club is based on the economy exhibiting certain desirable structural characteristics; not on income levels. Poor countries can join the club by making appropriate institutional changes; otherwise they risk falling into a non-convergence trap.

Convergence between developing and developed countries can occur from two sources:

- Capital deepening: Developing countries tend to operate at relatively low capital-labor ratios so the marginal productivity of capital in those countries is still relatively high. On the other hand, developed countries tend to operate at high capital-labor ratios, where marginal productivity of capital is relatively low. Therefore, developing countries can catch up to their developed peers simply through capital accumulation.
- By importing technologies from developed countries, developing countries can achieve faster economic growth and converge to the income levels of advanced economies.

Growth in an Open Economy

Opening up the economy to trade and financial flows has the following advantages:

- Investment is not constrained by domestic savings as the country can finance investments with foreign savings.
- Productivity improves as the country can focus on industries in which it has a comparative advantage.
- Domestic producers can exploit economies of scale as they attain access to larger overseas markets.
- TFP improves as countries are able to import latest technologies.
- Faced with competition from foreign producers, domestic companies strive to produce better products and improve productivity.

Convergence (as predicted by the neoclassical model) should occur more quickly if there is free trade and no restrictions on capital flows.

ECONOMICS OF REGULATION
Cross-Reference to CFA Institute Assigned Reading #13

Classifications of Regulations

- Statutes: Laws enacted by legislative bodies.
- Administrative regulations: Rules issued by government agencies and other regulators.
- Judicial law: Interpretations of courts.

Classifications of Regulators

Regulations can come from **government agencies** or **independent regulators**. Independent regulators get their regulatory authority through recognition from a government body or agency. Note that independent regulators do not receive government funding so they are politically independent.

Independent regulators include **self-regulatory organizations (SROs)**. These are private entities that represent their members and regulate them as well. While they may be immune from political pressure, SROs are subject to pressure from their members which can give rise to conflicts of interest. Not all SROs are independent regulators however. Those that are granted authority by government bodies obviously serve as independent regulators, but there are others that get their regulating authority from their members. These members agree to comply with the SROs rules and standards and to enforce them. Note that this authority does not have the force of law.

Reasons for Reliance on Self-Regulation

- Increases overall level of regulatory resources.
- Uses knowledge and expertise of industry professionals.
- Enables the regulator to focus on other priorities while relying on the SRO for front line supervision of members and markets.

Reasons for Decreased Reliance on Self-Regulation

- Privatization of securities exchanges.
- Intense competition.
- Uncertainty regarding effectiveness of self-regulation.
- Internationalization.
- Strengthening of government regulators.
- Trend toward consolidation of financial regulators.
- "Cooperative regulation."
- Pressure to increase efficiency and lower costs.

Economic Rationale for Regulatory Intervention

Regulatory intervention becomes essential due to the presence of **informational frictions** and **externalities**.

Informational frictions result in the following issues:

- **Adverse selection**, where some market participants have access to information that is unavailable to others.
- **Moral hazard**, where one party will have a tendency to take risks because the costs that could incur will not be felt by the party taking the risk.

Externalities in the context of regulation refer to the provision of public goods. Public goods give rise to the free-rider problem, as consumption of a public good by a person does not preclude another person from consuming it.

Regulatory Interdependencies

The **regulatory capture theory** argues that regulation can often actually advance the interests of the regulated.

Regulatory differences across jurisdictions can result in shift in location and the behavior of entities due to regulatory competition and regulatory arbitrage.

- **Regulatory competition** refers to competition between regulators to provide a regulatory environment designed to attract certain entities.
- **Regulatory arbitrage** refers to practices whereby firms capitalize on loopholes in regulatory systems in order to circumvent unfavorable regulation. It includes cases where companies shop around for locations that allow certain behavior rather than changing their own behavior.

Regulatory Tools

Price mechanisms (taxes and subsidies): Taxes are imposed to discourage certain behaviors (e.g., taxes on cigarettes to deter smoking), while subsidies are imposed to encourage certain behavior (e.g., subsidies for farmers on certain crops to increase domestic production).

Regulatory mandates and restrictions on behaviors: Governments can mandate certain activities (e.g., minimum capital requirements for banks) or restrict certain activities (e.g., insider trading).

Provision of public goods and financing for private projects: Governments can provide public goods (e.g., national defense, transportation infrastructure) or provide loans to individuals and businesses for specific activities that the government wants to promote.

Regulation of Commerce

- Government regulation plays an important role in various aspects of business such as protecting workers' and employers' rights and responsibilities, and consumer health and safety.
- Governments set the legal standards for the recognition and protection of different types of intellectual property.
- Other examples of government regulations covering commerce include company laws, tax laws, bankruptcy laws and banking laws.
- Governments take the steps they deem necessary to support and protect domestic business interests against unfair competition (e.g., by imposing anti-dumping duties).

Regulation of Financial Markets

Regulation of Securities Markets

Securities regulation is generally aimed at protecting investors, creating confidence in markets, and enhancing capital formation. Various aspects of securities regulation include:

- Securities registration requirements to develop investor confidence.
- Regulations geared towards mitigating the principal-agent problem.
- Protecting the interests of retail investors.

Regulation of Financial Institutions

Regulation of financial institutions focuses on protecting consumers and investors, ensuring the safety and soundness of financial institutions, promoting the smooth operation of the payments system, and maintaining availability to credit. Financial regulation also aims to tackle concerns relating to the overall economy such as price stability, unemployment, and economic growth.

Prudential supervision refers to regulation and monitoring of the safety and soundness of financial institutions for promoting financial stability, reducing system-wide risks, and protecting customers of financial institutions. This aspect of financial regulation is critical because a failure of a financial institution can have far-reaching consequences on the overall economy.

The financial crisis of 2008 highlighted two negative externalities that have recently been tackled by financial regulation. These are:

- Systematic risk: **The risk of failure of the financial system.**
- Financial contagion: **A situation in which financial shocks spread from their place of origin to other countries i.e., when faltering economies affect healthier ones.**

Increased globalization has led to increased concerns about contagion and regulatory competition.

Antitrust Risk

- In evaluating mergers and acquisitions regulators evaluate whether the merger will lead to monopolization of the market.
- Competition and anti-trust laws also prohibit other types of anticompetitive behavior. Examples of such behavior include exclusive dealings and refusals to deal, price discrimination, and predatory pricing.
- Large companies that operate in multiple markets need to simultaneously satisfy regulators from several countries when faced with antitrust issues.

EC

Costs of Regulation

- **Regulatory burden** refers to the costs of regulation for the regulated entity. It can be viewed as the private costs of regulation or government burden.
- **Net regulatory burden** results from subtracting private benefits of regulation from private costs.

When conducting cost-benefit analysis, analysts should consider direct and indirect costs of regulation. Further, there may be "unintended" costs associated with regulations. **Sunset provisions** require regulators to conduct a new cost-benefit analysis before the regulation is renewed.

STUDY SESSION 5: FINANCIAL REPORTING AND ANALYSIS (1)

INTERCORPORATE INVESTMENTS
Cross-Reference to CFA Institute Assigned Reading #14

Table 1: Summary of Accounting Treatment for Investments

	In Financial Assets	In Associates	Business Combinations	In Joint Ventures
Influence	Not significant	Significant	Controlling	Shared Control
Typical percentage interest	Usually < 20%	Usually 20%–50%	Usually > 50%	Varies
Current Financial Reporting Treatment (prior to IFRS 9 taking effect)	Classified as • Held-to-maturity • Available-for-sale • Fair value through profit or loss (held for trading or designated as fair value). • Loans and receivables.	Equity method	Consolidation	IFRS: Equity method or proportionate consolidation.
New Financial Reporting Treatment (post IFRS 9 taking effect)	Classified as • Fair value through profit or loss • Fair value through other comprehensive income. • Amortized cost	Equity method	Consolidation	IFRS: Equity method

INVESTMENTS IN FINANCIAL ASSETS: STANDARD IAS 39 (Prior to the Issuance of IFRS 9)

This standard can be applied until IFRS 9 takes effect and is no longer optional.

The accounting treatment of investments in financial assets is similar under IFRS and U.S. GAAP.

Under **IFRS**, financial assets may be classified as:

1. Held-to-maturity.
2. Available-for-sale.
3. Fair value through profit or loss; which includes
   • Held-for-trading, and
   • Designated as fair value through profit or loss.
4. Loans and receivables.

Held-to-Maturity (HTM) Investments

HTM investments are investments in financial assets with fixed or determinable payments and fixed maturities (debt securities) that the investor has a positive intent and ability to hold till maturity. HTM investments cannot be reclassified or sold prior to maturity except in unusual circumstances. Reclassification/sale of HTM investments can result in the investor being precluded from classifying investments under the HTM category going forward.

The initial and subsequent treatment of HTM securities is essentially the same under **IFRS** and **U.S. GAAP**. At each reporting date HTM securities are reported at **amortized cost** using the **effective interest method** (unless objective evidence of impairment exists).

- Interest income and realized gains/losses are recognized in the income statement.
- Unrealized gains/losses (due to changes in fair value) are ignored.

Fair Value through Profit or Loss (IFRS)

Under IFRS, investments classified as fair value through profit or loss include (1) held for trading (HFT) investments and (2) investments designated at fair value. U.S. GAAP is similar. The accounting treatment of both is similar:

- Investments are initially recognized at fair value.
- At each subsequent reporting date, investments are remeasured at fair value.
- Unrealized gains/losses, realized gains/losses, interest income and dividend income are all reported in profit or loss.

Available-for-Sale (AFS) Investments

AFS investments are debt and equity securities that are not classified as held-to-maturity or at fair value through profit or loss.

Under **IFRS**:

- AFS investments are initially recognized at fair value, and remeasured at each reporting date to reflect fair value.
- All unrealized gains/losses (except for gains/losses on AFS **debt** securities arising from exchange rate movements) are recognized (net of taxes) in equity under other comprehensive income. When they are sold, these (now realized) gains/losses are reversed out of other comprehensive income and reported in profit or loss as a reclassification adjustment.
- Unrealized gains/losses on AFS **debt** securities resulting from exchange rate movements are recognized on the income statement.
- Realized gains/losses, interest income and dividend income are also recognized on the income statement.

The accounting treatment of AFS securities is the same under **U.S. GAAP**, except that **all unrealized gains/losses** (including those on AFS debt securities caused by exchange rate movements) are reported in other comprehensive income.

Loans and Receivables

- IFRS has a **specific** definition for loans and receivables. Items that meet the definition are carried at amortized cost unless they are designated as (1) fair value through profit or loss or (2) available for sale.
- U.S. GAAP relies on **legal** form for the classification of debt securities. Loans and receivables that meet the definition of debt securities are classified as HFT, AFS or HTM, with HFT and AFS securities being measured at fair value.

Reclassification of Investments

Under **IFRS**:

- Reclassification of securities into and out of the "designated at fair value" category is generally prohibited.
- Reclassification out of the "held-for-trading" category is restricted.
- HTM (debt) securities can be reclassified as AFS securities if there is a change in intention or ability to hold the asset until maturity.
    - When HTM securities are reclassified as AFS securities, they are remeasured at fair value and any differences between fair value and carrying amount (amortized cost) are recognized in OCI.
    - Once a company has reclassified HTM securities, it may be prohibited from using the HTM classification for other existing debt securities and new purchases.
- Debt securities initially classified as AFS can be reclassified as HTM securities if there is a change in intention or ability to hold the asset until maturity.
    - When AFS debt securities are reclassified as HTM securities, their fair value at time of reclassification becomes their (new) amortized cost and any unrealized gains/losses previously recognized in OCI are amortized to profit or loss over the security's remaining life using the effective interest method.
    - Differences between the new amortized cost and par (maturity) value are also amortized over the remaining term of the securities using the effective interest method.
- Debt instruments may be reclassified from HFT or AFS to loans and receivables if (1) the definition is met; and (2) the company expects to hold them for the forseeable future.
- An investment classified as AFS may be measured at **cost** if there is no reliable measure of fair value and no evidence of impairment.
    - Note that once a reliable fair value estimate becomes available, the asset must be remeasured at fair value and any changes in value must be recognized in other comprehensive income.

U.S. GAAP generally allows reclassifications of securities between all categories when justified, with fair values being determined at the transfer date. However, if HTM securities are reclassified, the company may be precluded from using the HTM category for other investments.

The treatment of unrealized gains/losses on the transfer date depends on security's initial classification.

- For HFT securities that are being reclassified as AFS securities, any unrealized gains/losses (differences between carrying value and current fair value) have already been recognized in profit and loss.

- When securities are reclassified as HFT securities, any unrealized gains/losses are recognized immediately in profit and loss.
  - When AFS securities are reclassified as HFT, the cumulative amount of unrealized gains/losses previously recognized in other comprehensive income is recognized in profit and loss on the date of transfer.
- When HTM securities are reclassified as AFS, unrealized gains/losses (differences between fair value and amortized cost) at the date of the transfer are reported in other comprehensive income.
- When AFS debt securities are reclassified as HTM, the cumulative amount of unrealized gains/losses that have been recognized in other comprehensive income are amortized over the security's remaining life as an adjustment of yield (interest income) in the same manner as a premium or discount.

Impairments

Under **IFRS**, at the end of each reporting period, all financial assets that are not carried at fair value must be assessed for impairment, and any current impairment must be recognized in profit or loss immediately. Securities classified as fair value through profit or loss are reported at fair value so any impairment losses have already been recognized in profit or loss.

A **debt** security is considered impaired if at least one loss event (which has an impact on its estimated future cash flows that can be reliably estimated) has occurred.

An **equity** security is considered impaired if:

- There has been a substantial and extended decline in the fair value of the security below its cost.
- There have been significant changes in the technology, market, and/or legal environment that have had an adverse impact on the investee, and indicate that the initial cost of the investment may not be recovered.

For (1) HTM (debt) securities; and (2) loans and receivables that have become impaired, the impairment loss is calculated as the difference between the security's carrying value and the present value of its expected future cash flows discounted at the initial effective interest rate.

- The carrying amount of the security is reduced either directly, or indirectly through an allowance account.
- The impairment loss is recognized in profit or loss.
- Reversals of previously recognized impairment losses are allowed.
- A reversal of a previously recognized impairment charge results in an increase in the carrying value of the asset and an increase in net income.

For AFS securities that have become impaired, the cumulative loss recognized in other comprehensive income (as the security is remeasured at fair value at each successive reporting date) is transferred from other comprehensive income to the income statement as a reclassification adjustment.

- Reversal of impairment losses is only allowed for AFS debt securities, not for AFS equity securities.
- The amount of reversal is recognized in profit or loss.

Under **U.S. GAAP**, AFS and HTM securities must be assessed for impairment at each balance sheet date. A security is considered impaired if the decline in its value is "other than temporary."

For debt securities classified as HTM, impairment means that the investor will be unable to collect all amounts owed according to contractual terms at acquisition.

- If the decline in fair value is deemed other than temporary, the cost basis of the securities is written down to their fair value, which then becomes the new cost basis.
- The impairment loss is treated as a realized loss on the income statement.

For AFS debt and equity securities:

- If the decline in fair value is deemed other than temporary, the cost basis of the securities is written down to their fair value, which then becomes the new cost basis.
- The impairment loss is treated as a realized loss on the income statement.
- However, the new cost basis cannot be increased if there is a subsequent increase in fair value (i.e., reversals of impairment losses are not allowed).
- Subsequent increases in fair value (and decreases, of other than temporary) are treated as unrealized gains and included in other comprehensive income.

Investments in Financial Assets: IFRS 9

Both the IASB and the FASB have developed new standards for financial investments.

- The IASB issued the first phase of their project dealing with classification and measurement of financial instruments by including relevant chapters in IFRS 9, Financial Instruments. IFRS 9, which replaces IAS 39, became effective on January 1, 2018.
- The FASB issued ASC 825 in January 2016, with the standard being effective for periods after December 15, 2017. The new ASC has resulted in significant (but not total) convergence with IFRS with respect to financial instruments.

The new standard is based on an approach that considers (1) the contractual characteristic of cash flows, and (2) the management of the financial assets. The terms **available-for-sale** and **held-to-maturity** no longer appear in IFRS 9.

Another key change in IFRS 9, compared with the old standard IAS 39, relates to the approach to provisioning models for financial assets, financial guarantees, loan commitments, and lease receivables.

The criteria to use amortized cost are similar. In order to be measured at amortized cost, financial assets must meet two criteria:

1. **A business model test**: The financial assets are being held to collect contractual cash flows.
2. **A cash flow characteristic test**: The contractual cash flows are solely payments of principal and interest on principal.

FRA

Classification and Measurement of Financial Assets under IAS 9

All financial assets are measured at fair value when initially acquired. Subsequently, financial assets are measured at either fair value or amortized cost.

- Financial assets that meet the preceding two criteria are generally measured at **amortized cost**.
- If the financial asset meets the two criteria but may be sold (a "hold-to-collect and sell" business model), it may be measured at **fair value through other comprehensive income**.
- However, management may choose the **fair value through profit or loss** option to avoid an accounting mismatch.

Debt instruments are measured at amortized cost, fair value through other comprehensive income (FVOCI), or fair value through profit or loss (FVPL), depending upon the business model.

Equity instruments are measured at FVPL or at FVOCI.

- Equity investments held-for-trading must be measured at FVPL.
- Other equity investments can be measured at either FVPL or FVOCI, but the choice is irreversible. If the entity uses the FVOCI option, only the dividend income is recognized in profit or loss. Further, the requirements for reclassifying gains or losses recognized in other comprehensive income are different for debt and equity instruments.

Financial assets that are **derivatives** are measured at **fair value through profit or loss** (except for hedging instruments).

Reclassification of Investments

Under the new standards:

- Reclassification of **equity** instruments is not permitted (the initial classification as FVPL and FVOCI is irrevocable).
- Reclassification of **debt** instruments is permitted only if the objective for holding the assets (business model) has changed in a way that significantly affects operations.
  - When reclassification is deemed appropriate, there is no restatement of prior periods at the reclassification date.
  - If the financial asset is reclassified from amortized cost to FVPL, the asset is measured at fair value with gain or loss recognized in profit or loss.
  - If the financial asset is reclassified from FVPL to amortized cost, the fair value at the reclassification date becomes the carrying amount.

Analysis of Investments in Financial Assets

- Analysis of operating performance should exclude items related to investing activities (e.g., interest income, dividends, realized and unrealized gains/losses).
- Non-operating assets should be excluded from the calculation of return on operating assets.
- Use of market values of financial assets is encouraged when assessing performance ratios.

INVESTMENTS IN ASSOCIATES

Equity Method of Accounting

This method is used when the investor exercises significant influence, but not control over the investee.

- The investment is initially recognized on the investor's **balance sheet** at cost (within a single line item) under non-current assets.
  - The investor's proportionate share of investee earnings increases the carrying amount of the investment, while its proportionate share of losses and dividends decreases the carrying value of the investment.
- The investor's proportionate share of investee earnings is reported within a single line item on its **income statement**.
- If the value of the investment falls to zero (e.g., due to losses), use of the equity method to account for the investment is discontinued.
  - Use of the equity method may only be resumed if the investee subsequently reports profits and the investor's share of profits exceeds the losses not reported by it since abandonment of the equity method.

Excess of Purchase Price over Book Value and Amortization of Excess Purchase Price

- The excess amount is first allocated to specific assets whose fair value exceeds book value.
  - The excess related to inventory is expensed, while the excess related to PP&E is depreciated or amortized over an appropriate period of time.
  - Amounts allocated to land and other assets or liabilities that are not amortized continue to be reported at fair value as of the date of investment.
  - Since these expenses are not reflected in the investee's financials, the investor directly adjusts the carrying amount of the investment on its balance sheet by reducing its share of investee profits on the income statement.
- The remaining amount is treated as goodwill, which is not amortized but reviewed periodically for impairment.

Fair Value Option

Both U.S. GAAP and IFRS (with certain restrictions) now offer investors the option to account for their equity method investments using fair values. When the fair value method is applied:

- Unrealized gains/losses arising from changes in fair value, as well as interest and dividends received are included in the investor's income.
- The investment account on the investor's balance sheet does not reflect the investor's proportionate share in the investee's earnings, dividends, or other distributions.
- The excess of cost over the fair value of the investee's identifiable net assets is not amortized.
- Goodwill is not created.

FRA

Impairment

Under both IFRS and U.S. GAAP, equity method investments should be reviewed periodically for impairment. Since goodwill is included in the carrying amount of the investment (i.e., it is not separately recognized) under the equity method, it is not tested for impairment separately.

- Under IFRS, an impairment loss is recognized if there is objective evidence of a loss event and the recoverable amount of the investment is less than the carrying amount.
  - Recoverable amount is the higher of "value in use" and "net selling price."
- Under U.S. GAAP, an impairment loss is recognized if the fair value of the investment is less than the carrying amount and the decline is deemed to be permanent.
- Impairment results in a decrease in net income and reduces the investment's carrying amount on the balance sheet.
- Both IFRS and U.S. GAAP prohibit reversals of impairment losses.

Transactions with Associates

Profits from transactions between the investor and investee must be deferred until the profit is confirmed through use or sale to a third party.

Upstream sales (investee to investor): The profits on these sales are recognized on the investee's income statement, so a proportionate share of these profits is also included in the investor's income statement. Until these profits are confirmed, the investor must reduce its equity income by the amount of its **proportionate share** in profits from upstream sales. The investor may recognize these profits once they are confirmed.

Downstream sales (investor to investee): Associated profits are recognized on the investor's income statement. The investor's **proportionate share** in unconfirmed profits from sales made to the investee must be eliminated from the investor's equity income.

Analytical Issues

- Is use of the equity method of accounting appropriate given the ownership stake and degree of influence enjoyed by the investor over the investee?
- One-line consolidation results in significant assets and liabilities not being reported on the investor's balance sheet, which can distort debt ratios.
- Margin ratios may be overstated as a proportionate share of investee net income is included on the investor's income statement, but investee sales are not included.
- Earnings may be permanently reinvested. Earnings may not be available to the investor to the full extent of the investor's proportionate share in the investee's earnings.

JOINT VENTURES

A joint venture is a venture undertaken and controlled by two or more parties. IFRS identifies the following characteristics of joint ventures:

- A contractual agreement exists between two or more venturers; and
- The contractual arrangement establishes joint control.

Both **IFRS** and **U.S. GAAP** now require the use of the equity method to account for joint ventures (except under rare circumstances).

BUSINESS COMBINATIONS

- IFRS does not differentiate between business combinations based on the structure of the surviving entity.
- U.S. GAAP categorizes business combinations into the following:
  - Mergers: The acquiring firm absorbs all the assets of the acquired company which ceases to exist. The acquiring firm is the only surviving entity.
  - Acquisitions: Both entities continue to exist, and are connected through a parent-subsidiary relationship.
  - Consolidation: A new entity is formed that absorbs both the companies.

Historically, companies could use the pooling-of-interests method or the purchase method to account for business combinations. However, IFRS and U.S. GAAP now prohibit use of the pooling-of-interests method and require the acquisition method (which has replaced the purchase method).

Pooling of Interests Method (U.S. GAAP) / Uniting of Interests Method (IFRS)

- The assets and liabilities of the two firms are combined using book values.
- Operating results for prior periods are combined and presented as if the companies were always combined.
- Fair values play no role in this method and the actual price paid for an acquisition is not evident on the financial statements.

Acquisition Method for Business Combinations

- All the assets, liabilities, revenues, and expenses of the acquiree are combined with those of the parent.
  - All identifiable tangible and intangible assets and liabilities of the acquired entity are measured at fair value.
  - The acquirer must also recognize any assets and liabilities that the acquiree has not recognized on its financial statements.
- The acquirer must recognize any contingent liability assumed in the acquisition if (1) it is a present obligation that arises from past events, and (2) it can be measured reliably.
- The acquirer must recognize an indemnification asset if the acquiree contractually indemnifies the acquirer for (1) the outcome of a contingency, (2) an uncertainty related to a specific asset or liability of the acquiree, or (3) against losses above a specified amount on a liability arising from a particular contingency.
- If the purchase price is less than the fair value of the subsidiary's net assets, it is referred to as a bargain acquisition. Both IFRS and U.S. GAAP require the difference between the fair value of the acquired net assets and the purchase price to be recognized immediately as a gain in profit or loss.
- Transactions between the acquirer and acquiree are eliminated.
- The acquiree's shareholders' equity accounts are ignored.

Business Combinations with Less than 100 Percent Acquisition

If a parent controls a subsidiary, but owns less than a 100% equity interest in the company, it must also create a non-controlling interest account on the consolidated balance sheet and income statement to reflect the proportionate share in the net assets and net income of the subsidiary that belongs to minority shareholders.

FRA

Measuring Goodwill and Non-Controlling (Minority) Interests

U.S. GAAP requires the use of the full goodwill method, in which goodwill equals the excess of the **total fair value of the subsidiary** over the **fair value of its identifiable net assets**.

IFRS permits both the full goodwill method and the partial goodwill method. Under the partial goodwill method, goodwill equals the excess of the **purchase price** over the **fair value of the parent's proportionate share of the subsidiary's identifiable net assets**.

- If the full goodwill method is used, the non-controlling interest is measured based on its **proportionate share of the subsidiary's fair value**.
- If the partial goodwill method is used, the non-controlling interest is measured based on its **proportionate share of the fair value of the subsidiary's identifiable net assets**.
- The income statement is exactly the same under the full and partial goodwill methods.

Full versus Partial Goodwill Methods

Note that although net income is the same, return on assets and return on equity will be *lower* if the full goodwill method is used because it results in higher assets and higher equity than the partial goodwill method. Further, the value of the subsidiary will change over time due to (1) changes in equity or (2) net income. Therefore, the value of non-controlling interest on the consolidated balance sheet will also change.

Impairment of Goodwill

Since goodwill is an intangible asset with an **indefinite** life, it is not amortized. However, goodwill must be tested for impairment at least annually or more frequently if events and circumstances indicate that it may be impaired. Once an impairment charge has been made against goodwill, it cannot subsequently be reversed.

Under **IFRS**:

- At the time of acquisition, the total amount of goodwill recognized is allocated to each of the acquirer's **cash-generating units** that will benefit from the synergies expected from the business combination.
- There is a one-step approach: Goodwill is deemed impaired if the recoverable amount of the cash-generating unit is lower than its carrying amount (including goodwill).
- The impairment loss equals the difference between carrying value and recoverable amount of the unit.
- The impairment loss is first applied to the goodwill of the cash-generating unit. Once this has been reduced to zero, the remaining amount of the loss is allocated to all the other assets in the unit on a pro rata basis.

Under **U.S. GAAP**:

- At the time of acquisition, the total amount of goodwill recognized is allocated to each of the acquirer's **reporting units**.
- There is a two-step approach to goodwill impairment testing.
  - Test for impairment: If the carrying value of the reporting unit (including goodwill) exceeds its fair value, goodwill is deemed to be impaired.

- o Measurement of impairment loss: The impairment loss equals the difference between the implied fair value of the reporting unit's goodwill (implied goodwill) and its carrying amount.
  - Implied goodwill equals the fair value of the unit minus the fair value of the net assets of the unit.
- The impairment loss is applied to the goodwill allocated to the reporting unit. After the reporting unit's goodwill has been eliminated, no adjustments are made to the carrying amounts of the unit's other assets or liabilities.

Under both IFRS and U.S. GAAP, the impairment loss is recognized as a separate line item on the consolidated income statement.

Variable Interest Entities (U.S. GAAP) and Special Purpose Entities (IFRS)

Special purpose entities: Equity investors do not have a controlling financial interest. These entities are established for a particular purpose by the sponsoring company.

In the past, the structure of SPEs allowed sponsoring companies to:

- Avoid disclosures of significant guarantees to debt holders.
- Transfer assets and liabilities to the SPE and record revenues and gains related to these transactions.
- Avoid recognition of assets and liabilities of the SPE on their financial statements.

This resulted in improved asset turnover, higher profitability and lower levels of operating and financial leverage for sponsoring companies.

Now IFRS and U.S. GAAP require sponsoring companies to consolidate the SPE's financials with their own. Further, standards relating to measurement, reporting and disclosure of guarantees have been revised. For example, under U.S. GAAP, the primary beneficiary of a VIE must consolidate it as its subsidiary regardless of how much of an equity investment it has in the VIE.

- The primary beneficiary (which is often the sponsor) is defined as the entity that is (1) expected to absorb the majority of the VIE's expected losses, (2) receive the majority of the VIE's residual returns, (3) or both.
- If one entity will absorb a majority of the VIE's expected losses while another entity will receive a majority of the VIE's expected profits, the entity absorbing a majority of the losses must consolidate the VIE.
- If there are non-controlling interests in the VIE, these would also be shown in the consolidated balance sheet and consolidated income statement of the primary beneficiary.

Securitization of Assets

SPEs are often set up to securitize receivables held by the sponsor. The SPE issues debt to finance the purchase of these receivables from the sponsor, and interest and principal payments to debt holders are made from the cash flow generated from the pool of receivables.

FRA

The motivation for the sponsor to sell its accounts receivable to the SPE is to accelerate inflows of cash. However, an important aspect of the arrangement is whether the SPE's debt holders have recourse to the sponsor if sufficient cash is not generated from the pool of receivables. In this case, the transaction is basically just like taking a loan and collateralizing it with the receivables. If the receivables are not entirely realized, the loss is borne by the sponsor.

Adjusted Values Upon Reclassification of Sale of Receivables:

CFO	Lower
CFF	Higher
Total cash flow	Same
Current assets	Higher
Current liabilities	Higher
Current ratio	Lower

(Assuming it was greater than 1)

Table 2: Impact of Different Accounting Methods on Financial Ratios

	Equity Method	Acquisition Method
Leverage	Better (lower) as liabilities are lower and equity is the same	Worse (higher) as liabilities are higher and equity is the same
Net Profit Margin	Better (higher) as sales are lower and net income is the same	Worse (lower) as sales are higher and net income is the same
ROE	Better (higher) as equity is lower and net income is the same	Worse (lower) as equity is higher and net income is the same
ROA	Better (higher) as net income is the same and assets are lower	Worse (lower) as net income is the same and assets are higher

EMPLOYEE COMPENSATION: POST-EMPLOYMENT AND SHARE-BASED
Cross-Reference to CFA Institute Assigned Reading #15

Types of Post-Employment Benefits

Type of Benefit	Amount of Post-Employment Benefit to Employee	Obligation of Sponsoring Company	Sponsoring Company's Pre-funding of Its Future Obligation
Defined contribution pension plan	Amount of future benefit is not defined. Actual future benefit will depend on investment performance of plan assets. Investment risk is borne by employee.	Amount of the company's obligation (contribution) is defined in each period. The contribution, if any, is typically made on a periodic basis with no additional future obligation.	Not applicable.
Defined benefit pension plan	Amount of future benefit is defined, based on the plan's formula (often a function of length of service and final year's compensation). Investment risk is borne by company.	Amount of the future obligation, based on the plan's formula, must be estimated in the current period.	Companies typically pre-fund the DB plans by contributing funds to a pension trust. Regulatory requirements to pre-fund vary by country.
Other post-employment benefits (e.g., retirees' health care)	Amount of future benefit depends on plan specifications and type of benefit.	Eventual benefits are specified. The amount of the future obligation must be estimated in the current period.	Companies typically do not pre-fund other post-employment benefit obligations.

Measuring a Defined Benefit Pension Plan's Obligations

Under both IFRS and U.S. GAAP, a company's projected benefit obligation (PBO) is measured as the present value of all future benefits that its employees are entitled to (or have earned) for services provided to date.

Computing the pension obligation requires a company to make several estimates including:

- Future compensation increases and levels as they directly influence the dollar amount of the annual pension payment owed to an employee upon retirement.
- The discount rate, which is used to determine the present value of pension payments that must be paid in the future. The greater the discount rate, the lower the pension obligation (present value of promised future payments).

FRA

- The probability that some employees will not satisfy the company's vesting requirements.
  - If the employee leaves the company before satisfying these requirements, she would be entitled to none or only a portion of the benefits earned to date.
  - If the employee leaves the company after satisfying these requirements, she would be entitled to receive all the benefits earned to date.

Items that Directly Influence the Amount of a Company's Pension Obligation

- Current service costs refer to the increase in the present value of pension obligation as a result of an employee's service in the current period.
- Interest expense refers to accrued interest, or the increase in the value of the pension obligation (which represents the PV of promised payments) due to the passage of time.
- Past service costs (PSC)/ prior service costs refer to the increase in the pension obligation from retroactive benefits given to employees for years of service provided before the date of adoption or amendment of the plan.
- Changes in actuarial assumptions (e.g., discount rate, future compensation increases, life expectancy) result in changes in the value of pension obligation.
  - A change in actuarial assumptions that results in an increase in the pension obligation is an actuarial loss.
  - A change in actuarial assumptions that results in a decrease in the pension obligation is an actuarial gain.
- Benefits paid by the company decrease the pension obligation.

Items that Increase the Pension Obligation

- Current service costs.
- Interest costs accrued on the pension obligation.
- Prior service costs from plan amendments.
- Actuarial losses.

Items that Decrease the Pension Obligation

- Actuarial gains.
- Benefits paid.

Reconciling Beginning and Ending Pension Obligation

Pension obligation at the beginning of the period
+ Current service costs
+ Interest costs
+ Prior service costs
+ Actuarial losses
− Actuarial gains
− Benefits paid
Pension obligation at the end of the period

Measuring a Defined Benefit Pension Plan's Assets

The fair value of assets held in the plan will increase as a result of:

- A positive actual dollar return earned on plan assets; and
- Contributions made by the employer to the plan.

On the other hand, the fair value of plan assets will decrease when benefits are paid to employees.

Reconciling Beginning and Ending Balances of the Fair Value of Plan Assets

Fair value of plan assets at the beginning of the period
+ Actual return on plan assets
+ Contributions made by the employer to the plan
− Benefits paid to employees
Fair value of plan assets at the end of the period

Balance Sheet Presentation of Defined Benefit Pension Plans

Under both IFRS and U.S. GAAP, the defined-benefit liability (or asset) reported on the balance sheet equals the pension plan's funded status (FS). The funded status equals the difference between the fair value of plan assets (FVPA) and pension obligation (PO) so it represents a net amount.

$$\text{Funded status} = \text{Fair value of plan assets} - \text{Pension obligation}$$

- If the pension obligation is greater than the fair value of plan assets, the plan is said to be **underfunded**, and a **net pension liability** equal to the negative difference is recognized on the balance sheet.
- If the pension obligation is less than the fair value of plan assets, the plan is said to be **overfunded**, and a **net pension asset** equal to the positive difference is recognized on the balance sheet.
    - Note that the amount of net pension asset reported is subject to a **ceiling** equal to the present value of future economic benefits, such as refunds from the plan or reductions of future contributions.

It is very important for you to understand that the funded status represents the net pension asset:

- If Pension obligation > Fair value of plan assets:

    Plan is underfunded → Negative funded status → Net pension liability.

- If Pension obligation < Fair value of plan assets:

    Plan is overfunded → Positive funded status → Net pension asset.

Net Pension Liability (Asset)

The **net pension liability (asset)** is calculated as **pension obligation** minus the **fair value of plan assets**.

Periodic Pension Cost versus Periodic Pension Expense

- **Periodic pension cost** is the total cost related to a company's DB pension plan for a given period. Various components of this total cost can be recognized on the profit and loss (P&L) or in other comprehensive income (OCI) under IFRS and U.S. GAAP.
- **Periodic pension expense** (also known as **pension cost reported in P&L**) refers to the components of periodic pension cost that are recognized on the P&L (not OCI).

PERIODIC PENSION COST

Calculating Periodic Pension Cost

There are two approaches to calculating periodic pension cost. Further, for a particular company over a given period, periodic pension cost would come to the same amount whether it subscribes to IFRS or to U.S. GAAP when preparing its financial statements.

Approach 1: Adjusting the Change in Net Pension Liability (Asset) for Employer Contributions

The periodic cost of a company's DB pension plan equals the change in the net pension liability/asset excluding the effects of employer contributions to the plan.

Net periodic pension cost = Ending net pension liability − Beginning net pension liability + Employer contributions

- An increase in net pension liability or a decrease in net pension asset over the reporting period entails a pension-related cost for the company.
- A decrease in net pension liability or an increase in net pension asset over the reporting period results in a pension-related benefit for the company.

VERY Important: *Please note that the curriculum uses a (seemingly) different formula to compute periodic pension cost. That formula, along with the associated footnote (Footnote 10), will only confuse you. Every year candidates face an issue here, but the CFAI refuses to change the way it presents this formula. Please just stick to our formula and thought process and you will be fine for the exam.*

Approach 2: Aggregating Periodic Components of Cost

The components of periodic pension cost are basically items that result in changes in the net pension liability other than employer contributions. Changes in the net pension liability come from (1) changes in the pension obligation and/or (2) changes in the fair value of plan assets.

Changes in the pension obligation are caused by:

- Economic expenses for the period. These include:
  - Current service costs
  - Interest costs
  - Past service costs
  - Actuarial losses (gains)
- Benefits paid to employees.

Changes in the fair value of plan assets are caused by:

- The actual return on plan assets.
- Benefits paid to employees.

- Employer contributions.
- Benefits paid to employees reduce the pension obligation and the fair value of plan assets so they have no impact on the overall funded status.
- We have already shown that employer contributions have nothing to go with periodic pension cost.
- Therefore, the periodic pension cost of a company's DB pension plan equals the increase in the pension obligation (excluding the impact of benefits paid to employees) minus actual earnings on plan assets.

$$\text{Periodic pension cost} = \text{Current service costs} + \text{Interest costs} + \text{Past service costs}$$
$$+ \text{Actuarial losses} - \text{Actuarial gains} - \text{Actual return on plan assets}$$

Periodic Pension Cost Under IFRS and U.S. GAAP

While total periodic pension cost is the same under IFRS and U.S. GAAP, the manner in which total pension cost is divided between the P&L and OCI is different under the two sets of standards.

Under **IFRS**, periodic pension cost is divided into three components. Two of them are recognized in P&L, while one is recognized in OCI.

1. Service costs: Both current and past service costs are recognized as an expense on the P&L under IFRS.
2. Net interest expense/income: Net interest expense/income is also recognized on the P&L under IFRS.

$$\text{Net interest expense (income)} = \text{Net pension liability (asset)} \times \text{Discount rate}$$
$$= (\text{Pension obligation} - \text{Fair value of plan assets}) \times r$$
$$= \text{Pension obligation} \times r - \text{Fair value of plan assets} \times r$$

3. Remeasurement: This component of periodic pension cost is recognized in OCI under IFRS. Further, remeasurement amounts are **not subsequently amortized** into P&L. Remeasurement of the net pension liability/asset includes:
   - Actuarial gains and losses.
   - The difference between the actual return on plan assets and the return on plan assets (based on the discount rate, r) that has already been accounted for in the calculation of net interest expense/income.
     - Actual return on plan assets − (Fair value of plan assets × r)

Contrasting U.S. GAAP Treatment of Periodic Pension Cost with IFRS Treatment

Under U.S. GAAP:

- Service costs are recognized in P&L. However, past service costs are reported in OCI in the period during which the change that gave rise to the costs occurred. In subsequent years, these past service costs are amortized to P&L over the average service lives of affected employees. Under IFRS, past service costs are also recognized on the P&L as *pension expense* for the period.
- Periodic pension expense includes interest expense on pension obligations (which increases pension cost) and returns on plan assets (which decrease pension cost). However, unlike IFRS:
  - These two components are not presented in a single net amount. The second component of pension cost under IFRS (i.e., net interest expense/income, represents a single net amount.)

FRA

Note that generally speaking, actuarial gains and losses have an impact on the pension obligation and the funded status. However, this additional source of actuarial gains and losses under U.S. GAAP (from differences between actual and expected returns on plan assets) does not have an impact on the plan's funded status.

- ○ The return on plan assets is calculated based on an assumed expected return on plan assets. The difference between the actual return and the expected return on plan assets is *another* source (in addition to changes in assumptions that determine the value of the pension obligation e.g., discount rate and life expectancy) of actuarial gains and losses under U.S. GAAP.
- All actuarial gains and losses can be reported either in P&L or in OCI. Typically, companies report actuarial gains and losses in OCI and recognize gains and losses in P&L by applying the corridor method. Under IFRS, actuarial gains and losses are a part of the remeasurement component, which is never amortized into P&L from OCI.

Under the **corridor method**, if the net cumulative amount of unrecognized actuarial gains and losses at the beginning of the reporting period exceeds 10% of the greater of (1) the defined benefit obligation or (2) the fair value of plan assets, then the *excess* is amortized over the expected average remaining working lives of the employees participating in the plan and included as a component of periodic *pension expense* on the P&L.

Table 1: Components of a Company's Defined Benefit Pension Periodic Costs

IFRS Component	IFRS Recognition	U.S. GAAP Component	U.S. GAAP Recognition
Service costs	Recognized in P&L.	Current service costs	Recognized in P&L.
		Past service costs	Recognized in OCI and subsequently amortized to P&L over the service life of employees.
Net interest income/expense	Recognized in P&L as the following amount: Net pension liability or asset × interest rate[a]	Interest expense on pension obligation Expected return on plan assets	Recognized in P&L. Recognized in P&L as the following amount: Plan assets × expected return.
Remeasurements: Net return on plan assets and actuarial gains and losses	Recognized in OCI and not subsequently amortized to P&L. - Net return on plan **assets** = Actual return – (Plan assets × Interest rate). - Actuarial gains and losses = Changes in a company's pension obligation arising from changes in actuarial assumptions.	Actuarial gains and losses including differences between the actual and expected returns on plan assets	Recognized immediately in P&L or, more commonly, recognized in OCI and subsequently amortized to P&L using the corridor or faster recognition method.[b] - Difference between expected and actual return on assets = Actual return – (Plan assets × Expected return). - Actuarial gains and losses = Changes in a company's pension obligation arising from changes in actuarial assumptions.

(a) The interest rate used is equal to the discount rate used to measure the pension liability (the yield on high quality corporate bonds.)

(b) If the cumulative amount of unrecognized actuarial gains and losses exceeds 10 percent of the greater of the value of the plan assets or of the present value of the DB obligation (under U.S. GAAP, the projected benefit obligation), the difference must be amortized over the service lives of the employees.

Reporting the Periodic Pension Cost

For pension costs that are not capitalized (e.g., certain costs recorded in inventory as mentioned earlier):

- **IFRS** only differentiates between components included in P&L and in OCI. It does not specify where exactly the various components of pension cost must be presented.
- **U.S. GAAP** also differentiates between components included in P&L and in OCI. Further, it requires all components of pension expense recognized in P&L to be aggregated and presented within one net line item on the income statement.

Note that both IFRS and U.S. GAAP require total periodic pension cost to be disclosed in the notes to the financial statements.

Effects of Changes in Key Assumptions

The Discount Rate

An increase in the assumed discount rate:

- Decreases the opening pension obligation (as the PV of promised payments decreases).
- Typically decreases total periodic pension cost.
- Typically decreases the closing pension obligation.

Compensation Growth Rate

If the pension formula is based on the final year's salary, an increase in the assumed rate of growth in compensation:

- Increases the pension obligation.
- Increases periodic pension cost.

Expected Return on Plan Assets

Under U.S. GAAP, the expected return on plan assets reduces the periodic *pension expense*. An increase in the assumed expected return on plan assets:

- Has no impact on a company's net pension liability reported on the balance sheet.
- Decreases the company's *pension expense* (under U.S. GAAP). Note that total periodic pension cost is not affected by a change in the expected return on plan assets.

Expected Life Expectancy

If, under the terms of the plan, the sponsoring company must make pension payments to employees until their death, an increase in assumed life expectancy will result in an increase in the annual unit credit and the pension obligation. Further, service costs and interest costs will also increase so periodic pension cost will rise.

Table 2: Impact of Key Assumptions on Net Pension Liability and Periodic Pension Cost

Assumption	Impact of Assumption on Net Pension Liability (Asset)	Impact of Assumption on Periodic Pension Cost and Pension Expense
Higher discount rate	Lower obligation	Pension cost and pension expense will both typically be lower because of lower opening obligation and lower service costs
Higher rate of compensation increase	Higher obligation	Higher service and interest costs will increase periodic pension cost and pension expense
Higher expected return on plan assets	No effect, because fair value of plan assets are used on balance sheet	Not applicable for IFRS No effect on periodic pension cost under U.S. GAAP Lower periodic pension expense under U.S. GAAP

Disclosures of Pension and Other Post-Employment Benefits

When comparing financial results of different companies using ratios, analysts should consider the impact of pensions and other post-employment benefits on the financial statements. Comparisons across companies can be affected by:

- Differences in key assumptions.
- Amounts reported on the balance sheet are net amounts (net pension liability or asset). Adjustments to incorporate gross amounts would impact financial ratios.
- Non-comparability of periodic pension *expense*. Pension expense may not be comparable as IFRS and U.S. GAAP differ with regards to how periodic pension costs can be recognized on the P&L versus OCI.
- Differences across IFRS and U.S. GAAP regarding the reporting of components of pension expense on the income statement.
- Differences across IFRS and U.S. GAAP regarding the classification of pension contributions on the cash flow statement. Under IFRS, a portion of contributions may be treated as financing cash flows rather than operating cash flows. Under U.S. GAAP, all contributions are treated as operating cash flows.

Assumptions

Companies disclose their assumptions about discount rates, expected compensation increases, medical expense inflation rates and (for U.S. GAAP companies) expected return on plan assets. Analysts should examine these assumptions over time and across companies to assess whether a company is becoming increasingly conservative or aggressive in accounting for its DB obligations. A company could employ aggressive pension-related assumptions to improve reported financial performance by assuming:

- A higher discount rate.
- A lower compensation growth rate.
- A higher expected rate of return on plan assets.

Accounting for **other post-employment benefits** also requires companies to make several assumptions. All other things constant, each of the following assumptions will lead to an increase in the company's medical obligation and associated periodic cost:

- A higher health care inflation rate.
- A higher ultimate health care trend rate.
- A longer time to reach the ultimate health care trend rate.

Periodic Pension Costs Recognized in P&L versus OCI

Total periodic pension cost recognized under IFRS and U.S. GAAP is the same. However, the two sets of standards differ in their provisions regarding which components are recognized in P&L and which ones are recognized in OCI. These differences are important for analysts when evaluating companies that use different sets of standards.

- Under IFRS, current and past service costs are recognized in P&L. Under U.S. GAAP, the P&L only reflects current service costs (and amortization of any past service costs).
- Under IFRS, pension expense on the P&L incorporates a return on plan assets equal to the discount rate (used for measuring the pension obligation) times the value of plan assets. Under U.S. GAAP, pension expense on the P&L incorporates a return on plan assets equal to an estimated rate of return on plan assets times the value of plan assets.
- Under IFRS, the P&L would never show amortization of pension-related amounts previously recognized in OCI. Under U.S. GAAP, the P&L would reflect amortization of any past service costs, and may reflect amortization of actuarial gains and losses if they were initially recorded in OCI and if the "corridor" has been exceeded.

An analyst comparing the financial statements of a company that follows IFRS to one that follows U.S. GAAP would have to make adjustments to reported amounts to achieve comparability. To make a U.S. GAAP–following company's P&L comparable to the P&L of a company following IFRS, she would:

- Include past service costs on the P&L as pension expense.
- Exclude the effects of amortization of past service costs arising in previous periods.
- Exclude the effects of amortization of unrecognized actuarial gains and losses arising in previous periods.
- Incorporate the effects of the expected return on plan assets based on the discount rate (rather than the expected rate).

Alternatively, she could use total periodic pension cost as the basis for comparison by focusing on **comprehensive income** (which includes net income and other comprehensive income).

Classification of Periodic Pension Costs Recognized in P&L

Analysts should make the following adjustments to reflect a company's operating performance more accurately on the income statement:

1. Add back the entire amount of pension costs recognized on the P&L (pension expense) to operating income.
2. Subtract service costs before determining operating profit.
3. Add the interest component of pension expense to the company's interest expense.
4. Add the return on plan assets to non-operating income.

Further, analysts may also make adjustments to reflect the actual return on plan assets. Recall that:

- Under IFRS, net interest expense/income on the P&L incorporates a return on plan assets based on the discount rate. The difference between this return and the actual return is a part of remeasurement, which is included in OCI.
- Under U.S. GAAP, pension expense incorporates a return on plan assets based on an expected rate of return assumption. The difference between the actual and expected return is a source of actuarial gains (losses), which are typically initially reported in OCI.

Note that adjusting the P&L to incorporate the actual return on plan assets introduces an element of volatility in net income. However, reclassification of interest expense has no impact on net income.

Cash Flow Information

For a funded plan, the impact of the plan on the sponsoring company's cash flows is the amount of contributions the company makes to fund the plan. For an unfunded plan, the impact of the plan on the sponsoring company's cash flows is the amount of benefits paid. Note that in both cases, these cash flows are usually classified as operating cash flows. From an economic perspective however, classification of employer contributions to DB pension plans depends on how they relate to total pension costs for the period.

- If a company's contribution to the plan over the period is greater than total pension cost for the period, the excess may be viewed as a reduction in the overall pension obligation.
- If a company's contribution to the plan over the period is lower than total pension cost for the period, the shortfall results in an increase in the overall pension obligation.

If the amount of pension obligation is material, analysts may choose to reclassify the excess (shortfall) in contributions as a use (source) of cash from financing activities rather than operating activities.

Share-Based Compensation

Advantages

- Aligns interests of management along with those of shareholders.
- Requires no cash outlays.

Disadvantages

- The employee may have limited influence on the company's market value.
- Increased ownership may make management more risk averse.
- The option-like payoff may make management take excessive risks.
- Ownership dilution.

Accounting for Share-Based Compensation

- Both IFRS and U.S. GAAP require companies to **measure** share-based compensation expense based on the **fair value** of the compensation granted.
- Both IFRS and U.S. GAAP require companies to **disclose** the following:
  - The nature and extent of share-based compensation for the period.
  - The basis for determining the fair value of share-based compensation over the period.

○ The effects of share-based compensation on the company's net income for the period and its financial position.
- As far as **accounting** for share-based compensation is concerned, the specifics depend on the type of compensation.

Stock Grants

Stock grants include outright stock grants, restricted stock grants and performance shares. Compensation expense equals the fair value (typically market value) of the shares issued and is allocated over the employee's service period.

Stock Options

Compensation expense for stock options issued is also measured at fair value (as opposed to intrinsic value, which would result in lower reported compensation expense). Fair value of employee stock options must be estimated because they contain features that make them different from traded options.

- Assumptions of higher volatility, longer estimated life, lower dividend yield and higher risk-free rate increase the estimated fair value of employee stock options.
- If the number of shares and option price are known, compensation expense is measured at the grant date.
- If the fair value of options depends on events after the grant date, compensation expense is measured at the exercise date.

Accounting for Compensation Expense Related to Stock Options

- If stock options vest immediately, the entire cost (fair value) of options awarded is recognized on the grant date (in the current period).
- If stock options vest after a specified service period, compensation expense is allocated over the service period.
- If vesting of stock options is conditional (e.g., upon a target share price being reached), compensation expense is recognized over the estimated service period.

Stock Appreciation Rights (SARs)

SARs compensate employees based on the changes in the value of the company's shares without requiring employees to actually hold the shares.

- The potential for risk aversion is limited as SARs holders have asymmetrical upside and downside potential.
- Share ownership is not diluted.
- They require a current period cash outflow
- Compensation expense is measured at fair value and allocated over the service life of the employee.

Phantom Shares

Compensation expense is based on the performance of hypothetical stock rather than the company's actual stock. They can be used by private companies and highly illiquid companies.

MULTINATIONAL OPERATIONS
Cross-Reference to CFA Institute Assigned Reading #16

Definitions

- The presentation currency (PC) is the currency in which the parent company reports its financial statements. It is typically the currency of the country where the parent is located.
- The functional currency (FC) is the currency of the primary business environment in which an entity operates. It is usually the currency in which the entity primarily generates and expends cash.
- The local currency (LC) is the currency of the country where the subsidiary operates.

Foreign Currency Transaction Exposure to Foreign Exchange Risk

- For an import purchase, foreign exchange transaction exposure for the importing company arises when it defers a payment that must be made in foreign currency. The importer faces the risk that the value of the foreign currency will increase between the purchase date and the settlement date. Appreciation of the foreign currency would mean that the importer will have to spend more units of domestic currency to purchase the required amount of foreign currency to settle the obligation.
- For an export sale, foreign exchange transaction exposure for the exporting company arises when it allows the purchaser to make the payment sometime after the purchase date and agrees to be paid in foreign currency. The exporter faces the risk that the value of the foreign currency will decrease between the date of sale and the settlement date. Depreciation of the foreign currency would mean that the exporter will receive a lower number of units of domestic currency upon converting the foreign currency amount when it is received.

Note that foreign currency transaction risk only arises when the payment and settlement dates are different.

Both, U.S. GAAP and IFRS require that changes in the value of a foreign currency asset/ liability resulting from a foreign currency transaction be recognized as gains/losses on the income statement. The exact amount of gains/losses recognized depends on:

- Whether the company has an asset or a liability that is exposed to foreign exchange risk.
- Whether the foreign currency increases or decreases in value versus the domestic currency.

		Foreign Currency	
Transaction	Type of Exposure	Strengthens	Weakens
Export sale	Asset (account receivable)	Gain	Loss
Import purchase	Liability (account payable)	Loss	Gain

If the balance sheet date occurs between the transaction date and settlement date, foreign exchange gains/losses are still recognized (based on the difference between the spot rate at transaction date and the exchange rate on the balance sheet date). Once the transaction is settled, additional gains/losses are recognized (based on the difference between the exchange rate at balance sheet date and the exchange rate at settlement date).

Analytical Issues

- The calculation of operating profit margin is affected by where translation gains/losses are recorded on the income statement.
- The eventual translation gain/loss can be different from the amount recognized initially if the balance sheet date lies between the transaction and settlement dates.

Translation of Foreign Currency Financial Statements

- The current rate method (also known as the all-current method) is used to translate financial statements presented in the functional currency (FC) into amounts expressed in the parent's presentation currency (PC).
- The temporal method (also known as remeasurement) is used to translate financial statements presented in local currency (LC) into amounts expressed in the functional currency (FC).

The translation method that applies to a particular situation depends on the entity's functional currency.

- If the local currency is deemed to be the functional currency (LC = FC ≠ PC), the current rate method is used to translate foreign currency financial statements into the parent's presentation currency.
    - Such instances usually arise when the subsidiary is independent and its operating, investing, and financing activities are decentralized from the parent.
- If the presentation currency is deemed to be the functional currency (LC ≠ FC = PC), the temporal method is used to translate foreign currency financial statements into the parent's presentation currency.
    - Such instances usually arise when the subsidiary and parent are well-integrated.
- If local currency, functional currency, and presentation currency are different (LC ≠ FC ≠ PC), then:
    - The temporal method is used to convert local currency amounts into functional currency; and then
    - The current rate method is used to convert functional currency amounts into presentation currency.

Methods for Translating Foreign Currency Financial Statements of Subsidiaries

Current Rate/Temporal Method	Local Currency	T	Functional Currency	CR	Presentation Currency
Temporal Method	Local Currency	T	Functional Currency	=	Presentation Currency
Current Rate Method	Local Currency	=	Functional Currency	CR	Presentation Currency

The Current Rate Method

- The income statement and statement of retained earnings is translated first, and then the balance sheet is translated.
- All income statement accounts are translated at the historical rate (which for practical purposes is assumed to equal the average rate).
- All balance sheet accounts (except common equity) are translated at the current rate.
- Common equity is translated at the historical rate.
- Dividends are translated at the rate that applied when they were declared.
- The translation gain/loss for the period is included in shareholders' equity under the cumulative translation adjustment (CTA).

The Temporal Method

- The balance sheet is translated first, followed by the income statement and statement of retained earnings.
- Monetary assets and monetary liabilities are translated at the current rate.
  - Monetary assets include cash and receivables.
  - Monetary liabilities include accounts payable, accrued expenses, long-term debt, and deferred income taxes. Most liabilities are monetary liabilities.
- Nonmonetary assets and liabilities measured at historical cost are translated at historical rates.
  - Nonmonetary assets measured at historical cost include inventory measured at **cost** under the lower of cost or market rule, PP&E, and intangible assets.
  - Nonmonetary liabilities measured at historical cost include deferred revenue.
- Nonmonetary assets and liabilities measured at current value are translated at the exchange rate that existed when current value was determined.
  - Nonmonetary assets measured at current cost include marketable securities and inventory measured at **market** under the lower of cost or market rule.
- Shareholders' equity accounts are translated at historical rates.
- Revenues and expenses (other than expenses related to nonmonetary assets) are translated at the average rate.
- Expenses related to nonmonetary assets (e.g., COGS, depreciation, and amortization) are translated at historical rates prevailing at time of purchase of the related nonmonetary assets.
- The translation gain/loss is reported on the income statement.

Note that the historical exchange rate used to translate inventory and COGS under the temporal method will differ according to the cost flow assumption (FIFO, LIFO, AVCO) used.

- If FIFO is used:
  - Ending inventory is composed of recent purchases so inventory will be translated at relatively recent exchange rates.
  - Units sold are from the older purchases so COGS will be translated at relatively old exchange rates.
- If LIFO is used:
  - Ending inventory is composed of older purchases so inventory will be translated at relatively old exchange rates.
  - Units sold are from the more recent purchases so COGS will be translated at relatively recent exchange rates.

Differences in the Results of the Temporal and Current Rate Method

- Income before translation gain/loss is different under the two methods.
  - ○ The current rate method uses the average rate for depreciation and COGS.
  - ○ The temporal method uses historical rates.
- The translation gain/loss is different between the two methods.
  - ○ Exposure under the current rate method equals the subsidiaries' net assets.
  - ○ Exposure under the temporal method equals the subsidiaries' net monetary assets.
- Net income is different between the two methods.
  - ○ COGS and depreciation are converted at different rates under the two methods.
  - ○ Under the current rate method, the translation gain/loss is reported in shareholders' equity. Under the temporal method, it is reported on the income statement.
- Total assets are different between the two methods.
  - ○ Inventory and fixed assets are translated at current rates under the current rate method, but at historical rates under the temporal method.

Rules for Foreign Currency Translation

Income Statement Component	Current Rate Method FC = LC	Temporal Method FC = PC
	Exchange Rate Used	
Sales	Average rate	Average rate
Cost of goods sold	Average rate	Historical rate
Selling expenses	Average rate	Average rate
Depreciation expense	Average rate	Historical rate
Amortization expense	Average rate	Historical rate
Interest expense	Average rate	Average rate
Income tax	Average rate	Average rate
Net income before translation gain (loss)		Computed as Rev – Exp
Translation gain (loss)	N/A	Plug in Number
Net income	Computed as Rev – Exp	Computed as ΔRE + Dividends
Less: Dividends	Historical rate	Historical rate
Change in retained earnings	Computed as NI – Dividends Used as input for translated B/S	From B/S

FRA

Balance Sheet Component	Current Rate Method FC = LC	Temporal Method FC = PC
	Exchange Rate Used	
Cash	Current rate	Current rate
Accounts receivable	Current rate	Current rate
Monetary assets	Current rate	Current rate
Inventory	Current rate	Historical rate
Nonmonetary assets measured at current value	Current rate	Current rate
Property, plant, and equipment	Current rate	Historical rate
Less: Accumulated depreciation	Current rate	Historical rate
Nonmonetary assets measured at historical cost	Current rate	Historical rate
Accounts payable	Current rate	Current rate
Long-term notes payable	Current rate	Current rate
Monetary liabilities	Current rate	Current rate
Nonmonetary liabilities:		
Measured at current value	Current rate	Current rate
Measured at historical cost	Current rate	Historical rate
Capital stock	Historical rate	Historical rate
Retained earnings	From I/S	To balance Used as input for translated I/S
Cumulative translation adjustment	Plug in Number	N/A

Balance Sheet Exposure under the Current Rate and Temporal Methods

Exposure to translation adjustment is referred to as balance sheet translation, or accounting exposure.

- A foreign operation will have a net asset balance sheet exposure when the value of assets translated at the current exchange rate is greater than the value of liabilities translated at the current exchange rate.
- A foreign operation will have a net liability balance sheet exposure when the value of liabilities translated at the current exchange rate is greater than the value of assets translated at the current exchange rate.

Whether the current period's translation adjustment results in a gain or loss depends on (1) the nature of the balance sheet exposure (net asset versus net liability) and (2) the direction of change in the value of the foreign currency (appreciating or depreciating).

Balance Sheet Exposure	Foreign Currency (FC)	
	Strengthens	Weakens
Net asset	Positive translation adjustment	Negative translation adjustment
Net liability	Negative translation adjustment	Positive translation adjustment

Under the current rate method:

- The parent's foreign currency exposure equals its **net asset position** in the subsidiary.
- If the subsidiary has a net asset (liability) exposure, an appreciating foreign currency will result in a translation gain (loss), which will be reflected in an increasing (decreasing) cumulative translation adjustment on the balance sheet.
- The current rate method usually results in a net asset balance sheet exposure (unless the entity has negative shareholders' equity, which is very rare).
- Elimination of balance sheet exposure under the current rate method is rather difficult as it would require total assets to equal total liabilities (or zero shareholders' equity in the foreign subsidiary).

Items Translated at Current Exchange Rate
Total assets > Total Liabilities → Net asset balance sheet exposure

Under the temporal method:

- The parent's exposure is limited to the subsidiary's **net monetary assets (liabilities)**.
- If the subsidiary has a net monetary asset (liability) exposure, an appreciating foreign currency will result in a translation gain (loss) on the income statement.
- Most liabilities are monetary liabilities (which are translated at the current exchange rate and entail exposure to translation adjustment), while most assets are nonmonetary assets (which are translated at historical exchange rates and do not entail exposure to translation adjustment). Therefore, liabilities translated at the current exchange rate usually exceed assets translated at the current exchange rate, which results in a net monetary liability exposure under the temporal method.
- Elimination of balance sheet exposure under the temporal method is relatively easy as the parent simply has to ensure that the monetary assets of the foreign subsidiary equal its monetary liabilities.

Items Translated at Current Exchange Rate
Exposed assets > Exposed liabilities → Net asset balance sheet exposure
Exposed assets < Exposed liabilities → Net liability balance sheet exposure

Financial Statement Ratios (Originally in Local Currency versus Current Rate Method)

- Pure income statement and balance sheet ratio remain unaffected by the method used.
- If the foreign currency is appreciating (depreciating) mixed ratios (based on end-of-year balance sheet values) will be smaller (larger) after translation.

Effects of Direction of Change in the Exchange Rate on Translated Amounts

Current Rate Method

Compared to a scenario where the exchange rate remains stable:

- If the foreign currency appreciates against the parent's presentation currency, revenues, assets, liabilities, and total equity reported on the parent's consolidated financial statements will be higher.
- If the foreign currency depreciates against the parent's presentation currency, revenues, assets, liabilities, and total equity reported on the parent's consolidated financial statements will be lower.

FRA

Temporal Method

Compared to a scenario where the exchange rate remains stable:

- If the foreign currency appreciates against the parent's presentation currency, revenues, assets, and liabilities reported on the parent's consolidated financial statements will be higher. However, net income and shareholders' equity will translate into lower amounts (assuming that the subsidiary has a net monetary liability exposure) because of the translation loss.
- If the foreign currency depreciates against the parent's presentation currency, revenues, assets, and liabilities reported on the parent's consolidated financial statements will be lower. However, net income and shareholders' equity will translate into higher amounts (assuming that the subsidiary has a net monetary liability exposure) because of the translation gain.

Effects of Exchange Rate Movements on Financial Statements

	Temporal Method, Net Monetary Liability Exposure	**Temporal Method, Net Monetary Asset Exposure**	**Current Rate Method**
Foreign currency strengthens relative to parent's presentation currency	↑ Revenues ↑ Assets ↑ Liabilities ↓ Net income ↓ Shareholders' equity Translation loss	↑ Revenues ↑ Assets ↑ Liabilities ↑ Net income ↑ Shareholders' equity Translation gain	↑ Revenues ↑ Assets ↑ Liabilities ↑ Net income ↑ Shareholders' equity Positive translation adjustment
Foreign currency weakens relative to parent's presentation currency	↓ Revenues ↓ Assets ↓ Liabilities ↑ Net income ↑ Shareholders' equity Translation gain	↓ Revenues ↓ Assets ↓ Liabilities ↓ Net income ↓ Shareholders' equity Translation loss	↓ Revenues ↓ Assets ↓ Liabilities ↓ Net income ↓ Shareholders' equity Negative translation adjustment

Hyperinflationary Economies

- U.S. GAAP defines a high inflationary economy as one where the cumulative three-year inflation rate exceeds 100%, which equates to an average of approximately 26% per year.
- IFRS provides no specific definition of high inflation, but does indicate that a cumulative three-year inflation rate approaching or exceeding 100% indicates high inflation.

Under **U.S. GAAP**, the functional currency is assumed to be the parent's presentation currency and the temporal method is used to translate the subsidiary's financial statements. The translation gain/loss is included in net income.

Under **IFRS**, the subsidiary's foreign currency accounts are restated for inflation (using the procedures described below) and then translated into the parent's presentation currency using the current exchange rate.

- Nonmonetary assets and liabilities are restated for changes in the general purchasing power of the local currency.
  - Nonmonetary items carried at historical cost are restated for inflation by multiplying their values by the change in the general price index from the date of acquisition to the balance sheet date.
  - Nonmonetary items carried at revalued amounts are restated for inflation by multiplying their revised values by the change in the general price index from the date of revaluation to the balance sheet date.
- Monetary assets and liabilities (e.g., cash, receivables, and payables) are not restated for inflation.
- Shareholders' equity accounts are restated for inflation by multiplying their values by the change in the general price index from the beginning of the period, or from the date of contribution (if later), till the balance sheet date.
- Income statement items are restated for inflation by multiplying their values by the change in the general price index from the dates when the items were originally recorded to the balance sheet date.
- All items are then translated into the parent's presentation currency using the current exchange rate.
- The gain/loss in purchasing power is recorded on the income statement.

Under this method, a company's net monetary asset (liability) position is exposed to inflation risk as monetary assets and liabilities are not restated for inflation. In an inflationary environment, borrowers (who have payables) gain while lenders (who hold receivables) lose out. Therefore, a company will recognize a purchasing power gain (loss) if it holds more monetary liabilities (assets) than monetary assets (liabilities).

Translation Disclosures and Analysis

Under both IFRS and U.S. GAAP, companies are required to disclose:

- The total amount of exchange differences (foreign currency transaction and translation gains and losses) recognized in net income.
- The total amount of cumulative translation adjustment classified as a separate component of shareholders' equity, as well as a reconciliation of the amount of cumulative translation adjustment at the beginning and end of the period.

Further, note that:

- Disclosures relating to foreign currency translation are typically found in the MD&A section and the notes to the financial statements in the annual report.
- Multinational companies typically have several subsidiaries in different regions so the translation gain/loss on the income statement and cumulative translation adjustment on the balance sheet include the effects of translation of foreign currency accounts of all the parent's subsidiaries.
- In order to facilitate comparisons across companies, analysts may add the change in CTA over the year to net income for the year. This adjustment where gains/losses that are reported directly in equity, are instead reported in net income, is known as clean surplus accounting.

> **FRA**

> Under dirty surplus accounting certain gains/losses are included in shareholders' equity directly under comprehensive income. Examples of dirty surplus items include unrealized gains and losses on available-for-sale securities.

Multinational Operations and a Company's Effective Tax Rate

Entities with operations in multiple countries with different tax rates have an incentive to set transfer prices (i.e., the prices at which divisions within the company transact with each other) such that a higher portion of profits is allocated to lower tax rate jurisdictions. This has prompted countries to establish various laws and practices to prevent aggressive transfer pricing practices.

Accounting standards require companies to explain the relationship between tax expense and accounting profit in a detailed reconciliation between the average effective tax rate (tax expense divided by pretax accounting profits) and the relevant statutory tax rate. Changes in impact of foreign taxes on the parent's effective tax rate can be caused by (1) changes in applicable tax rates and/or (2) changes in the mix of profits earned in different countries (with different tax rates).

Additional Disclosures on the Effects of Foreign Currency

Disclosures Related to Sales Growth

Companies often include disclosures related to the impact of exchange rate movements on sales growth in (1) the MD&A and sometimes in (2) other financial reports such as company presentations to investors and earnings announcements. For multinationals, sales growth can be attributed to changes in price, volumes, and/or exchange rates. Analysts should consider organic sales growth (excluding foreign currency effects on sales growth) when forecasting future performance or evaluating management performance.

Disclosures Related to Major Sources of Foreign Exchange Risk

In order to assist users of financial statements, a multinational may:

- Describe the source(s) of its currency risks and approach to measuring and managing those risks (usually in MD&A); and
- Present a sensitivity analysis on the effects of currency fluctuations (usually in the additional disclosures sections of the notes).

ANALYSIS OF FINANCIAL INSTITUTIONS

Important Aspect of Basel III

1. Minimum capital requirement
   - Specifies the minimum percentage of a bank's risk-weighted assets that must be funded with equity capital.
   - Prevents a bank from using excessive financial leverage such that its ability to tolerate loan losses is critically impaired.
2. Minimum liquidity
   - Specifies that a bank must have enough high-quality liquid assets to meet its liquidity requirements in a 30-day liquidity stress scenario.
   - Ensures that a bank has adequate cash in the event that it loses access to some of its funding sources or if it has to meet off-balance-sheet funding requirements.

3. Stable funding
   ○ Specifies the minimum amount of stable funding in relation to the liquidity needs of a bank over a one-year time horizon.
   ○ Longer maturity deposits are considered more stable than shorter maturity deposits.
   ○ Consumer deposits are considered more stable than funding from the interbank market.

Analyzing a Bank (The CAMELS Approach)

A bank is given a score between 1 and 5 on each factor, as well as an overall score that combines the bank's scores on each of the individual factors. Factors considered include:

- Capital adequacy
  ○ Common Equity Tier 1 Capital – Includes common stock, any surplus resulting from the issue of common stock, retained earnings, accumulated other comprehensive income, and certain regulatory adjustments and deductions applied in the calculation of Common Equity Tier 1 Capital.
  ○ Other Tier 1 Capital – Includes instruments that meet certain criteria, such as subordination to bank deposits and other debt obligations, bear no fixed maturity, and have no requirement to pay dividends or interest that is not fully at the bank's discretion.
  ○ Tier 2 Capital – Includes instruments that are subordinate to bank deposits and general creditors, as well as portions of the allowance for loan losses.
- Asset quality
  ○ Analysis of credit quality
    ▪ Credit risk associated with a bank's loan portfolio (usually the largest proportion of assets).
    ▪ Credit risk associated with a bank's investments.
    ▪ Counterparty credit risk associated with trading activities.
    ▪ Potential credit risk linked to off-balance-sheet obligations such as guarantees and letters of credit.
    ▪ Diversification of credit risk exposure across a bank's financial assets.
    ▪ Liquidity and other factors that affect asset value and marketability.
- Ratio analysis
  ○
    ▪ Ratio of loan loss (or impairment) allowance to impaired loans.
    ▪ Ratio of loan loss allowance to actual loan losses (actual loan losses equal charge-offs net of recoveries).
    ▪ Ratio of loan loss provision to actual loan losses.
    ▪ Management capabilities. Key roles of bank management are:
  ○ Identifying and exploiting profitable business opportunities.
  ○ Ensuring compliance with applicable laws and regulations.
  ○ Implementing a strong corporate governance framework that includes an independent board and reduces agency risk.
  ○ Identifying and controlling the wide range of risks faced by the bank.

- Earnings
    - Accounting estimates must be scrutinized.
    - Net interest income and net fee and commission income are typically less volatile than net trading income.
    - Net interest income can be further analyzed by interest margin and average cost of funding.
- Liquidity position
    - Liquidity Coverage Ratio (LCR)
        - This is calculated as highly liquid assets divided by expected cash outflows.
        - Highly liquid assets consist of cash and assets that can be easily converted into cash.
        - Expected cash flows are the anticipated one-month liquidity needs in a stress scenario.
        - Basel III sets a minimum LCR of 100%.
    - Net Stable Funding Ratio (NSFR)
        - This is calculated as available stable funding (ASF) divided by required stable funding.
        - ASF is dependent on the composition and maturity of a bank's funding sources (capital, deposits, and other liabilities).
        - Required stable funding is dependent on the composition and maturity of a bank's asset base.
        - The NSFR assesses the liquidity needs of a bank's assets against the liquidity provided by its funding sources.
        - On the asset side, longer-maturity loans require more stable funding than short-term liquid assets.
        - With funding sources, long-dated deposits are deemed to be more stable than short-dated deposits, whereas retail deposits are deemed to be more stable than deposits by other entities of the same maturity.
        - Basel III sets a minimum NSFR of 100%.
- Sensitivity to market risk
    - Mismatches in maturity, repricing frequency, reference rates, and currency of its balance sheet assets and liabilities.
    - Off-balance-sheet guarantees and derivatives positions linked to interest rates, equities, exchange rates, and commodities.

Factors not considered include:

- Government support/ownership.
- Mission of bank.
- Corporate culture.

Analytical considerations relevant to all types of companies not covered by CAMELS:

- Competitive environment.
- Off-balance-sheet items.
- Segment information.
- Currency exposure.
- Risk disclosures.

Analyzing an Insurance Company

- Business profile and operations
- Earnings characteristics. Ratios considered include:
  - Loss and loss adjustment expense ratio.
    - This is calculated as the sum of loss expense and loss adjustment expense divided by net premiums earned.
    - A lower ratio indicates that an insurer is better at estimating the risks that it is insuring.
  - Underwriting expense ratio
    - This is calculated as underwriting expense divided by net premiums written.
    - A lower ratio indicates that an insurer is more efficient at generating new insurance premiums.
  - Combined ratio
    - This is calculated as the sum of the loss and loss adjustment expense ratio and the underwriting expense ratio.
    - This ratio is used to assess the overall efficiency of an insurer's underwriting business.
    - A combined ratio of less than 100% is considered efficient, while a combined ratio of greater than 100% indicates an underwriting loss.
  - Dividends to policyholders (or shareholders) ratio
    - This is calculated as dividends paid divided by net premiums earned.
    - This ratio is a liquidity measure, as it compares dividends paid and premiums earned in the same accounting period.
  - Combined ratio after dividends
    - This is calculated as the sum of the combined ratio and the dividends to policyholders (or shareholders) ratio.
    - This is a more stringent measure of overall efficiency than the combined ratio as it includes the cash return to policyholders (or shareholders).

FRA

EVALUATING QUALITY OF FINANCIAL REPORTS
Cross-Reference to CFA Institute Assigned Reading #18

Conceptual Framework for Assessing the Quality of Financial Reports

- Financial reporting quality refers to the usefulness of information contained in the financial reports, including disclosures in the notes.
  - High-quality reporting provides information that is useful in investment decision-making in that it is relevant and faithfully represents the company's performance and position.
- Earnings quality (or results quality) pertains to the earnings and cash generated by the company's core economic activities and its resulting financial condition.
  - High-quality earnings (1) come from activities that the company will be able to sustain in the future, and (2) provide an adequate return on the company's investment.
  - Note that the term, **earnings** quality, encompasses quality of earnings, cash flow, and balance sheet items.

Relationship between Financial Reporting Quality and Earnings Quality

| | | Financial Reporting Quality | |
		Low	High
Earnings (Results) Quality	High	LOW financial reporting quality impedes assessment of earnings quality and impedes valuation.	HIGH financial reporting quality enables assessment. HIGH earnings quality increases company value.
	Low		HIGH financial reporting quality enables assessment. LOW earnings quality decreases company value.

Quality Spectrum of Financial Reports

GAAP, Decision-Useful, Sustainable, and Adequate Returns: These are high-quality reports that provide useful information about high-quality earnings.

GAAP, Decision-Useful, but Sustainable? This level refers to a situation where high-quality reporting provides useful information, but the economic reality being depicted is not of high quality (i.e., earnings do not provide an adequate rate of return or they are not expected to recur).

Within GAAP, but Biased Accounting Choices: This level refers to a situation where high-quality reporting provides useful information, but biased choices result in financial reports that do not faithfully represent the company's true economic situation.

- Management can make aggressive or conservative accounting choices, both of which go against the concept of neutrality as *unbiased* financial reporting is the ideal.

- Aside from biases in determining reported amounts, biases can also creep into the way information is *presented*. A company may choose to present information in a manner that obscures unfavorable information and/or highlights favorable information.

Within GAAP, but "Earnings Management": This level refers to a situation where high-quality reporting provides useful information, but where earnings are "managed." Earnings can be managed by taking real actions or through accounting choices.

Departures from GAAP Non-Compliant Accounting: This level reflects financial information that deviates from GAAP. Such financial information cannot be used to assess earnings quality, as comparisons with other entities or earlier periods cannot be made.

Departures from GAAP Fictitious Transactions: The level reflects the lowest quality of financial reports, where actual transactions are omitted and/or fictitious transactions are reported.

POTENTIAL PROBLEMS THAT AFFECT THE QUALITY OF FINANCIAL REPORTS

Reported Amounts and Timing of Recognition

While the choice regarding the reported amount and timing of recognition may focus on a single financial statement element (assets, liabilities, owners' equity, revenues and gains, or expenses and losses), it can affect other elements as well.

- Aggressive, premature, and fictitious revenue recognition results in overstated income and, consequently, overstated equity. Further, assets (typically accounts receivable) are also overstated.
- Conservative revenue recognition, such as deferred recognition of revenue, results in understated net income, understated equity, and understated assets.
- Omission and delayed recognition of expenses result in understated expenses and overstated income, overstated equity, overstated assets, and/or understated liabilities.
  - An understatement of bad debt expense results in overstated accounts receivable.
  - Understated depreciation or amortization results in overstated long-lived assets.
  - Understated interest, taxes, or other expenses result in understated related liabilities (accrued interest payable, taxes payable, or other payables).
- Understatement of contingent liabilities comes with overstated equity resulting from understated expenses and overstated income or overstated other comprehensive income.
- For financial assets and liabilities that must be reported at fair value, overstatement of financial assets and understatement of financial liabilities are associated with overstated equity resulting from overstated unrealized gains or understated unrealized losses.
- Cash flow from operations may be increased by deferring payments on payables, accelerating payments from customers, deferring purchases of inventory, and deferring other expenditures (e.g., maintenance and research).

Classification

While choices relating to reported amounts and timing of recognition usually affect more than one financial statement element, classification choices typically relate to how an item is classified within a particular financial statement.

Accounting Warning Signs[1]

Potential Issues	Possible Actions/Choices	Warning Signs

• Overstatement or non-sustainability of operating income and/or net income
  ○ Overstated or accelerated revenue recognition
  ○ Understated expenses
  ○ Misclassification of revenue, gains, expenses, or losses
	• Contingent sales with right of return, "channel stuffing" (the practice of inducing customers to order products they would otherwise not order or order at a later date through generous terms), "bill and hold" sales (encouraging customers to order goods and retain them on seller's premises)
	• Lessor use of finance (capital) leases
	• Fictitious (fraudulent) revenue
	• Capitalizing expenditures as assets
	• Lessee use of operating leases
	• Classifying non-operating income or gains as part of operations
	• Classifying ordinary expenses as non-recurring or non-operating
	• Reporting gains through net income and losses through other comprehensive income
		• Growth in revenue higher than that of industry or peers
		• Increases in discounts to and returns from customers
		• Higher growth rate in receivables than revenue
		• Large proportion of revenue in final quarter of year for a non-seasonal business
		• Cash flow from operations is much lower than operating income
		• Inconsistency over time in the items included in operating revenues and operating expenses
		• Increases in operating margin
		• Aggressive accounting assumptions, such as long, depreciable lives
		• Losses in non-operating income or other comprehensive income and gains in operating income or net income
		• Compensation largely tied to financial results

(Table continued on next page...)

---

1 - 2018 CFA Program Curriculum Volume 2, Exhibit 4.

Potential Issues	Possible Actions/Choices	Warning Signs

• Misstatement of balance sheet items (may affect income statement)
  ○ Over- or understatement of assets
  ○ Over- or understatement of liabilities
  ○ Misclassification of assets and/or liabilities
	• Choice of models and model inputs to measure fair value
	 • Classification from current to non-current
	 • Over- or understating reserves and allowances
	 • Understating identifiable assets and overstating goodwill
		• Models and model inputs that bias fair value measures
		 • Inconsistency in model inputs when measuring fair value of assets compared with that of liabilities
		 • Typical current assets, such as accounts receivable and inventory, included in non-current assets
		 • Allowances and reserves that fluctuate over time or are not comparable with peers
		 • High goodwill value relative to total assets
		 • Use of special purpose vehicles
		 • Large changes in deferred tax assets and liabilities
		 • Significant off-balance-sheet liabilities

• Overstatement of cash flow from operations	• Managing activities to affect cash flow from operations • Misclassifying cash flows to positively affect cash flow from Operations	• Increase in accounts payable and decrease in accounts receivable and inventory • Capitalized expenditures in investing activities • Sales and leaseback • Increases in bank overdrafts

Quality Issues and Mergers and Acquisitions

- Companies that are finding it difficult to generate cash may acquire other companies to increase cash flow from operations.
- A potential acquisition may create an incentive for management to use aggressive choices or even misreport.
- Misreporting can also be an incentive to make an acquisition.
- Acquisitions also provide opportunities to make choices that affect (1) the initial consolidated balance sheet and (2) consolidated income statements in the future.

GAAP Compliant Financial Reporting that Diverges from Economic Reality

- Recognition of asset impairments and restructuring charges in a single accounting period is consistent with most GAAP, even though they are both likely the results of past activities over an extended period.
- Other items that are commonly encountered by analysts include the following:
  - Revisions to estimates, such as the remaining economic lives of assets
  - Sudden increases in allowances and reserves
  - Large accruals for losses (e.g., environmental or litigation-related liabilities)
- Some economic assets and liabilities may not be reflected on the financial statements (e.g., leases classified as operating leases, research and development (R&D) expenses, sales order backlogs).
- Certain items presented in other comprehensive income should be included in an analysis of net income.

Quantitative Tools to Assess the Likelihood of Misreporting

Beneish Model

$$\text{M-score} = -4.84 + 0.920(\text{DSR}) + 0.528(\text{GMI}) + 0.404(\text{AQI}) + 0.892(\text{SGI}) \\ + 0.115(\text{DEPI}) - 0.172(\text{SGAI}) + 4.670(\text{Accruals}) - 0.327(\text{LEVI})$$

M-score = Score indicating probability of earnings manipulation.

- The higher the M-score (i.e., the less negative the number) the higher the probability of earnings manipulation.
- Generally speaking, a probability of earnings manipulation greater than 3.75% (corresponding to an M-score greater than −1.78) is considered a higher-than-acceptable probability of manipulation.

INDICATORS OF EARNINGS QUALITY

Recurring Earnings

- Generally speaking, reported earnings that contain a high proportion of non-recurring items (e.g., discontinued operations, one-off asset sales, one-off litigation settlements, one-off tax settlements) are less likely to be sustainable and are therefore, considered low quality.
  - For the purpose of analysis, it is important to include non-recurring items when making historical comparisons and in developing input estimates for valuation. However, analysts should always keep an eye out for classification shifting when estimating recurring or core earnings.
- Companies also understand that investors focus on recurring or core earnings. Therefore, in addition to reporting net income (on the face of the income statement), many companies voluntarily disclose pro forma income (also known as adjusted income or as non-GAAP measures) that excludes non-recurring items.
  - Analysts must recognize that some companies may be motivated to classify an item non-recurring if it improves a performance metric that is important to investors.

FRA

Earnings Persistence and Related Measures of Accruals

The higher the persistence of a company's earnings, the higher its intrinsic value.

$$\text{Earnings}_{t+1} = \alpha + \beta_1 \text{Cash flow}_t + \beta_2 \text{Accruals}_t + \varepsilon$$

- The cash component of earnings is more persistent than the accruals component so β_1 tends to be greater than β_2. The larger the accruals component of earnings, the lower the level of persistence and therefore, the lower the quality of earnings.

Discretionary versus Non-Discretionary Accruals

- Discretionary accruals arise from transactions or accounting choices outside the normal, which are possibly made with the intent to manage earnings.
- Non-discretionary accruals arise from normal transactions.

Identifying Abnormal Discretionary Accruals

- Model the company's normal accruals and then identify outliers.
- Compare the magnitude of total accruals across companies.

Other Important Points

- A relatively strong signal that earnings are being manipulated is when a company reports positive net income, but with negative operating cash flows.
- However, note that although significant accruals can suggest earnings manipulation, it is not necessary for all fraudulent companies to have sizeable accruals.
- Research has shown that extreme levels of earnings, both high and low, are mean reverting, i.e., they tend to revert to normal levels over time. Therefore, extremely high/low earnings should not simply be extrapolated into the future when constructing forecasts. If earnings have a significant accruals component, they will be expected to revert towards the mean more quickly.
- Analysts should be wary of companies that consistently report earnings that exactly meet or only narrowly beat forecasts as they may be managing reported earnings.
- Two external indicators of poor-quality earnings are (1) enforcement actions by regulatory authorities and (2) restatements of previously-issued financial statements.

Looking for Quality in Revenues[2]

Start with the Basics

- The first step should be to fully understand the revenue recognition policies as stated in the most recent annual report. Without context for the way revenue is recognized, an analyst will not understand the risks involved in the proper reporting of revenue. For instance, analysts should determine the following:
  - What are the shipping terms?
  - What rights of return does a customer have: limited or extensive?
  - Do rebates affect revenues, and if so, how are they accounted for? What estimates are involved?

    ○ Are there multiple deliverables to customers for one arrangement? If so, is revenue deferred until some elements are delivered late in the contract? If there are multiple deliverables, do deferred revenues appear on the balance sheet?

Age Matters

- A study of DSO can reveal much about their quality. Receivables do not improve with age. Analysts should seek reasons for exceptions appearing when they
  - Compare the trend in DSOs or receivables turnover over a relevant time frame.
  - Compare the DSO of one company with the DSOs of similar competitors over similar time frames.

Is It Cash or Accrual?

- A high percentage of accounts receivable to revenues might mean nothing, but it might also mean that channel-stuffing has taken place, portending high future returns of inventory or decreased demand for product in the future. Analysts should
  - Compare the percentage of accounts receivable to revenues over a relevant time frame.
  - Compare the company's percentage of accounts receivable to revenues with that of competitors or industry measures over similar time frames.

Compare with the Real World When Possible

- If a company reports non-financial data on a routine basis, try relating revenues to those data to determine whether trends in the revenue make sense. Examples include
  - Airlines reporting extensive information about miles flown and capacity, enabling an analyst to relate increases in revenues to an increase in miles flown or capacity.
  - Retailers reporting square footage used and number of stores open.
  - Companies across all industries reporting employee head counts.
- As always, analysts should compare any relevant revenue-per-unit measure with that of relevant competitors or industry measures.

Revenue Trends and Composition

- Trend analysis, over time and in comparison with competitors, can prompt analysts to ask questions of managers, or it can simply evoke discomfort with the overall revenue quality. Some relationships to examine include
  - The relationships between the kinds of revenue recognized. For example, how much is attributable to product sales or licenses, and how much is attributable to services? Have the relationships changed over time, and if so, why?
  - The relationship between overall revenue and accounts receivable. Do changes in overall revenues make sense when compared with changes in accounts receivable?

Relationships

- Does the company transact business with entities owned by senior officers or shareholders? This is a particularly sensitive area if the manager/shareholder-owned entities are private and there are revenues recognized from the private entity by a publicly owned company; it could be a dumping ground for obsolete or damaged inventory while inflating revenues.

FRA

Looking for Quality in Expense Recognition[3]

Start with the Basics

- The first step should be to fully understand the cost capitalization policies as stated in the most recent annual report. Without context for the costs stored on the balance sheet, analysts will not be able to comprehend practice exceptions they may encounter. Examples of policies that should be understood include the following:
  - What costs are capitalized in inventory? How is obsolescence accounted for? Are there reserves established for obsolescence that might be artificially raised or lowered?
  - What are the depreciation policies, including depreciable lives? How do they compare with competitors' policies? Have they changed from prior years?

Trend Analysis

- Trend analysis, over time and in comparison with competitors, can lead to questions the analyst can ask managers, or it can simply evoke discomfort with overall earnings quality because of issues with expenses. Some relationships to examine include the following:
  - Each quarter, non-current asset accounts should be examined for quarter-to-quarter and year-to-year changes to see whether there are any unusual increases in costs. If present, they might indicate that improper capitalization of costs has occurred.
  - Profit margins—gross and operating—are often observed by analysts in the examination of quarterly earnings. They are not often related to changes in the balance sheet, but they should be. If unusual buildups of non-current assets have occurred and the profit margins are improving or staying constant, it could mean that improper cost capitalization is taking place. Recall WorldCom and its improper capitalization of "line costs": Profitability was maintained by capitalizing costs that should have been expensed. Also, the overall industry environment should be considered: Are margins stable while balance sheet accounts are growing and the industry is slumping?
  - Turnover ratio for total assets; property, plant, and equipment; and other assets should be computed (with revenues divided by the asset classification). Does a trend in the ratios indicate a slowing in turnover? Decreasing revenues might mean that the assets are used to make a product with declining demand and portend future asset write-downs. Steady or rising revenues and decreasing turnover might indicate improper cost capitalization.
  - Compute the depreciation (or amortization) expense compared to the relevant asset base. Is it decreasing or increasing over time without a good reason? How does it compare with that of competitors?
  - Compare the relationship of capital expenditures with gross property, plant, and equipment over time. Is the proportion of capital expenditures relative to total property, plant, and equipment increasing significantly over time? If so, it may indicate that the company is capitalizing costs more aggressively to prevent their recognition as current expenses.

---

3 - 2018 CFA Program Curriculum Volume 2, page 332–333.

Relationships

- Does the company transact business with entities owned by senior officers or shareholders? This is a particularly sensitive area if the manager/shareholder-owned entities are private. Dealings between a public company and the manager-owned entity might take place at prices that are unfavorable for the public company in order to transfer wealth from the public company to the manager-owned entity. Such inappropriate transfers of wealth can also occur through excessive compensation, direct loans, or guarantees. These practices are often referred to as "tunneling."
- In some cases, sham dealings between the manager-owned entity and the public company might be falsely reported to improve reported profits of the public company and thus enrich the managers whose compensation is performance based. In a different type of transaction, the manager-owned entity could transfer resources to the public company to ensure its economic viability and thus preserve the option to misappropriate or to participate in profits in the future. These practices are often referred to as "propping."

Bankruptcy Protection Models

Altman Model

$$Z\text{-score} = 1.2 \text{ (Net working capital/Total assets)} + 1.4 \text{ (Retained earnings/Total assets)}$$
$$+ 3.3 \text{ (EBIT/Total assets)} + 0.6 \text{ (Market value of equity/Book value of liabilities)}$$
$$+ 1.0 \text{ (Sales/Total assets)}$$

- A higher Z-score is better.

CASH FLOW QUALITY

Indicators of Cash Flow Quality

For more established companies high-quality cash flow has the following characteristics:

- Positive OCF
- OCF derived from sustainable sources
- OCF adequate to cover capital expenditures, dividends, and debt repayment
- OCF with relatively low volatility (relative to industry participants)

FRA

Generally speaking, OCF is viewed as being less easily manipulated than operating income and net income. However, the importance of OCF to investors creates a strong incentive for managers to manipulate amounts reported. Examples of issues relating to cash flow reporting quality are:

- Boosting OCF by selling receivables to a third-party.
  - A decrease in a company's days of sales outstanding may suggest this is happening.
- Boosting OCF by delaying repayment of payables.
  - An increase in a company's days of payables may suggest this is happening.
- Misclassifying cash flows. Management may try to shift inflows of cash from investing or financing activities into the operating section of the cash flow statement to inflate reported OCF.

BALANCE SHEET QUALITY

When it comes to the balance sheet, high financial *results* quality (i.e., a strong balance sheet) is indicated by an optimal amount of leverage, adequate liquidity, and optimal asset allocation. High financial *reporting* quality is indicated by (1) completeness, (2) unbiased measurement, and (3) clear presentation.

SOURCES OF INFORMATION ABOUT RISK

- The company's financial statements
- Auditor's opinion
- Notes to the financial statements
- Management commentary (management discussion and analysis, or MD&A)
- Other required disclosures
- Financial press as a source of information about risk

INTEGRATION OF FINANCIAL STATEMENT ANALYSIS TECHNIQUES
Cross-Reference to CFA Institute Assigned Reading #19

A Financial Statement Analysis Framework:[1]

Phase	Sources of Information	Examples of Output
1. Define the purpose and context of the analysis.	• The nature of the analyst's function, such as evaluating an equity or debt investment or issuing a credit rating. • Communication with client or supervisor on needs and concerns. • Institutional guidelines related to developing specific work product.	• Statement of the purpose or objective of analysis. • A list (written or unwritten) of specific questions to be answered by the analysis. • Nature and content of report to be provided. • Timetable and budgeted resources for completion.
2. Collect input data.	• Financial statements, other financial data, questionnaires, and industry/economic data. • Discussions with management, suppliers, customers, and competitors. • Company site visits (e.g., to production facilities or retail stores)	• Organized financial statements. • Financial data tables. • Completed questionnaires, if applicable.
3. Process input data, as required, into analytically useful data.	• Data from the previous phase.	• Adjusted financial statements. • Common-size statements. • Forecasts.
4. Analyze/interpret the data.	• Input data and processed data	• Analytical results
5. Develop and communicate conclusions and recommendations (e.g., with an analysis report).	• Analytical results and previous reports • Institutional guidelines for published reports	• Analytical report answering questions posed in Phase 1 • Recommendations regarding the purpose of the analysis, such as whether to make an investment or grant credit.
6. Follow-up.	• Information gathered by periodically repeating above steps as necessary to determine whether changes to holdings or recommendations are necessary	• Update reports and recommendations

1 - 2018 CFA Program Curriculum Volume 2, Exhibit 1.

Integrated Financial Statement Analysis

- The extended Dupont decomposition is used to identify the company's key performance drivers. Equity income from associates should be removed from net income to evaluate the company's performance on a stand-alone basis.
- The company's asset base is analyzed to look for changes in the composition of the balance sheet.
- The capital structure is evaluated to determine if the company can support its strategic objectives and fulfill payment obligations.
- Segment disclosures are examined to attribute the company's overall performance to different components of the business.
- Earnings should be broken down into their cash flow and accruals components to assess their persistence and sustainability.
- The company's market value should be adjusted for the market value of the company's ownership interests in associates. The implied value of the company on a stand-alone basis should be evaluated in light of peer company valuation ratios.
- The effects of sources of off balance sheet financing on the company's operating and leverage ratios should be measured.
- The impact of proposed changes in accounting standards should be assessed as these may have a significant impact on the company's valuation.

STUDY SESSION 7: CORPORATE FINANCE (1)

CAPITAL BUDGETING
Cross-Reference to CFA Institute Assigned Reading #20

Capital Budgeting Analysis

Initial investment

Initial investment for a new investment = FCInv + NWCInv

- NWCInv = ΔNon-cash current assets − ΔNon-debt current liabilities

Initial investment for a replacement project = FCInv + NWCInv − Sal_0 + T (Sal_0 − B_0)

Annual after-tax operating cash flows

For a new investment: CF = (S − C − D) (1 − T) + D or CF = (S − C) (1 − T) + TD

For a replacement project: ΔCF = (ΔS − ΔC) (1 − t) + tΔD

Terminal year after-tax non-operating cash flows

TNOCF = Sal_T + NWCInv − T (Sal_T − B_T)

When calculating terminal year after-tax non-operating cash flow for replacement project only consider the changes in cash flows that result from the replacement.

Important:

- Accelerated depreciation methods result in greater tax savings in the early years of a capital project compared to the straight-line method. Therefore, all other factors remaining the same, accelerated depreciation methods result in a greater net present value (NPV) for a project compared to straight-line depreciation.
- Spreadsheets are commonly used to evaluate capital budgeting proposals as they provide an effective way of building complex models that allow analysts to examine the effects of changes in assumptions on valuations.

Inflation and Capital Budgeting Analysis

Analysts should use a nominal discount rate to discount nominal cash flows and a real discount rate to discount real cash flows.

(1 + Nominal rate) = (1 + Real rate) × (1 + Inflation rate)

- Inflation reduces the value of depreciation tax savings.
- If inflation is higher (lower) than expected, then the profitability of the project will be lower (higher) than expected.
- If inflation is higher (lower) than expected, real payments to bondholders are lower (higher) than expected.
- Inflation does not affect all revenues and costs uniformly.

Mutually Exclusive Projects with Unequal Lives

Least Common Multiple of Lives Approach

The lives of both the projects are extended by replicating them until both the project chains extend over the same time horizon. Given equal time horizons, the two projects are compared based on the NPVs of all the cash flows in the chain and the chain with higher NPV is chosen.

Equivalent Annual Annuity Approach

This approach calculates the annuity payment over the project's life that is equivalent in value to the project's NPV. The investment project with the higher EAA is chosen.

Capital Rationing

In an ideal situation, companies would want to invest in all available projects that generate a positive NPV. Typically however, a company will have to choose its investments in a manner that will maximize shareholder wealth given the budget constraint. This is known as capital rationing.

- Under hard capital rationing, the budget is fixed. In such situations, managers should use the NPV or PI valuation methods.
- Under soft capital rationing, the managers may be allowed to exceed their budgets if they can invest the additional funds in a profitable manner.

Risk Analysis of Capital Investments

Stand-Alone Methods

Sensitivity analysis determines the effect of a change in one input variable at a time on the NPV of the project.

Scenario analysis calculates the NPV of a project in a number of different scenarios.

Simulation (Monte Carlo) analysis estimates the probability distribution of outcomes for the NPV of a project.

Market Risk Methods

The discount rate used to calculate a project's NPV should reflect the risk associated with the project. Analysts typically use the capital asset pricing model (CAPM) to calculate this discount rate.

Required return for a project = Risk-free rate of return + Beta of the project (Market risk premium)

The required rate of return can be used in two ways. It can either be used to calculate the:

- NPV of the project and positive NPV projects are accepted; or
- IRR of the project and projects whose IRR exceeds the required rate of return are accepted.

Real Options

Real options are just like financial options and give their holders the right, but not the obligation, to make a capital budgeting decision in the future. Real options are contingent upon future events and provide managers with greater flexibility, which enhances the NPV of projects. There are several types of real options:

- Timing options give the company an option to delay investment.
- Sizing options give the company an option to either abandon a project if market conditions deteriorate, or to expand it if market conditions improve.
- Flexibility options give the company an option to either set a different price, or change the number of units produced depending on market conditions.
- Fundamental options are projects that behave as options as their payoffs are contingent on the price of an underlying asset.

Evaluating Capital Budgeting Projects with Real Options

- Use DCF analysis without considering real options.
- Use DCF analysis and add an estimated value of the real option.
- Use decision trees.
- Use option pricing models.

Common Capital Budgeting Pitfalls

- Not incorporating economic responses into the investment analysis.
- Misusing capital budgeting templates.
- Undertaking pet projects of senior managers.
- Basing investment decisions on EPS, net income, or return on equity instead of incremental cash flows.
- Using IRR instead of NPV to make investment decisions.
- Accounting for cash flows inaccurately.
- Over- or under-estimating of overhead costs.
- Not using the appropriate risk-adjusted discount rate.
- Spending the entire investment budget just because it was available.
- Failing to consider investment alternatives.
- Handling sunk costs and opportunity costs incorrectly.

Other Income Measures

Economic Income

Economic income is measured as an investment's after-tax cash flows plus the change in the investment's market value.

$$\text{Economic income} = \text{After-tax cash flows} + \text{Increase in market value}$$

$$\text{Economic income} = \text{After-tax cash flows} - \text{Economic depreciation}$$

Economic income does not explicitly deduct interest expense when calculating cash flows; interest expense is reflected in the discount rate.

Accounting Income

Accounting income refers to a company's reported net income. It differs from economic income in the following two ways:

- Accounting income subtracts interest expenses to arrive at net income.
- Unlike economic depreciation, which is based on the market value of the investment, accounting depreciation is based on the original cost of the investment.

Valuation Models

Economic Profit

Economic profit = [EBIT (1 − Tax rate)] − $WACC = NOPAT − $WACC

Future economic profit should be discounted at the weighted average cost of capital to calculate NPV.

Residual Income

Residual income = Net income for the period − Equity charge for the period

Equity charge for the period = Required return on equity × Beginning-of-period book value of equity

Future residual income should be discounted at the required return on equity to calculate NPV.

Claims Valuation

This approach values a firm based on the values of claims of debt and equity holders against the firm's assets. Cash flows available to debt and equity holders are separated and the cash flows available to debt holders are discounted at the cost of debt, while cash flows available to equity holders are discounted at the cost of equity. The present values of the two are added to calculate the NPV.

CAPITAL STRUCTURE
Cross-Reference to CFA Institute Assigned Reading #21

The Capital Structure Decision

A company's capital structure refers to the combination of debt and equity capital it uses to finance its business. The goal is to determine the capital structure that results in the minimum weighted average cost of capital and consequently, in the maximum value of the company.

$$r_{WACC} = \left(\frac{D}{V}\right) r_D (1-t) + \left(\frac{E}{V}\right) r_E$$

MM Assumptions

- Investors have homogeneous expectations.
- Capital markets are perfect.
- Investors can borrow and lend at the risk-free rate.
- There are no agency costs.
- The financing decision and the investment decision are independent of each other.

MM Proposition I without Taxes: Capital Structure Irrelevance

Given the assumptions listed above and no taxes, changes in capital structure do not affect company value.

$$V_L = V_U$$

MM Proposition II without Taxes: Higher Financial Leverage Raises the Cost of Equity

Debt finance is cheaper than equity finance. However, increased use of debt leads to an increase in the required rate of return on equity. The higher required return on equity is exactly offset by the cheaper cost of debt and therefore, there is no change in the company's weighted average cost of capital. Basically, the company's cost of capital is not determined by its capital structure but by business risk.

$$r_E = r_0 + (r_0 - r_D)\frac{D}{E}$$

$$V = \frac{Interest}{r_D} + \frac{EBIT - Interest}{r_E}$$

Relaxing the Assumption of no Taxes

MM Proposition I with Taxes

Use of debt would actually increase the value of a company. Interest paid is tax deductible in most countries, so the use of debt results in tax savings for the company. Therefore, the value of a levered company is greater than that of an unlevered company by an amount equal to the marginal tax rate multiplied by the value of debt:

$$V_L = V_U + tD$$

In this scenario (with no costs of financial distress), the value of a company would be maximized if its capital structure comprised of 100% debt.

MM Proposition II with Taxes

The cost of equity would still increase with increased debt financing, but not fast enough to exactly offset the use of (cheaper) debt, thereby decreasing the company's weighted average cost of capital. Under this scenario, a company's weighted average cost of capital is minimized at 100% debt.

$$r_{WACC} = \left(\frac{D}{V}\right)r_D(1-t) + \left(\frac{E}{V}\right)r_E$$

$$r_E = r_0 + (r_0 - r_D)(1-t)\left(\frac{D}{E}\right)$$

$$V_L = \frac{Interest}{r_D} + \frac{EBIT - Interest}{r_E}$$

MM Propositions

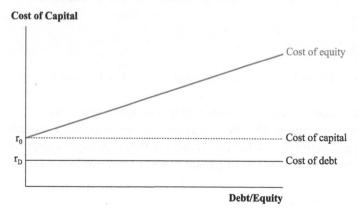

Figure 07.1a:
Cost of Capital with No Taxes.

MM Proposition II (without taxes) states that the use of cheaper debt increases the cost of equity. The increase in the cost of equity exactly offsets the benefit of adding cheaper debt to the capital structure, resulting in a constant WACC (cost of capital).

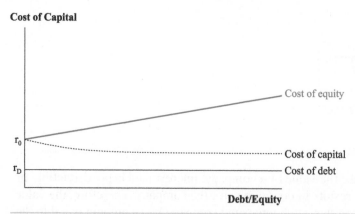

Figure 07.1b:
Cost of Capital with Taxes

Under MM Proposition II (with taxes) the cost of equity still increases, but not fast enough to completely undo the benefit of using cheaper debt (since debt also results in an interest tax shield), resulting in a decrease in the company's weighted average cost of capital.

Costs of Financial Distress

The expected cost of financial distress equals the actual cost of financial distress times the probability that the company will face financial distress. Leverage increases the costs of financial distress and the probability of financial distress.

Agency Costs

The conflicts of interest between owners and managers in all public and large private companies give rise to agency costs, which include:

- Monitoring costs
- Bonding costs
- Residual loss

Using more debt in the capital structure reduces net agency costs of equity.

Costs of Asymmetric Information

Information asymmetry arises from the fact that a company's managers generally have more information about its performance than outsiders. Managers prefer internal financing and debt over equity as sources of raising capital (pecking order theory). Costs of asymmetric information decrease as more debt is issued.

The Optimal Capital Structure—Static Trade-Off Theory

Managers must balance the use of debt in a way that its tax shield benefits are exactly offset by its associated costs of financial distress.

$$V_L = V_U + tD - PV \text{ (Costs of financial distress)}$$

The capital structure at which company value is maximized is the same as the capital structure at which the cost of capital (WACC) is minimized. Further, note that the WACC curve is U-shaped:

- Initially as more debt is added to the capital structure, the WACC falls due to the lower cost of debt (compared to equity).
- Eventually, WACC increases as the cost of equity and the cost of debt both rise to compensate for the higher risk associated with high debt levels.

CF

Trade-Off Theory with Taxes and Costs of Financial Distress

Value of Company and the D/E Ratio

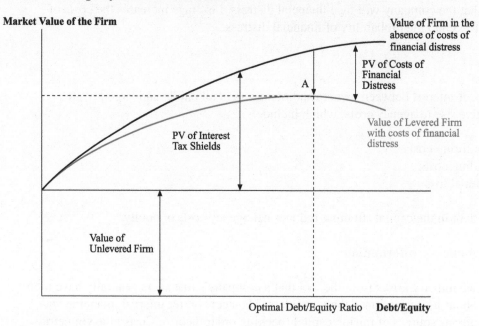

Cost of Capital and the D/E Ratio

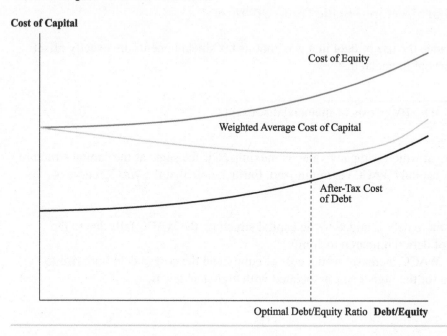

The weight of debt in an optimal capital structure is less than 100%. Companies usually adopt their optimal capital structure as their target capital structure with periods during which they temporarily deviate from their target capital structure due to the following reasons:

- It may make sense to exploit short-term opportunities in another source of financing.
- Changes in market values of debt and equity result in a change in the company's capital structure.
- It might be impractical or expensive to maintain the target capital structure.

Practical Issues in Capital Structure Policy

Debt Ratings

Higher financial leverage lowers a company's debt ratings, which results in higher costs of raising additional debt. Companies therefore strive to maintain a level of debt which would not result in a downgrade in their credit rating.

Capital Structure Policy

When evaluating a company's capital structure policy an analyst should consider:

- Changes in the company's capital structure over time.
- The capital structure of competitors that have similar business risks.
- Company specific factors that may affect agency costs (e.g., corporate governance).

Leverage in an International Setting

Differences in capital structures across countries may be explained by:

- Institutional and legal environment.
- Financial markets and banking sector.
- Macroeconomic environment.

The impact of these factors is summarized in the following table:

Country-Specific Factor	D/E Ratio	Maturity of Debt
Institutional Framework		
Efficient legal system	Lower	Longer
Common law as opposed to civil law	Lower	Longer
Lower information asymmetry	Lower	Longer
Favorable taxes on equity	Lower	N/A
Financial Markets and Banking System		
Active bond and stock market	N/A	Longer
Bank-based financial system	Higher	N/A
Large institutional investors	Lower	Longer
Macroeconomic Environment		
High inflation	Lower	Shorter
High GDP growth	Lower	Longer

CF

DIVIDENDS AND SHARE REPURCHASES: ANALYSIS
Cross-Reference to CFA Institute Assigned Reading #22

Dividend Policy and Company Value: Theory

CASH DIVIDENDS

Regular Cash Dividends

- A record of consistent dividends over an extended period of time indicates that the company is consistently profitable.
- A trend of increasing regular dividends over time indicates that the company is doing well and is willing to share profits with shareholders. This suggests that the company's shares are of high investment quality.
- An increase in a company's regular dividend, especially if unexpected, can send a very strong message out to investors and usually has a positive effect on share price.

Dividend Reinvestment Plans (DRPs)

A dividend reinvestment plan (DRP) is a system that allows investors to reinvest all or a portion of cash dividends received from a company in shares of the company. There are three types of DRPs:

- Open market DRPs, in which the company purchases shares (on behalf of plan participants) from the open market.
- New-issue DRPs or scrip dividend schemes, in which the company issues additional shares instead of repurchasing them.
- Plans where companies are permitted to obtain additional shares through open-market purchases or new issuances.

Advantages to the Company

- The shareholder base is diversified as smaller investors gain easier access to additional shares in the company. Companies usually prefer a broad and diversified shareholder base.
- They may encourage long-term investment in the company by building investor loyalty to the company.
- New issue DRPs allow companies to raise equity capital without incurring flotation costs.

Advantages to Shareholders

- Shareholders can accumulate shares in the company using dollar-cost averaging.
- DRPs are a cost-effective means for small investors to purchase additional shares in the company.
- There are no transaction costs associated with obtaining shares through a DRP.
- Shares offered in a DRP are sometimes issued to shareholders at a discount to the market price.

Disadvantages to Shareholders

- In jurisdictions where capital gains are taxed, investors must keep records of the cost basis of shares received to accurately compute gains and losses when shares are sold. If the shares are obtained at a price that is higher (lower) than the purchase price of the shares originally held, the investor's average cost basis will increase (decrease).
- Cash dividends are fully taxed in the year they are received (even if reinvested). As a result, an investor who participates in a DRP may have to pay tax on cash that he actually does not receive.
- If new shares are issued at a discount, shareholders that do not participate in the DRP tend to suffer dilution.

Extra or Special (Irregular) Dividends

A special dividend refers to a dividend payment by a company that does not usually pay dividends, or a dividend payment on top of the company's regular dividend. Companies use special dividends to distribute more earnings in strong years and to distribute excess cash to shareholders.

Liquidating Dividends

A dividend payment is known as a liquidating dividend when:

- A company goes out of business and its net assets are distributed to shareholders.
- A company sells off a portion of its business and distributes the proceeds to shareholders.
- A company pays out a dividend that is greater than its retained earnings. Such a payment reduces (impairs) the company's stated capital.

STOCK DIVIDENDS

A stock dividend or a bonus issue occurs when a company issues additional common shares in the company (instead of cash) to shareholders.

- The investor ends up with more shares, which she did not have to pay for.
- The company issues a dividend without spending any cash.
- The market value of the company does not change in response to a stock dividend.
- The investor's average cost per share falls, but the total cost remains unchanged.

Stock dividends do not affect an investor's proportionate ownership of a company. A stock dividend basically just divides the market value of a firm's equity into smaller pieces, but the percentage of the company owned by each shareholder remains the same, as does the market value of each investor's holding. Stock dividends are generally not taxable.

Advantages of Paying Out Stock Dividends

- With more shares outstanding there is a greater chance of more small shareholders owning the stock, which broadens the company's shareholder base.
- Stock dividends could bring the stock's market price into the "optimal range" (believed to lie somewhere between $20 and $80 for U.S. companies), where investors are attracted to the stock.

CF

Differences between Stock Dividends and Cash Dividends for the Company

Cash dividends reduce assets (cash) and shareholders' equity (retained earnings). When a company pays out cash dividends, not only do liquidity ratios deteriorate, but leverage ratios (e.g., debt-assets and debt-equity ratios) also worsen. On the other hand, stock dividends do not have any effect on a company's capital structure. Retained earnings fall by the value of stock dividends paid, but there is an offsetting increase in contributed capital so there is no change in shareholders' equity. Therefore, stock dividends have no impact on a company's liquidity and solvency ratios.

STOCK SPLITS

Stock splits are similar to stock dividends in that they increase the total number of shares outstanding and have no economic effect on the company. If a company announces a 3-for-1 stock split, it means that each investor will get an additional 2 shares (to make a total of 3) for each share originally held.

- The investor ends up with more shares, which she did not have to pay for.
- The company issues a dividend without spending any cash.
- The market value of the company does not change in response to a stock split.
- The investor's average cost per share falls, but the total cost remains unchanged.

A stock dividend results in a transfer of retained earnings to contributed capital, whereas a stock split has no impact on any shareholders' equity accounts.

Companies typically announce stock splits after a period during which the stock price has appreciated significantly to bring it down into a more marketable range. Many investors however, see a stock split announcement as a signal for future stock price appreciation.

A reverse stock split increases the share price and reduces the number of shares outstanding. Similar to stock splits, the aim of a reverse stock split is to bring the stock price into a more marketable range.

DIVIDEND POLICY AND COMPANY VALUE: THEORY

Dividend Policy Does Not Matter

Miller and Modigliani proposed that under the assumptions of perfect capital markets a company's dividend policy should have no impact on its cost of capital or on shareholders' wealth because:

- A company's dividend policy is independent of its investment and financing decisions.
- If shareholders needed investment income, they could construct their own cash flow stream by selling a sufficient number of shares without incurring any costs (homemade dividends).

Note that under the MM assumptions, there is no distinction between dividends and share repurchases.

Market imperfections make it difficult to apply this theory in the real world.

- Companies and individuals incur transactions costs.
- Stock price volatility creates difficulties in creating homemade dividends.

Dividend Policy Matters: The Bird in Hand Argument

- Even under perfect capital markets, shareholders prefer current dividends over uncertain capital gains in the future.
- Shareholders require a lower return from companies that pay dividends, which lowers the cost of capital for those companies and increases their share prices.

MM counter: Paying dividends does not affect the risk of future cash flows; it only lowers the ex-dividend price of the stock with no impact on shareholder wealth.

Dividend Policy Matters: The Tax Argument

- Many countries impose a higher tax on dividends than on capital gains.
- Taxable investors therefore prefer companies that pay lower cash dividends and reinvest their earnings in profitable growth opportunities.
- In cases where companies do not have profitable growth opportunities, those investors would prefer share repurchases over cash dividends.

Other Theoretical Issues

Clientele Effect

- Different groups of investors prefer different dividend policies and are attracted to companies that match their desired policies.
- Investors' marginal tax rates also have an effect on their preference for dividends.
- Some institutional investors prefer to invest only in companies that pay dividends.

The clientele effect does not lead to the conclusion that dividend policy affects shareholder wealth; it only asserts that dividend policy attracts investors who prefer that particular policy. Therefore, a change in a company's dividend policy would have no effect on shareholders' wealth and would only result in a switch in its clientele.

More on tax considerations:

The expected decrease in share price when a stock goes ex-dividend can be calculated using the following expression:

$$P_w - P_x = \frac{1 - T_D}{1 - T_{CG}} \times D$$

- If the investor's marginal tax rate on dividends is equal to that on capital gains, the decrease in share price when it goes ex-dividend should be equal to the amount of the dividend.
- If the investor's marginal tax rate on dividends is higher (lower) than that on capital gains, the decrease in share price when it goes ex-dividend should be less (more) than the amount of the dividend.

Signalling Effect

- Dividend initiations or increases are usually taken as positive signals and lead to an increase in stock price.
    - A dividend declaration can reduce some of the information asymmetry between insiders and outsiders and close the gap between the market price and intrinsic value of the stock.
    - A dividend initiation or increase tends to be associated with share price increases because it attracts more attention to the company.
    - In contrast, managers of overvalued companies have little reason to mimic such a signal because increased scrutiny would presumably result in a downward price adjustment to their shares.
- Companies that consistently increase their dividends seem to share the following characteristics:
    - Dominant or niche positions in their industry.
    - Global operations.
    - Relatively less volatile earnings.
    - Relatively high returns on assets.
    - Relatively low debt ratios.

Controlling Agency Costs

- Shareholders are often concerned about management investing in projects that may increase the size of the company, but reduce shareholder wealth. In such cases, payment of cash dividends constrains management's ability to overinvest.
- Excessive dividends reduce the amount of cash available to the company to make payments to its bondholders. Bondholders often restrict the amount of dividends that can be paid by a company during the term of their bonds through covenants.

Factors Affecting Dividend Policy

- **Investment opportunities:** All else being equal, companies that have greater profitable investment opportunities tend to pay lower dividends.
- **Expected volatility of future earnings:** All else being equal, companies with high expected volatility of future earnings tend to be more cautious in the size and frequency of dividend increases.
- **Financial flexibility:** A company's management may omit or cut dividends to keep substantial cash in hand to deal with any unforeseen circumstances.
- **Tax considerations:** The lower an investor's marginal tax rate on dividends relative to her marginal tax rate on capital gains, the stronger her preference for dividends. However, an important factor that works in favour of income from capital gains is that capital gains taxes do not have to be paid until shares are sold, while taxes on dividends must be paid when dividends are received.

- Flotation costs: Internally generated funds are the cheapest source of finance for a company. Companies with profitable investment opportunities tend to pay lower dividends and reinvest cash as opposed to issuing equity (with high associated flotation costs) when cash needs arise.
- Contractual and legal restrictions: Companies may be contractually or legally obligated to pay out dividends or to restrict the amount of dividends paid. This may be due to government regulations or bond covenants.

Taxation Methods

- Double taxation: A company's earnings are first taxed at the corporate level and then again at the shareholder level when distributed as dividends.

$$ETR = CTR + [(1 - CTR) \times MTR_D]$$

- Split-rate: A company's earnings that are distributed as dividends are taxed at a lower rate than earnings that are retained by the company. Dividends are then taxed again at the shareholder level as ordinary income.
- Imputation: A company's earnings that are distributed as dividends are taxed only once, at the shareholder's marginal tax rate.

$$ETR = CTR_D + [(1 - CTR_D) \times MTR_D]$$

Payout Policies

Stable Dividend Policy

Companies attempt to pay a regular stream of dividends (unaffected by short-term earnings volatility) and increase dividends only when forecasts suggest that the increase will be sustainable. Companies following this policy usually set a target payout ratio based on long-term sustainable earnings and make dividend increases accordingly.

$$\text{Expected increase in dividends} = (\text{Expected earnings} \times \text{Target payout ratio} - \text{Previous dividend}) \times \text{Adjustment factor}$$

Constant Dividend Payout Ratio Policy

This policy is followed by companies that want to reflect the cyclical nature of their business in the payment of dividends. They aim to pay out a constant percentage of net income as dividends.

CF

Residual Dividend Policy

Companies following this policy pay out dividends only if there is sufficient cash after accounting for investment opportunities in positive NPV projects.

- This policy results in significant fluctuations in the amount of dividends paid.
- To smooth their dividend payments, companies usually forecast earnings and capital expenditure requirements for a number of years in the future. This helps them determine residual dividends, which are then paid evenly over the forecast period.

> Dividend = Residual earnings = Earnings − (Capital budget × Equity percent in capital structure), or zero, whichever is greater.

SHARE REPURCHASES

A share repurchase occurs when a company buys back its own shares. Shares that are repurchased by the company are known as Treasury shares and once repurchased, are not considered for dividends, voting or calculating earnings per share.

Share Repurchases versus Cash Dividends

- Just because a company authorizes a share repurchase, it does not necessarily mean that the company is obligated to go through with the purchase. For cash dividends, once a company announces a dividend, it is committed to paying them.
- Cash dividends are distributed to shareholders in proportion to their ownership percentage. However, repurchases generally do not distribute cash in such a manner.

Share Repurchase Methods

Buy in the open market: Under this method, the company repurchases shares from the open market. Buying in the open market offers the company flexibility and is also cost-effective.

Buy back a fixed number of shares at a fixed price: This type of repurchase is known as a fixed price tender offer. The company offers to purchase a fixed number of shares at a fixed price (typically at a premium to the current market price) at a fixed date in the future. Fixed price tender offers can be accomplished very quickly.

Dutch Auction: Instead of specifying a fixed price for all the shares that the company wants to buy back (as is the case in a fixed price tender offer), under a Dutch Auction the company specifies a range of acceptable prices. Shareholders who are interested in selling their shares specify their selling price and the amount of shares that they want to sell. The company accepts the lowest bids first and then accepts higher and higher bids until it has repurchased the desired number of shares. Dutch auctions can also be accomplished relatively quickly.

Repurchase by direct negotiation: This occurs when a company negotiates directly with a major shareholder to buy back its shares. This may occur in the following situations:

- A large shareholder wants to sell off its shares and the company wants to prevent the large block of shares from overhanging the market and depressing the share price.
- The company wants to buy out a large shareholder to prevent it from gaining representation on the company's board of directors.

Effects of Share Repurchases

Share repurchases have an effect on a company's balance sheet and its income statement. If the repurchase is financed with cash, assets (cash) and shareholders' equity decline, and result in an increase in reported debt ratios. On the income statement, repurchases can increase or decrease EPS depending on how and at what cost the repurchase is financed.

- If the funds used to finance the repurchase are generated internally, a repurchase will increase EPS only if the funds would not have earned the company's cost of capital if they were retained by the company.
- If borrowed funds are used to finance the repurchase, and the after-tax cost of borrowing is greater than the company's earnings yield, EPS will fall.
- If borrowed funds are used to finance the repurchase, and the after-tax cost of borrowing is lower than the company's earnings yield, EPS will rise.

It would be incorrect to infer that an increase in EPS indicates an increase in shareholder wealth. The cash used to finance the repurchase could as easily have been distributed as a cash dividend. Any capital gains resulting from an increase in EPS from share repurchases may be offset by a decrease in the stock's dividend yield.

Effects of Share Repurchases on Book Value

- When the market price is greater than the book value per share, book value per share will decrease after the repurchase.
- When the market price is lower than the book value per share, book value per share will increase after the repurchase.

Impact on Shareholder Wealth of Cash Dividends and Share Repurchases

The impact on shareholder wealth of distributing cash to shareholders through a share repurchase or a cash dividend is the same. However, the above analysis assumes that:

- Dividends are received as soon as the shares go ex-dividend.
- Tax implications of dividends and repurchases are the same.
- The information content of the two policies does not differ.
- The company can purchase any number of shares at the current market price. If the company must repurchase stock at a premium to the current market price, shareholders whose shares are repurchased benefit, while remaining shareholders suffer a decrease in their wealth.

CF

Cash Dividends versus Share Repurchases

All else being equal, the impact of share repurchases on shareholders' wealth is the same as that of cash dividends. Managers often prefer share repurchases over cash dividends because of the following reasons:

- Potential tax advantages.
- Share price support / signalling that the company considers its shares a good investment.
- Added managerial flexibility.
- Offset dilution from employee stock options.
- Increasing financial leverage.

Share repurchases can signal that:

- Management thinks that the company's shares are undervalued.
- The company has few positive NPV investment opportunities.

Analysis of Dividend Safety

All else being equal, a *higher* dividend payout ratio or a *lower* dividend coverage ratio *increases* the risk of a dividend cut or omission.

A comprehensive measure of dividend safety is the FCFE-coverage ratio:

$$\text{FCFE coverage ratio} = \text{FCFE} / [\text{Dividends} + \text{Share repurchases}]$$

- If the ratio equals 1, the company is distributing all available cash to shareholders.
- If the ratio is greater than 1, the company is retaining some earnings to enhance liquidity.
- If the ratio is less than 1, the company is borrowing cash to pay dividends.

Past financial data is not always an accurate determinant of future dividend safety. Unforeseen circumstances may force dividend-paying companies to cut or even omit their dividends altogether.

CORPORATE PERFORMANCE, GOVERNANCE, AND BUSINESS ETHICS
Cross-Reference to CFA Institute Assigned Reading #23

A company's stakeholders are individuals or groups with an interest, claim, or stake in the company. Internal stakeholders include stockholders and employees (including managers, executives, and board members), while external stakeholders include customers, suppliers, creditors, governments, unions, local communities, and the general public.

Stakeholder Impact Analysis

In making choices between stakeholder groups, the company should prioritize the interests of its most important stakeholders. In order to identify its most important stakeholders, companies perform stakeholder impact analysis (SIA). This exercise has typically led companies to the conclusion that their three most important stakeholder groups are customers, employees, and stockholders.

Improving a company's profitability and profit growth rate goes a long way in satisfying stockholders as well as the claims of several stakeholder groups (other than just stockholders). However, not all stakeholder groups want the company to maximize its long-run profitability and profit growth (e.g., suppliers and customers)

Agency Theory

Agency theory seeks to explain why managers might engage in behavior that is either illegal or, at the very least, not in the interests of the company's stockholders.

Information asymmetry arises because stockholders delegate decision-making authority to the CEO, who by virtue of his or her position inside the company is likely to know far more than stockholders do about the company's operations. While stockholders are aware of this information asymmetry, they have no choice but to trust that the agent will serve their interests. Principals try to deal with these challenges through a series of governance mechanisms that:

- Shape the behavior of agents so that they act in line with the goals set by principals.
- Reduce the information asymmetry between agents and principals.
- Remove agents who do not prioritize the goals of principals and mislead them.

Ethical Issues in Strategy

Those who take the stakeholder view of business ethics often argue that managers should behave in an ethical manner because doing so will ensure the support of stakeholders and thus ultimately benefit the firm and its managers (i.e, managers who behave ethically only do so in "enlightened self-interest"). Others go a step further and argue that businesses need to recognize their noblesse oblige and give something back to the society that made their success possible.

The Roots of Unethical Behavior

- An agent who lacks a strong sense of personal ethics is more likely to behave in an unethical manner in a business setting.
- An agent may not realize that she is behaving unethically, probably because the decision-making process used does not incorporate ethical considerations.
- An organizational culture that encourages making all decisions purely on economic grounds.
- Pressure from senior management to meet unrealistic performance goals.
- Unethical leadership that sets a precedent within the company that leads to violations.

Behaving Ethically

Managers should:

- Favor hiring and promoting people with a well-grounded sense of personal ethics.
- Build an organizational culture that places a high value on ethical behavior.
- Establish systematic decision-making processes that provide managers with a moral compass.
- Appoint ethics officers who (1) train employees to always be ethically aware, (2) review decisions to make sure that are ethically responsible, and (3) handle confidential inquiries/complaints from employees.
- Establish strong corporate governance procedures to ensure that managers adhere to ethical norms.
- Strengthen the moral courage of employees by supporting employees who exercise moral courage, say no to superiors, or otherwise complain about unethical actions.

Philosophical Approaches to Ethics

The Friedman Doctrine

- The only social responsibility of business is to increase profits, as long as the company stays within the **rules of law**.
- Businesses have no responsibility to make social investments. If stockholders wish to undertake social expenditures, they can do it with their own money.
- Businesses should behave in an ethical manner, and not engage in deceit or fraud.
- Businesses should remain "within the rules of the game." Unfortunately, rules of the game are not always well-established, and tend to be different across cultures.

Utilitarian Ethics

- The best decisions are those that produce the greatest good for the greatest number of people.
- While it is theoretically appealing, this philosophy has its drawbacks.
  - First, measuring the benefits, costs, and risks of an action is not always straightforward.
  - Second, the philosophy does not consider justice.

Kantian Ethics

- People should be treated as ends and never purely as means to the ends of others.
- While the argument here is widely accepted, it is still an incomplete ethical framework.

Rights Theories

- People have certain fundamental rights that take precedence over a collective good. These rights form the basis for the moral compass that managers should apply in evaluating the ethical component of business decisions.
- The obligation to ensure that the rights of others are secured falls on more than one moral agent (a person or institution that is capable of moral action, including the government and corporations).

Justice Theories

- There should be a just (i.e., fair and equitable) distribution of economic goods and services.
- In a system where everyone is under the veil of ignorance (i.e., if everyone is ignorant of his or her particular characteristics, e.g., race, sex, intelligence, nationality, family background, etc.), people would unanimously agree on two fundamental principles of justice.
  - First, that each person should be permitted the maximum amount of basic liberty.
  - Second, that once equal basic liberty is ensured, inequality in basic social goods (income, wealth, and opportunities) is acceptable only if it benefits the least-advantaged person (differencing principle).

CORPORATE GOVERNANCE
Cross-Reference to CFA Institute Assigned Reading #24

Objectives of Corporate Governance

- Eliminate or reduce conflicts of interest, especially those between managers and shareholders, and
- Ensure that the company's assets are used in the best interests of its investors and other stakeholders.

An Effective Corporate Governance System

- Describes the rights of shareholders and other important stakeholders.
- Defines to stakeholders the responsibilities of managers and directors.
- Identifies measurable accountabilities for the performance of responsibilities.
- Ensures fairness and equitable treatment in all dealings between managers, directors, and shareholders.
- Ensures complete transparency and accuracy in disclosures regarding operations, performance, risk, and financial position.

The system of corporate governance is affected by the way a business is structured. Three main forms of businesses are discussed below:

Conflicts of Interest in Agency Relationships

- **Manager-shareholder conflicts:** Managers are entrusted with the capital provided by shareholders. Conflicts arise when, instead of using those funds for the benefit of shareholders, managers may use them for their own welfare. Managers may only invest in projects that increase the size of the firm or the firm's revenue, but are not in the best interests of shareholders in the long-term.
- **Director-shareholder conflicts:** The board of directors of a company serves as an intermediary between the managers and owners. Directors act as agents of shareholders, entrusted with the responsibility of keeping a check on management. Conflicts arise when directors identify with the interests of management and prioritize those interests ahead of those of shareholders.

Responsibilities of the Board of Directors

- Establish corporate values and governance structures in the company to ensure that the business is conducted in an ethical, competent, fair and professional manner.
- Ensure that all legal and regulatory requirements are met and complied with fully in a timely manner.
- Establish long-term strategic objectives for the company with the goal of ensuring that the interests of shareholders come first and that the company's obligations to others are met in a timely and complete manner.
- Establish clear lines of responsibility and a strong system of accountability and performance measurement in all areas of the company's operations.
- Hire the chief executive officer, determine the compensation package, and periodically evaluate the officer's performance.

- Ensure that management has supplied the board with sufficient information for it to be fully-informed and prepared to make the decisions that are its responsibility, and to be able to adequately monitor and oversee the company's management.
- Meet frequently enough to adequately perform its duties, and meet in extraordinary sessions as required by events.
- Acquire adequate training so that members are able to perform their duties properly.

Desirable Characteristics of an Effective Board of Directors

An effective board of directors should have the following characteristics:

- 75% of the board should consist of independent members.
- The CEO and the chairman of the board should be separate.
- Directors should possess the appropriate skills and experience to fulfil their fiduciary responsibilities to stakeholders.
- The whole board should either be elected annually or only a portion of directors should be up for re-election each year (staggered board).
- The board of directors should conduct a self-evaluation at least annually.
- The directors should meet at least annually without management being present.
- There should be an audit committee consisting of independent board members responsible for complete oversight of the company's audit practices.
- There should be a nominations committee consisting of independent board members responsible for identifying and evaluating candidates for the board of directors and senior management.
- There should be a compensation committee consisting of independent board members responsible for setting directors' and managers' compensation.
- The board should have access to independent or expert legal counsel.
- There should be a statement of governance policies.

Environmental, Social, and Governmental Risk Exposures

- Legislative and regulatory risk
- Legal risk
- Reputational risk
- Operating risk
- Financial risk

Valuation Implications of Corporate Governance

Studies show that the quality of the corporate governance system of a company is directly related to shareholder wealth. Weak corporate governance systems pose the following risks to investors:

- Accounting risk
- Asset risk
- Liability risk
- Strategic policy risk

MERGERS AND ACQUISITIONS
Cross-Reference to CFA Institute Assigned Reading #25

An acquisition refers to the purchase of some portion of one company by another.

A merger occurs when a company purchases an entire company.

- In a statutory merger, all the assets and liabilities of the acquired company become part of the purchasing company and the acquired company ceases to exist as an identifiable entity.
- In a subsidiary merger, the acquired company becomes a subsidiary of the purchasing company.
- In a consolidation, both companies terminate their previous legal existence and form a new company.

Types of Mergers

- A horizontal merger occurs when two companies operating in the same kind of business merge.
- A vertical merger occurs when a company merges with another company in the same chain of production.
- A conglomerate merger occurs when a company merges with another company operating in a completely different line of business.

Motives for Mergers

- Synergy
- Growth
- Increasing market power
- Acquiring unique capabilities
- Diversification
- Bootstrapping earnings
- Managers' personal incentives
- Tax considerations
- Unlocking hidden value
- Cross-border motivations
  - To exploit market imperfections, e.g., lower cost of labor.
  - To overcome adverse government policies, such as protective tariffs, quotas, or other barriers to free trade.
  - To transfer superior technology to new markets.
  - To differentiate products from those of competitors as well as to acquire a good reputation.
  - To follow clients globally.

Mergers and Industry Life Cycles

Industry Life Cycle Stage	Industry Description	Motives for Merger	Types of Merger
Pioneering development	• Low but slowly increasing sales growth. • Substantial development costs.	• Younger, smaller companies may sell themselves to larger firms in mature or declining industries to enter into a new growth industry. • Young companies may merge with firms that allow them to pool management and capital resources.	• Conglomerate • Horizontal
Rapid accelerating growth	• High profit margins. • Low competition.	• To meet substantial capital requirements for expansion.	• Conglomerate • Horizontal
Mature growth	• Decrease in the entry of new competitors. • Growth potential remains.	• To achieve economies of scale, savings, and operational efficiencies.	• Horizontal • Vertical
Stabilization and market maturity	• Increasing capacity constraints. • Increasing competition.	• To achieve economies of scale in research, production, and marketing to match low costs and prices of competitors. • Large companies may buy smaller companies to improve management and provide a broader financial base.	• Horizontal
Deceleration of growth and decline	• Overcapacity. • Eroding profit margins.	• Horizontal mergers to ensure survival. • Vertical mergers to increase efficiency and profit margins. • Conglomerate mergers to exploit synergy. • Companies in the industry may acquire companies in young industries.	• Horizontal • Vertical • Conglomerate

Transaction Characteristics

Forms of Acquisition

- **Stock purchase:** This occurs when the acquirer purchases the target company's stock from its shareholders.
- **Asset purchase:** This occurs when the acquirer purchases the target company's assets by making a direct payment to the target company.

Major Differences of Stock versus Asset Purchases

	Stock Purchase	Asset Purchase
Payment	Target shareholders receive compensation in exchange for their shares.	Payment is made to the selling company rather than directly to shareholders.
Approval	Shareholder approval required.	Shareholder approval might not be required.
Tax: Corporate	No corporate-level taxes.	Target company pays taxes on any capital gains.
Tax: Shareholder	Target company's shareholders are taxed on their capital gain.	No direct tax consequence for target company's shareholders.
Liabilities	Acquirer assumes the target's liabilities.	Acquirer generally avoids the assumption of liabilities.

Methods of Payment

An acquirer may pay for the merger either with cash, by offering its own securities, or through a mixed offering.

- A stock offering transfers a portion of the risks and rewards of the acquisition to target company's shareholders. Therefore, if the acquirer is highly confident about the benefits of the merger, it would prefer to pay cash (in order to enjoy all the benefits of acquisition). Further, the more strongly target shareholders believe that the merger will create value, the more they will push for a stock offering.
- If the acquirer's shares are considered overvalued by the market relative to the target company's shares, the acquirer would prefer to pay in stock.
- The method of payment also depends on the acquirer's preference regarding the capital structure. Cash payment requires the issuance of debt which increases financial leverage. On the other hand, issuance of new shares for a stock offering dilutes the ownership interests of existing shareholders.

Mind-Set of Target Management

Friendly Mergers

Before reaching a formal deal, both parties conduct due diligence in which they both examine the others' books and records to confirm the accuracy of their statements in negotiations. After the completion of due diligence and successful negotiations, the parties enter into a definitive merger agreement, which contains the details of the transaction. This is the stage at which the parties publicly announce their intention to merge and the merger is now subject to shareholder approval.

Hostile Mergers

A hostile merger is one that is opposed by the target company's management. In this case, the acquirer may bypass management to make the offer directly to the target company's board of directors in a tactic known as a bear hug. If the company's directors consider the offer to be high enough, they may appoint a special committee to negotiate the sale.

In some situations, the acquirer may directly approach the shareholders of the target company through a tender offer. A tender offer can be made with cash, shares of the acquirer's own stock, other securities, or some combination of securities and cash.

An acquirer may also try to take control of the target company through a proxy fight. Shareholders are asked to vote for the acquirer's proposed list of directors. If elected, the new board of directors may change the target company's management and the takeover may turn friendly.

Takeovers

Pre-Offer Takeover Defense Mechanisms

- Poison pills
- Poison puts
- Incorporation in a state with restrictive laws
- Staggered board of directors
- Restricted voting rights
- Supermajority voting provisions
- Fair price amendments
- Golden parachutes

Post-Offer Takeover Defense Mechanisms

- "Just say no" defense
- Litigation
- Greenmail
- Share repurchase
- Leveraged recapitalization "Crown Jewel" defense
- "Pac-man" defense
- White knight defense
- White squire defense

Regulation

Antitrust Laws

These laws ensure that markets remain competitive. A common measure of market power is the Herfindahl-Hirschman Index (HHI). It measures market concentration by summing the squares of the market shares for each company in an industry.

$$HHI = \sum_{i}^{n} \left(\frac{\text{Sales or output of firm } i}{\text{Total sales or output of market}} \times 100 \right)^2$$

A higher HHI means that the industry is highly concentrated and there is little competition. Regulatory authorities are not only concerned with the HHI before the merger, but also with the change in HHI due to the merger.

HHI concentration level

Post-Merger HHI	Concentration	Change in HHI	Government Action
Less than 1,000	Not concentrated	Any amount	No action
Between 1,000 and 1,800	Moderately concentrated	100 or more	Possible challenge
More than 1,800	Highly concentrated	50 or more	Challenge

Additional considerations used in evaluating market power:

- Responsiveness of consumers to price changes.
- Efficiency of companies in the industry.
- Financial viability of merger candidates.
- Ability of U.S. companies to compete in foreign markets.

Securities Laws

These laws aim to maintain both fairness in merger activities and confidence in financial markets. The most important securities law is the Williams Act.

Merger Analysis

Target Company Valuation

Discounted Cash Flow Analysis

In discounted cash flow (DCF) models, analysts estimate the future cash flows expected to be generated by a company and discount these cash flows to the present in order to estimate the value of the company. These models require careful estimation of the growth rate in cash flows and the required rate of return.

Calculating FCFF:

	Net income
+	Net interest after tax
=	Unlevered income
+	Changes in deferred taxes
=	NOPLAT (net operating profit less adjusted taxes)
+	Net non-cash charges
–	Change in net working capital
–	Capital expenditures (capex)
	Free cash flow to the firm (FCFF)

Net interest after tax = (Interest expense – Interest income) (1 – tax rate)
Working capital = Current assets (excl. cash and equivalents) – Current liabilities (excl. short-term debt)

Calculating terminal value:

The terminal value may either be calculated using the constant growth formula or by applying a multiple for which the analyst expects the average company to sell at the end of the forecasting horizon.

$$\text{Terminal value}_T = \frac{\text{FCFF}_T(1+g)}{(\text{WACC}-g)}$$

Advantages of DCF analysis:

- It is easy to model expected changes in the target company's cash flows.
- The estimated intrinsic value is based on forecasted fundamentals.
- It is easy to change assumptions and estimates.

Disadvantages of DCF analysis:

- It is difficult to apply when free cash flows do not align with profitability.
- Estimates of earnings entail a great deal of uncertainty.
- Changes in discount rates due to capital market developments can have a significant impact on valuation.
- Terminal value estimates may vary across calculation methods.

Comparable Company Analysis

Under this approach, relative valuation measures are used to estimate the market value of the target company, and then a takeover premium is added to determine a fair acquisition price.

The following steps are followed in comparable company analysis:

- Identify a set of comparable companies.
- Calculate different relative value measures based on current market prices of comparable companies.
- Calculate specific relative value metrics and apply these to the target firm.
- Estimate the takeover premium.

  $$TP = \frac{(DP-SP)}{SP}$$

Advantages:

- The target company's value is estimated using similar companies in the market.
- Most of the required data is readily available.
- Value estimates are derived directly from the market.

Disadvantages:

- A mispricing in one of the companies will cause the estimated value to be incorrect as well.
- The takeover premium needs to be estimated separately.
- It is difficult to incorporate any specific plans for the target company into the analysis.
- The data available for past premiums may not be suitable for the target company.

CF

Comparable Transaction Analysis

This approach utilizes recent merger transactions involving comparable companies to determine a fair acquisition price (directly) for the target company. It requires the following steps:

- Identification of relevant merger transactions.
- Based on completed deals and transaction prices, relative valuation metrics are calculated for the companies in sample.
- Apply multiples to the target company.

Advantages of comparable transaction analysis:

- There is no need to estimate the takeover premium separately as it is built into the transaction prices used to calculate valuation multiples.
- Actual (and recent) transaction values are used in deriving the target's value, as opposed to the subjective estimates and assumptions used in DCF analysis.
- Challenges to valuation (litigation risk for target board members or management) are less likely given that recent comparable transaction prices are used.

Disadvantages of comparable transaction analysis:

- Recent transaction prices can be influenced by market conditions. In such instances, these inaccuracies flow through to the estimates of target company value.
- A lack of recent and relevant transaction data for companies in the same industry may force the use of data from related sectors. As a result, the value derived for the target may not be accurate.
- It is difficult to incorporate any anticipated target capital structure changes and merger synergies into the analysis.

Bid Evaluation

Target shareholders' gain = Premium = Price paid for the target company – Pre-merger value of the target company

Acquirers' gain = Synergies – Premium

The post-merger value of the combined company can be calculated as:

$$V_A{}^* = V_A + V_T + S - C$$

$V_A{}^*$ = Post-merger value of the combined company
V_A = Pre-merger value of the acquirer
V_T = Pre-merger value of the target company
S = Synergies created by the business combination
C = Cash paid to target shareholders

When evaluating a merger offer, the minimum bid that target shareholders would accept is the pre-merger market value of the target company, while the maximum amount that any acquirer would be willing to pay is the pre-merger value of the target plus the value of potential synergies.

CF

Bidding prices therefore generally lie between these two amounts. This also implies that analysis of a merger not only depends on the assessment of pre-merger target value, but also assessments of estimated synergies.

Factors Affecting Choice of Payment

- The more confident the counterparties are that estimated synergies will be realized from the merger, the more the acquiring company would want to pay in cash, and the more the target shareholders would prefer receiving stock.
  - The greater the proportion of the acquisition price represented by stock, the more that the risk and rewards of the merger will be passed on to target shareholders.
- The more confident the acquiring company is in its estimates of the target's value, the more it would prefer to pay in cash and the more the target would prefer to receive stock.

Who Benefits from Mergers?

- Empirical studies show that over the short-term, merger transactions benefit target company shareholders, while acquiring company shareholders suffer.
- In the long-term, acquiring companies tend to underperform comparable companies.

Based on empirical results, the characteristics of mergers and acquisitions that create value are:

- The buyer is strong.
- The transaction premiums are relatively low.
- The number of bidders is low.
- The initial market reaction is favorable.

Corporate Restructuring

Corporate restructuring typically refers to when a company gets smaller by selling, splitting off, or shedding operating assets. When a company sells a division or a subsidiary, it is referred to as a divestiture. Common reasons for restructuring are:

- Change in strategic focus.
- Poor fit.
- Reverse synergy.
- Financial or cash flow needs.

Forms of Restructuring

- Equity carve-out: A company separates one of its divisions to create a new legal entity offering its equity to outsiders.
- Spin-off: A company separates one of its divisions to create a new legal entity offering its current shareholders a proportional number of shares in the new entity. A spin-off does not result in a cash inflow to the parent.
- Split-off: A company separates one of its divisions to create a new legal entity offering its current shareholders shares in the newly formed entity in exchange for their shares of the parent.
- Liquidation: A company is broken and sold in parts.

EV

EQUITY VALUATION: APPLICATIONS AND PROCESSES
Cross-Reference to CFA Institute Assigned Reading #26

Intrinsic Value

Intrinsic value is the actual or "true" value of an asset based on its underlying investment characteristics. Estimates of intrinsic value depend on an analyst's forecasts as well as the valuation model used.

Efficient market hypothesis assumes that market price is the best available estimate of a security's intrinsic value. Active management is based on the notion that various factors can cause market price to diverge from intrinsic value. Active investment managers expect to earn abnormal risk-adjusted returns by trading on perceived mispricings (differences between a security's market price and intrinsic value).

There are two possible sources of mispricing:

- The difference between the unobservable true intrinsic value and the observed market price.
- The difference between the intrinsic value estimate and the unobservable true intrinsic value.

  Perceived mispricing = True mispricing + Error in the estimate of intrinsic value.

$$V_E - P = (V - P) + (V_E - V)$$

V_E = Estimate of intrinsic value
P = Market price
V = True (unobservable) intrinsic value

Going-Concern Value and Liquidation Value

- The going-concern value of a company is based on the going-concern assumption i.e., the company will continue to exist for the foreseeable future.
- The liquidation value is based on the assumption that the company will immediately be dissolved and its assets sold individually.

The difference between the going-concern and liquidation values for a company depends on:

- The amount of value created by the application of human capital to the assets' productive capacity.
- The time frame available for liquidating assets.

Fair Market Value and Investment Value

- Fair market value is the price at which an asset or a liability can be exchanged between knowledgeable, willing parties in an arm's length transaction. Market prices should in the long run generally reflect fair market values.
- There might be instances when investors are willing to pay more than the fair market value for an asset (e.g., due to potential synergies). This unique value to the particular buyer based on its requirements and expectations is known as investment value.

EV

Applications of Equity Valuation

- Selecting stocks.
- Inferring market expectations regarding company fundamentals (profitability, risk, etc.).
- Evaluating corporate events (mergers, acquisitions, divestures, etc.).
- Rendering fairness opinions from third parties (e.g., on the terms of a merger).
- Evaluating business strategies and models.
- Communicating with analysts and shareholders.
- Appraising private businesses for transactional and tax reporting purposes.
- Estimating value of share-based payments (compensation).

Steps in the Valuation Process

1. Understanding the business.
2. Forecasting company performance.
3. Selecting the appropriate valuation model.
4. Converting forecasts to a valuation.
5. Applying the valuation conclusions.

Industry and Competitive Analysis

How attractive are the industries in which the company operates?

- Intra-industry rivalry: Low rivalry among the industry participants enhances overall industry profitability.
- New entrants: High barriers to entry result in higher industry profitability.
- Substitutes: A few potential substitutes and high switching costs increase industry profitability.
- Supplier power: A large number of suppliers for inputs benefit the industry.
- Buyer power: A large number of customers for an industry's product is generally better for the industry.

What is the company's corporate strategy?

- Cost leadership: A company following this strategy aims to become the lowest cost producer of a specific product.
- Differentiation: A company following this strategy charges premium prices in return for its unique products and services that are valued by customers.
- Focus: A company following this strategy aims to seek competitive advantage in a particular target segment or segments either based on cost leadership or differentiation.

How well has the company executed its strategy and what are its prospects for future execution?

- Evaluate qualitative factors (e.g., ownership structure, economic value of intangible assets, etc.).
- Do not assume that past performance will be replicated going forward.

How persistent are the company's earnings?

- Identify those aspects of reported performance that are not likely to recur.
- Decompose income into its cash and accrual components. Accrual components are less persistent and result in lower ROA in the future.

Forecasting Company Performance

The top-down forecasting approach starts with international and national macroeconomic forecasts followed by industry forecasts and finally, individual company and asset forecasts.

The bottom-up forecasting approach aggregates individual company forecasts into industry forecasts, which in turn are aggregated to macroeconomic forecasts.

Valuation Models

Absolute valuation models look to estimate an asset's intrinsic value which can then be compared with its market price (e.g., dividend discount models and asset-based valuation models). Relative valuation models are based on the assumption that similar assets should be priced similarly and estimate an asset's value relative to that of another asset. Relative valuation is typically implemented using price multiples, the most common of which is the price-to-earnings ratio (P/E).

Instead of valuing a company as a single entity, analysts may estimate the values of its various businesses individually as going-concerns and then add them up to arrive at a value for the company. This method is known as sum-of-the-parts valuation. Conglomerate discounts may need to be applied when using this approach.

Criteria for Model Selection

The model must be:

- Consistent with the characteristics of the company being valued.
- Appropriate, given the availability and quality of data.
- Consistent with the purpose of valuation, including the analyst's perspective.

Converting Forecasts to a Valuation

- Sensitivity analysis aims to determine how changes in an assumed input would alter the outcome of the analysis.
- Situational adjustments include:
    - **Control premiums:** An investor willing to acquire a controlling interest in a company will need to pay a premium for control.
    - **Lack of marketability discount:** An investor requires a greater return from securities that are not traded publicly to compensate her for the lack of marketability.
    - **Illiquidity discount:** Securities that are not traded very frequently often reflect an illiquidity discount.

Analysts

- Sell-side analysts issue research reports that are widely distributed to current and prospective retail and institutional brokerage clients.
- Buy-side analysts work at investment management firms, trust, and bank trust departments where they issue reports that are used by the portfolio manager or investment committee as inputs in investment decision making.

Analysts' Role and Responsibilities

In performing valuations, analysts should hold themselves accountable to (1) standards of competence and (2) standards of conduct.

- Analysts help clients achieve their investment objectives.
- Analysts contribute to the efficient functioning of capital markets.
- Analysts benefit the suppliers of capital by effectively monitoring management performance.

Characteristics of an Effective Research Report

- Contains timely information.
- Is written in clear, incisive language.
- Is objective and well researched, with key assumptions clearly identified.
- Distinguishes clearly between facts and opinions.
- Contains analysis, forecasts, valuation, and a recommendation that are internally consistent.
- Presents sufficient information to allow a reader to critique the valuation.
- States the key risk factors involved in an investment in the company.
- Discloses any potential conflicts of interests faced by the analyst.

RETURN CONCEPTS
Cross-Reference to CFA Institute Assigned Reading #27

Holding Period Return (HPR)

HPR is the return earned on an investment over the entire investment horizon and consists of two components—investment income and price return. It is calculated as:

$$\text{Holding period return} = \frac{P_1 - P_0 + D_1}{P_0}$$

- Holding period returns based on past information (in which the selling price and dividends are known) are referred to as realized holding period returns.
- Holding period returns in a forward-looking context (in which the selling price and dividends are not known) are referred to as expected holding period returns.

Required Return

The required return is the minimum level of return required by an investor to invest in a particular asset (given the level of risk) over a specified period of time.

- If the expected return is equal to the investor's required return, the asset is fairly valued.
- If the expected return exceeds the investor's required return, the asset is undervalued.
- If the expected return is lower than the investor's required return, the asset is overvalued.

The difference between an asset's expected return and required return is called the asset's expected alpha or expected abnormal return. The difference between actual holding period return and the required return for the same period is called realized alpha.

- If an asset's current price *equals* its intrinsic value, the expected return is the same as the required return and the expected alpha is zero.
- If an asset's current price *exceeds* its intrinsic value, the expected return is less than the required return and the expected alpha is negative.
- If an asset's current price is *lower* than its intrinsic value, the expected return is greater than the required return and the expected alpha is positive.

When an asset's current price is lower than its intrinsic value, an investor would expect the market price to converge to intrinsic value over time. In such a situation, the investor's expected return has two components; the required return and a return from convergence of price to intrinsic value. However, the convergence component of expected return can be risky because:

- The analyst's estimates may not be accurate.
- The price may not converge to its intrinsic value over the investor's time horizon.

Discount Rate

The discount rate is used by investors to calculate the present value of a future stream of cash flows. It is based on the characteristics of the investment.

Internal Rate of Return (IRR)

The internal rate of return on an investment is the discount rate that equates the present value of all expected inflows from the investment to its current price. If an asset is assumed to be efficiently priced (i.e., market price equals its intrinsic value), the IRR can be calculated using the dividend discount model as follows:

$$\text{Required return (IRR)} = \frac{\text{Next year's dividend}}{\text{Market price}} + \text{Expected dividend growth rate}$$

The Equity Risk Premium (ERP)

ERP refers to the additional return (premium) required by investors to invest in equities rather than a risk-free asset.

The required rate of return on a particular stock can be computed using either of the following two approaches. Both these approaches require the equity risk premium to be estimated first.

1. Required return on share i = Current expected risk-free return + β_i (Equity risk premium)
   - A beta greater (lower) than 1 indicates that the security has greater-than-average (lower-than-average) systematic risk.
2. Required return on share i = Current expected risk-free return + Equity risk premium $\pm$ Other risk premia/discounts appropriate for i
   - This method of estimating the required return is known as the build-up method. It is discussed later in the reading and is primarily used for valuations of private businesses.

The equity risk premium may be estimated based on:

- Historical estimates of the difference between broad-based equity market-index returns and government debt returns over the same time period.
  - Use of the geometric mean is preferred over use of the arithmetic mean.
  - Use of the long-term government bond rate is preferred to use of a short-term rate as a proxy for the risk-free rate.
  - Estimates may be adjusted for survivorship bias, and to bring them in line with independent forward-looking estimates.
- Forward-looking estimates, which can be drawn from:
  - The Gordon growth model.
  - Macroeconomic models.
  - Surveys.

Estimating the Required Return on Equity

The required return on equity may be estimated using anyone of the following models:

1. The Capital Asset Pricing Model (CAPM)

   Required return on a stock = Expected risk-free rate + Beta × Equity risk premium

   The CAPM uses only one factor and is therefore very simple. However, choosing the appropriate factor can be problematic and the model may have low explanatory power in some cases.

2. Multifactor Models

   Required return = Risk-free rate + (Risk premium)$_1$ + (Risk premium)$_2$ + … + (Risk premium)$_k$
   - Fama-French Model
     - $r_i = RF + \beta_i^{mkt} RMRF + \beta_i^{size} SMB + \beta_i^{value} HML$
   - The Pastor-Stambaugh model adds a liquidity factor to the Fama-French model.
   - Macroeconomic multifactor models use economic variables that affect the value of companies as factors.
   - Statistical factor models use statistical methods to determine a portfolio of securities (serving as factors) that explain historical returns.

   Multifactor models generally have higher explanatory power but are more complex and costly.

3. Build-Up Method

   The build-up method starts with the risk-free rate and adds premiums for different risks, but does not use betas to adjust factor risk premiums.

   r_i = Risk-free rate + Equity risk premium + Size premium + Specific-company premium

   Another example of this method is the bond-yield plus risk premium approach.

   BYPRP cost of equity = YTM on the company's long-term debt + Risk premium

   Build-up models tend to be very simple and can be applied to closely held companies. However, they use historical estimates that may no longer be relevant.

Methods of Estimating Beta

- Through a regression of the return of a stock on the return of the market. The value obtained is called "raw" or unadjusted beta and needs to be adjusted for beta drift.

   Adjusted beta = (2/3) (Unadjusted beta) + (1/3) (1.0)

- For thinly traded stocks or non-public companies, beta may be estimated using the pure-play method:
  - Identify a comparable public company.
  - Estimate the beta of the comparable public company.
  - Un-lever the beta of the public company to estimate the beta of its assets.
  - Re-lever the asset beta of the public company based on the financial leverage of the subject company.

Issues in Estimating the Required Return on Equity in an International Context

- Analysts should incorporate exchange rate forecasts into their expectations of the local currency performance of the equity market and the risk-free asset.
- It is difficult to estimate the required return and risk premium in emerging markets.
  - The country spread and country risk rating models can be used to estimate the equity risk premium.

The Weighted Average Cost of Capital (WACC)

$$WACC = \frac{MVD}{MVD + MVCE}\, r_d\,(1 - \text{Tax rate}) + \frac{MVCE}{MVD + MVCE}\, r$$

- The cost of debt is adjusted downwards by a factor of $(1 - t)$ to reflect the tax deductibility of corporate interest payments.
- Use of the marginal tax rate is preferred over use of the effective tax rate in adjusting the cost of debt.
- Analysts often use target weights instead of current market value-weights of equity and debt in the capital structure when calculating the WACC.

Discount Rate Selection in Relation to Cash Flows

- When a cash flow to equity is discounted, the nominal required return on equity is the appropriate discount rate.
- When a cash flow to the firm is discounted, the nominal after-tax WACC is the appropriate discount rate.

INDUSTRY AND COMPANY ANALYSIS
Cross-Reference to CFA Institute Assigned Reading #28

APPROACHES TO PROJECTING FUTURE REVENUE

- Under a **top-down approach**, the analyst begins with the overall economy and then moves to more narrowly defined levels (sector, industry, or specific product) before eventually arriving at a revenue forecast for a particular company. There are two common top-down approaches to modeling revenue:
  - In the growth relative to GDP growth approach, the analyst considers how a company's growth rate will compare with growth in nominal GDP.
  - In the market growth and market share approach, the analyst first forecasts growth for a particular market, and then considers how the company's current market share is likely to grow over time.
- Under a **bottom-up approach**, an analyst begins at the individual company level or the individual unit level (product line, segment, or location) within the company, and then aggregates those forecasts to project total revenue for the company. Subsequently, revenue projections for individual companies are aggregated to develop forecasts for the sector, industry, or overall economy. Bottom-up approaches to forecasting revenue include:
  - Time series, where forecasts are based on historical growth rates or time series analysis.
  - Return on capital, where forecasts are based on balance sheet accounts.
  - Capacity-based measures, e.g., same-store sales growth or sales related to new stores in the retail industry.

Under a **hybrid approach**, elements of both the top-down and bottom-up approach are combined. Hybrid approaches are the most commonly used approaches as they are useful (1) in uncovering implicit assumptions made, and (2) in identifying any errors made when using a single approach.

Income Statement Modeling

When forecasting costs, analysts must carefully consider fixed and variable costs.

- **Variable costs** are usually directly linked to revenue growth and are often modeled as (1) a percentage of revenue or (2) projected unit volumes multiplied by variable costs per unit.
- **Fixed costs** are not related to revenue; instead they are typically linked to (1) future investment in PP&E and (2) total capacity growth.

Economies of scale occur when average cost per unit declines as total output increases. Factors that can lead to economies of scale include:

- Greater bargaining power with suppliers.
- Lower cost of capital.
- Lower per-unit marketing costs.

If a company/industry is benefiting from economies of scale, its gross and/or operating margins would be positively correlated with sales levels. An analysis of common-size income statements would show that larger companies in the industry would have lower COGS and/or SG&A as a percentage of sales compared to smaller companies.

Cost of Goods Sold (COGS)

Generally speaking, COGS tends to be the largest component of total cost for manufacturing and merchandising companies.

$$\text{Future COGS} = (\text{Historical COGS} / \text{Revenue}) \times \text{Projected sales}$$

$$\text{Future COGS} = (1 - \text{Historical GP margin}) \times \text{Projected sales}$$

- Given that COGS comprises the bulk of operating costs, analysts may find it useful to break down these costs (e.g., by segment, by product category, or by volume and price components) to improve forecasting accuracy.
- Analysts should also consider the company's general strategy regarding hedging various input costs.
- Finally, analysts should also check their gross margin assumptions against those of the company's competitors.

Selling, General, and Administrative Expenses (SG&A)

Generally speaking, SG&A have less of a correlation with revenue than COGS. While some components may be forecasted as a percentage of sales (e.g., wages and salaries), others tend to be less variable in nature (e.g., R&D expense and employee overheads).

Financing Expenses

- Interest income depends on (1) the amount of cash and cash equivalents held by the company, and (2) the rate of return earned on investments.
- Interest expense depends on (1) the amount of debt in the company capital structure, and (2) the interest rate associated with the debt.

Corporate Income Tax

- The statutory tax rate, which is the legally applicable rate charged in the country where the company is located.
- The effective tax rate, which is calculated as the reported tax amount (income tax expense) on the income statement divided by pre-tax income.
- The cash tax rate, which is calculated as tax actually paid divided by pre-tax income.

Differences between cash taxes and reported taxes result from (temporary) timing differences in the recognition of certain items between the tax return and the financial statements of a company. These differences are reflected in deferred tax assets and liabilities. On the other hand, differences between the statutory tax rate and the effective tax rate arise from permanent differences. Examples include tax credits, withholding taxes on dividends, adjustments to prior years, and expenses not deductible for tax purposes. A reconciliation of these two is typically contained in the notes to the financial statements.

- Effective tax rates can differ if a company operates in multiple jurisdictions with different statutory tax rates.
- In order to minimize taxes, some companies create special purpose entities to minimize profits reported in high-tax rate countries.

- Analysts should adjust the effective tax rate for one-time events. Further, if income from investments in subsidiaries accounted for using the equity method forms a substantial and volatile part of pre-tax income, analysts should exclude this item in estimating the future tax expense.
- Generally speaking, analysts project future tax expense using a tax rate based on normalized operating income (i.e., income before special items and income from associates).
- While the effective tax rate is used for forecasting earnings, it is the cash tax rate that is used for forecasting cash flows. Any differences between the tax amount on the P&L (income tax expense) and the amount on the cash flow statement (cash taxes) should be reconciled through a change in deferred tax assets/liabilities.

Other Items

- A company's stated dividend policy can be used to project future dividends. Typically, analysts assume that dividends grow each year (1) by a particular dollar amount, or (2) as a proportion of net income.
- If a company owns more than 50% of an affiliate, it will generally consolidate the affiliate's results with its own and report the portion of income that does not belong to it as minority interest.
- If a company owns less than 50% of an affiliate, it will report its share of income from the affiliate using the equity method.
- Share count (shares issued and outstanding) is a key input in the calculation of an intrinsic value estimate and earnings per share. Changes in a company's share count may come from (1) dilution related to exercise of stock options, convertible bonds, and similar securities, (2) issuance of new shares, and (3) share repurchases.
- Analysts usually exclude unusual charges from their forecasts as they are very difficult to predict. However, if a company has a history of classifying certain recurring costs as "unusual," analysts may want to include a "normalized" level of unusual charges in their forecasts.

Balance Sheet and Cash Flow Statement Modeling

Working capital accounts are typically forecast using efficiency ratios.

Long-term assets such as net PP&E are not strongly linked to the income statement. Net PP&E changes are linked to capital expenditures and depreciation (which are both important components of the cash flow statement).

- Depreciation forecasts are based on historical depreciation and disclosures relating to depreciation schedules.
- Capital expenditure forecasts depend on estimated future need for new PP&E. Capital expenditure includes:
  - Maintenance capital expenditures, which are required to sustain current business.
  - Growth capital expenditures, which are required to expand the business.

In order to project future debt and equity levels, analysts must make assumptions regarding leverage ratios (e.g., debt-capital, debt-equity and debt-EBITDA). Analysts must also consider the company's historical practices, current financial strategy and capital requirements when projecting future capital structure.

Return on Invested Capital (ROIC)

Return on invested capital (ROIC) measures the profitability of capital invested by the company.

$$\text{ROIC} = \text{NOPLAT} / \text{Invested capital}$$

- NOPLAT = Net operating profit less adjusted taxes.
- Invested capital = Operating assets − Operating liabilities.

ROIC is a better measure of profitability than return on equity (ROE) as it is not affected by the company's financial leverage/capital structure. Generally speaking, a sustainably high ROIC indicates a competitive advantage.

Return on Capital Employed (ROCE)

Return on capital employed (ROCE) is similar to ROIC, but focuses on pretax operating profit.

$$\text{ROCE} = \text{Operating profit} / \text{Capital employed}$$

- Operating profit is a pretax measure of profitability.
- Capital employed = Debt capital + Equity capital.

Since it is a pretax measure, ROCE is useful in performing comparisons across companies in different countries with different tax structures.

INFLATION AND DEFLATION

Industry Sales and Inflation or Deflation

The relationship between increases in input costs and increases in the price of final products depends on the following factors:

- Industry structure.
- Price elasticity of demand.
- Reaction of competitors and availability of substitutes.

Company Sales and Inflation or Deflation

In order to forecast revenue for a company that faces rising input costs, analysts must consider the following:

- Price elasticity of demand for its products.
- The different rates of cost inflation in countries where the company operates.
- Likely inflations in costs for individual product categories.
- Pricing strategy and market position.

Industry Costs and Inflation or Deflation

In order to forecast industry costs, analysts must consider the following:

- Specific purchasing characteristics.
- Underlying drivers of input prices.
- The competitive environment.

Company Costs and Inflation or Deflation

In order to forecast company costs, analysts should:

- Break down costs by category and geography, and evaluate the impact of inflation or deflation on each individual item.
- Consider whether the company can find cheaper substitutes or increase efficiency to offset the impact of higher input prices.

Technological Developments

Since the impact of technological innovation can be so unpredictable and significant, analysts typically employ a variety of assumptions and use scenario and/or sensitivity analysis to project future earnings.

- If a new innovation threatens to cannibalize sales of an existing product, a unit sales forecast for the new product must be combined with an expected cannibalization factor to project demand for the existing product.
- Technological developments can affect demand, supply, or both.

Longer-Term Forecasting

In determining the appropriate forecasting horizon, analysts must consider the following:

- Investment strategy for which the stock is being considered.
- Industry cyclicality.
- Company-specific factors.
- Valuation methods mandated by supervisor.

Longer-term projections typically provide a better reflection of normalized earnings than short-term forecasts. Normalized earnings reflect mid-cycle earnings for a company after excluding any unusual or temporary factors that (favorably or unfavorably) affect profitability.

Considerations in Deriving a Terminal Value Estimate

- If historical multiples are used to estimate terminal value, the implicit assumption is that the past is a good reflection of future expectations regarding growth and required returns. If the future growth and/or profitability of the company is likely to be significantly different from the historical average, a premium/discount should be applied to the historical multiple to reflect those differences.
- If the discounted cash flow (DCF) approach is used to estimate terminal value, the analyst should first determine whether the terminal year free cash flow forecast actually reflects normalized (mid-cycle) cash flows. If it does not, then an adjustment to reflect the normalized amount must be performed.

  Further, the analyst should also consider how the future long-term growth rate may be different from the historical growth rate.

- A final challenge for analysts in long-term forecasting is anticipating **inflection points**, where the future will significantly differ from the recent past. Such abrupt changes can come from:
  - ○ Economic disruption (e.g., the 2008 financial crisis).
  - ○ Changes in business cycle stage.
  - ○ Government regulation.
  - ○ Technological advances.

Building a Model

1. Collect industry information.
2. Collect company information including segment-wise financial information.
3. Construct the pro forma financial income statement.
   a. Forecast revenues for each individual segment using a top-down, bottom-up, or hybrid approach.
      - Under the top-down approach, any of the market growth plus market share, trend growth rate, or growth relative to GDP growth approaches can be used.
      - In the bottom-up approach, sales revenues are forecast based on assumptions of future prices, volumes, and exchange rates.
   b. Estimate COGS. COGS can be estimated based on a percentage of sales, or on a more detailed method which examines the company's business strategy, and competitive environment.
   c. Estimate SG&A. SG&A can be assumed to be fixed, or be related to sales.
   d. Estimate financing costs. Financing costs require making assumptions regarding future interest rates, debt levels, capital structure, and capital expenditure requirements.
   e. Estimate income tax expense. This is based on the historical effective tax rate (with adjustments if necessary).
   f. Estimate cash taxes. This requires consideration of changes in deferred tax items.
4. Construct the pro forma balance sheet.
   a. Most balance sheet accounts (retained earnings, accounts receivable, accounts payable, and inventory) are related to the income statement.
   b. Net PP&E is estimated based on depreciation estimates and capital expenditures (for maintenance and growth) which are typically estimated based on sales.
   c. Liability and capital accounts are influenced by the target capital structure, dividend payments, share repurchases, and debt redemptions/issues.
5. Construct the pro forma cash flow statement. Most of the inputs for the pro forma cash flow statement (e.g., operating profit, capital expenditures, working capital estimates, and capital structure changes) are estimated while constructing the pro forma income statement and balance sheet.

Analysts must use sensitivity analysis or scenario analysis to come up with a range of potential outcomes and assign probabilities to each outcome when appropriate.

DISCOUNTED DIVIDEND VALUATION
Cross-Reference to CFA Institute Assigned Reading #29

Present Value Models

Dividend Discount Models

The advantage of using dividends as a measure of cash flow is that dividends are less volatile than earnings and other return measures. The use of dividends as a measure of cash flow is appropriate when:

- The firm has a history of paying dividends.
- The company has an established dividend policy where dividends are related to the firm's earnings.
- The investor takes a non-control perspective.

Discounting Free Cash Flow

- Free cash flow to the firm (FCFF): The cash flow generated from a firm's operations less capital expenditure (investments in new assets and working capital).
- Free cash flow to equity (FCFE): The cash flow generated from a firm's operations less capital expenditures and net payments to debt holders.

The advantage of using DCF approaches is that they can be used for most companies, even those that do not currently pay dividends. However, free cash flows may sometimes be negative, which makes the application of the model difficult. The use of discounted free cash flow models is appropriate when:

- The firm does not have a history of paying dividends.
- The firm does pay dividends, but dividends significantly deviate from FCFE.
- The firm's free cash flow is related to its profitability.
- The investor takes a control perspective.

Residual Income Models

Residual income is calculated as the firm's earnings over a given period minus the investors' required rate of return on the beginning-of-period investment. The model asserts that the value of a company equals its book value plus the present value of expected future residual earnings. Use of the residual income is appropriate when:

- The firm does not have a history of paying dividends.
- The firm's expected free cash flows are negative for the foreseeable future.
- The firm's quality of accounting disclosures is good.

The Dividend Discount Model

One-Period DDM

$$V_0 = \frac{D_1}{(1+r)^1} + \frac{P_1}{(1+r)^1} = \frac{D_1 + P_1}{(1+r)^1}$$

Multiple-Year Holding Period DDM

$$V_0 = \frac{D_0(1+g)}{(r-g)}, \text{ or } V_0 = \frac{D_1}{(r-g)}$$

Infinite Period DDM (Gordon Growth Model)

$$V_0 = \frac{D_0(1+g)}{(r-g)}, \text{ or } V_0 = \frac{D_1}{(r-g)}$$

The relation between r and g is critical:

- As the difference between r and g increases, the intrinsic value of the stock falls.
- As the difference narrows, the intrinsic value of the stock rises.
- Small changes in either r or g can cause large changes in the value of the stock.

For the infinite-period DDM model to work, the following assumptions must hold:

- Dividends grow at a rate, g, which is not expected to change.
- r must be greater than g; otherwise, the model breaks down because of the denominator being negative.

The long-term constant growth rate can be calculated as earnings retention rate times return on equity.

$$g = \text{Retention rate} \times \text{Net profit margin} \times \text{Asset turnover} \times \text{Financial leverage}$$

The Gordon growth formula can be rearranged to calculate either the implied required rate of return on equity or the implied growth rate, given the other variables.

$$r = D_1/P_0 + g$$

$$g = r - D_1/P_0$$

DDM models can also be used to value companies that repurchase stock as long as the effect of expected repurchases on the dividend growth rate is taken into account.

If the firm distributes all of its earnings to shareholders in the form of dividends, the growth rate would equal zero. In this case, the value of the firm would equal current dividend divided by the required rate of return.

$$V_0 = \frac{D_0}{r}$$

Present Value of Growth Opportunities

The value of a stock can be broken down into two components:

- The value of the company without the earnings reinvestment (E_1/r) – known as no-growth value per share.
- The present value of growth opportunities (PVGO).

$$V_0 = \frac{E_1}{r} + PVGO$$

PVGO is determined by:

- The company's options or opportunities to invest.
- The company's available real options and managerial flexibility.

Explaining Negative PVGO

- There may be an expectation that management's current competitive and investment strategy will destroy value.
- The stock may be severely undervalued (possibly as a result of a significant recent market crash).
- The estimate of the no-growth value may be too high (i.e., the earnings estimate is too high and/or required return estimate is too low).

Gordon Growth Model and the Price-to-Earnings Ratio

The P/E ratio derived from the Gordon growth model is referred to as the justified P/E ratio as it is "justified" on the basis of fundamentals.

The P/E ratio based on forecasted next year's earnings is called leading P/E.

$$\text{Justified leading P/E ratio} = \frac{P_0}{E_1} = \frac{D_1/E_1}{r-g} = \frac{(1-b)}{r-g}$$

The P/E ratio based on earnings over the last four quarters is called trailing P/E.

$$\text{Justified trailing P/E} = \frac{P_0}{E_0} = \frac{D_1/E_0}{r-g} = \frac{D_0(1+g)/E_0}{r-g} = \frac{(1-b)(1+g)}{r-g}$$

Strengths and Limitations of the Gordon Growth Model

Strengths

- The model is applicable to stable, mature, and dividend-paying companies.
- It is applicable to broadly developed market equity indices.
- It is very simple and easy to implement.
- It can be used to determine the growth rate, cost of equity, and the present value of growth opportunities implied by a security's current market price.
- As you will see in the next section of this reading, it is used in multistage DDMs to compute company value in the mature phase.

Weaknesses

- Valuations are very sensitive to estimates of the required return on equity and the growth rate.
- The model cannot be applied to non-dividend-paying stocks.
- It cannot be applied to companies whose growth patterns are not expected to remain constant indefinitely.

Value of Non-Callable Fixed-Rate Perpetual Preferred Stock

$$V_0 = \frac{D_0}{r}$$

Terminal Value

The value estimated at the end of the high-growth stages, based on the assumption of a constant future growth rate, is referred to as the terminal value of the stock (also known as continuing value).

The terminal value of a stock may be calculated by either:

- Using the Gordon growth model; or
- Applying a multiple (e.g., P/E) to a forecasted value of a fundamental (e.g., earnings).

Multistage Dividend Discount Models

Companies usually go through the following phases:

- Growth phase: High growth in earnings, low or zero dividend payout ratios, and heavy reinvestments.
- Transition phase: Relatively lower earnings growth rate, declining capital requirements, and increasing dividend payout ratios.
- Mature phase: Earnings growth rates, dividend payout ratios, and return on equity stabilize at their long-run levels.

Two-Stage DDM

This model assumes that a company experiences a relatively high growth rate in the short-run (the first stage) and then growth stabilizes in the long run (the second stage).

$$V_0 = \sum_{t=1}^{n} \frac{D_0(1+g_s)^t}{(1+r)^t} + \frac{D_0(1+g_s)^n(1+g_L)}{(1+r)^n(r-g_L)}$$

g_S = Short-term supernormal growth rate
g_L = Long-term sustainable growth rate
r = required return
n = Length of the supernormal growth period

H-Model

The H-Model employs a more realistic assumption (relative to the 2-stage DMM) that the growth rate declines linearly from a temporary short-run extraordinarily high rate to a long-run constant sustainable growth rate.

$$V_0 = \frac{D_0(1+g_L)}{r-g_L} + \frac{D_0 H(g_s - g_L)}{r-g_L}$$

g_S = Short-term high growth rate
g_L = Long-term sustainable growth rate
r = required return
H = Half-life = 0.5 times the length of the high growth period

The above equation can also be rearranged to calculate the required rate of return as follows:

$$r = \left(\frac{D_0}{P_0}\right)[(1+g_L) + H(g_s - g_L)] + g_L$$

Three-Stage Dividend Discount Models

There are two versions of the three-stage DDM. The difference between the two lies in the modeling of the second stage.

In the first version, the company is assumed to have three stages of growth, where the growth rate during each stage is different but constant. For example, Stage 1 may have 25% growth for 3 years, Stage 2 may have 15% growth for 5 years, and Stage 3 could have 5% growth thereafter. Valuing the company under this DDM model requires the following steps:

- Estimate dividends for each year during the first 2 stages of growth and then discount them to the present.

- Estimate the dividend for the first year of the 3rd (constant growth into perpetuity) stage.
- Compute the terminal value at the beginning of the 3rd stage.
- Compute the present value of the terminal value.
- Add up the present values of the dividends over the first 2 stages and the present value of the terminal value.

In the second version of the three-stage DDM, the middle stage is similar to the first stage of the H-model. For example, Stage 1 may have 25% growth for 3 years, Stage 2 may see a linear decline in the growth rate to 5% over 5 years, and Stage 3 could have 5% growth into perpetuity. Valuing the company under this DDM model requires the following steps:

- Estimate dividends for each year during the first stage of growth and then discount them to the present.
- Apply the H-model to the second and third stages to obtain an estimate of value as of the beginning of the second stage. Then discount this estimated value to the present.
- Add up the present values of the dividends over the first stage, and the present value of value obtained from applying the H-model to the second and third stages.

The Sustainable Growth Rate

The sustainable growth rate (SGR) is defined as the growth rate of dividends (and earnings) that the company can sustain for a given return on equity, assuming that the capital structure remains unchanged over time, and no new equity is issued. The long-term sustainable growth rate can be calculated as earnings retention rate times return on equity:

$$g = b \times ROE$$

$$b = \text{Earnings retention rate, calculated as } 1 - \text{Dividend payout ratio}$$

- The higher the return on equity, the higher the sustainable dividend (earnings) growth rate.
- The higher the earnings retention rate, the higher the sustainable dividend (earnings) growth rate. This relationship is referred to as dividend displacement of earnings.

FREE CASH FLOW VALUATION
Cross-Reference to CFA Institute Assigned Reading #30

The use of free cash flow as the definition of return is appropriate when:

- The company does not pay dividends.
- The company does pay dividends, but dividends paid deviate significantly from the ability of the firm to pay dividends.
- The company's free cash flows are in line with profitability over the forecasting horizon.
- The perspective is that of an investor with a controlling interest in the company.
- There is a high probability of the company being acquired.

Definition of Free Cash Flow

Free Cash Flow to the Firm (FCFF): This is the cash flow generated from a firm's operations after operating expenses (and taxes) have been paid, and investments in fixed and working capital have been made. In other words, it is the cash flow available to be distributed to a firm's bondholders and stockholders. In order to calculate the value of the firm, FCFF must be discounted at the weighted average cost of capital.

$$\text{Firm Value} = \sum_{t=1}^{\infty} \frac{FCFF_t}{(1+WACC)^t}$$

- Free Cash Flow to Equity (FCFE): This is the cash flow available to holders of common equity after all operating expenses, interest, and principal payments have been paid, and necessary investment in fixed and working capital have been made. In order to calculate the value of a firm's equity, FCFE is discounted at the required rate of return on equity.

$$\text{Equity Value} = \sum_{t=1}^{\infty} \frac{FCFE_t}{(1+r)^t}$$

Analysts prefer the use of FCFF and FCFE over other cash-flow concepts as they can be used directly in a DCF framework without any adjustments. Other measures, such as CFO, net income, EBIT and EBITDA require a few adjustments before they can be used as proxies for free cash flow.

FCFE versus FCFF

- If the company's capital structure is relatively stable, using FCFE is more direct and simple than using FCFF.
- FCFE may sometimes be negative. In such cases, the value of the firm's equity can be calculated as the difference between the value of the firm (estimated using FCFF) and the market value of the firm's debt.
- The growth in FCFF may reflect a company's fundamentals more accurately than FCFE, which is affected by fluctuating amounts of net borrowings.

Computing FCFF

Computing FCFF from Net Income

$$FCFF = NI + NCC + Int(1 - Tax\ rate) - FCInv - WCInc$$

- Non-cash charges are subtracted from revenue to arrive at a firm's net income. These need to be added back as they do not result in any cash outflows.
  - Depreciation, amortization, and losses on sale of assets must be added back to net income. Similarly, gains on sales of investments must be subtracted from net income.
  - Restructuring charges must be added back to net income, while any income from reversals of restructuring charges must be subtracted from net income.
  - Amortization of bond discounts must be added back to net income, while accretion of bond premiums must be subtracted from net income.
  - Increases in deferred tax liabilities that are not expected to reverse must be added back to net income, while increases in deferred tax assets that are not expected to reverse must be subtracted from net income.
- Interest expense is subtracted from a firm's earnings in order to arrive at net income. Interest expense is a financing cash outflow and therefore, must be added back to net income in order to arrive at FCFF. However, only the after-tax portion of interest expense is added back. Similarly, any dividends on preferred stock must be added back to net income to arrive at FCFF.
- Investment in fixed assets is a non-operating cash outflow and therefore, must be subtracted from net income to arrive at FCFF.
  - FCInv = Capital expenditures − Proceeds from sales of long-term assets
- Investments in working capital can be estimated as the increase in working capital from year to year excluding cash, cash equivalents, notes payable, and the current portion of long-term debt.

Computing FCFF from CFO

$$FCFF = CFO + Int(1 - Tax\ rate) - FCInv$$

When computing FCFF from CFO, do not make any adjustments related to non-cash charges and investments in working capital as they have already been made in the calculation of CFO.

Computing FCFF from EBIT

$$FCFF = EBIT(1 - Tax\ rate) + Depreciation - FCInv - WCInv$$

When calculating FCFF from EBIT, do not make any adjustments for interest expense. Further, the above formula assumes that apart from depreciation, non-cash charges in the income statement are made after the calculation of operating earnings (EBIT).

Computing FCFF from EBITDA

$$FCFF = EBITDA(1 - Tax\ rate) + Depreciation(Tax\ rate) - FCInv - WCInv$$

Computing FCFE

Computing FCFE from FCFF

$$FCFE = FCFF - Int(1 - Tax\ rate) + Net\ borrowing$$

Computing FCFE from Net Income

$$FCFE = NI + NCC - FCInv - WCInv + Net\ borrowing$$

Computing FCFE from CFO

$$FCFE = CFO - FCInv + Net\ borrowing$$

Computing FCFE from EBIT

$$FCFE = EBIT(1 - Tax\ rate) - Int(1 - Tax\ rate) + Depreciation - FCInv - WCInv + NB$$

Computing FCFE from EBITDA

$$FCFE = EBITDA(1 - Tax\ rate) - Int(1 - Tax\ rate) + Dep(Tax\ rate) - FCInv - WCInv + NB$$

Computing FCFF and FCFE on a Uses-of-Free-Cash-Flow Basis

A firm generally has the following uses of positive FCFF:

- Retain it to increase its balances of cash and marketable securities.
- Make payments to providers of debt capital.
- Make payments to providers of equity capital (e.g., cash dividends or share repurchases).

Increases in cash balances
Plus: Net payments to providers of debt capital
     + Interest expense (1 – tax rate)
     + Repayment of principal
     – New borrowings
Plus: Net payments to providers of equity capital
     + Cash dividends
     + Share repurchases
     – New equity issues
     = Uses of FCFF

FCFE is usually only used to make payments to providers of equity capital.

Increases in cash balances
Plus: Net payments to providers of equity capital
     + Cash dividends
     + Share repurchases
     – New equity issues
     = Uses of FCFE

Forecasting FCFF and FCFE

- Calculate the current level of free cash flow and apply a specific growth rate assuming that free cash flow will grow at a constant growth rate, and that the historical relationship between free cash flow and fundamental factors is expected to continue.
- Forecast the individual components of free cash flow. For example, analysts may forecast EBIT, net non-cash charges, investments in fixed capital, and working capital and use these figures to calculate free cash flow.

Important

- Dividends, share repurchases, and share issues have no effect on FCFF and FCFE.
- Changes in leverage have a minor effect on FCFE and no impact on FCFF.

Net Income as a Proxy for Cash Flow

Net income is a poor proxy for FCFE for use in valuation because it:

- Includes the effects of non-cash charges like depreciation that should be added back to compute cash flow available to equity holders.
- Ignores cash outflow for investment in fixed and working capital.
- Ignores cash inflow from net borrowings.

EBITDA as a Proxy for Cash Flow

EBITDA is a poor proxy for FCFF for use in valuation because it:

- Does not account for cash outflow from taxes paid.
- Does not account for the contribution of the depreciation tax shield to FCFF.
- Ignores cash outflow for investment in fixed and working capital.

Free Cash Flow Model Variations

Single-Stage Valuation Model

$$\text{Value of the firm} = \frac{\text{FCFF}_1}{\text{WACC} - g}$$

$$\text{Value of equity} = \frac{\text{FCFE}_1}{r - g}$$

Multistage Valuation Models

There can be many different patterns of future growth rates depending on a firm's prospects. However, the same discounting principles are applied for valuing firms over multiple holding periods. In order to estimate the value of the firm, we first estimate the free cash flows that will be generated by the firm each year and then discount these expected cash flows at the appropriate rate.

Non-operating assets (e.g., excess cash and marketable securities) are separated from the company's operating assets. They are valued separately and their value is then added to the calculated value of the company's operating assets to determine total firm value.

General expression for the two-stage FCFF model:

$$\text{Firm value} = \sum_{t=1}^{n} \frac{FCFF_t}{(1+WACC)^t} + \frac{FCFF_{n+1}}{(WACC-g)} \frac{1}{(1+WACC)^n}$$

Firm value = PV of FCFF in Stage 1 + Terminal value × Discount Factor

General expression for the two-stage FCFE model:

$$\text{Equity value} = \sum_{t=1}^{n} \frac{FCFE_t}{(1+r)^t} + \frac{FCFF_{n+1}}{r-g} \frac{1}{(1+r)^n}$$

Equity value = PV of FCFE in Stage 1 + Terminal value × Discount Factor

Importance of Sensitivity Analysis

There are two major sources of errors in the valuation exercise.

1. Errors in estimating growth rates of FCFE and FCFF. These growth forecasts are dependent on a variety of factors including the company's sales growth, net profit margins, capital requirements, and industry profitability.
2. Errors in estimating the base-year values of FCFF and FCFE. Given the same set of growth forecasts, the estimate of value obtained from the model will vary with different base year values for FCFF and FCFE.

ESG Considerations in Free Cash Flow Models

Environmental, social, and governance (ESG) factocs, both quantitative or qualitative, can have a material impact on a company's value. Quantitative ESG-related information (e.g., the effects of projected environmental fines/penalties) is relatively easy to integrate into valuation models. Qualitative ESG-related information, however, is more difficult to integrate. The typical (albeit subjective) approach is to adjust the cost of equity by adding a risk premium in a valuation model.

Non-Operatinve Assets and Firm Value

Value of firm = Value of operating assets + Value of non-operating assets

MARKET-BASED VALUATION: PRICE AND ENTERPRISE VALUE MULTIPLES
Cross-Reference to CFA Institute Assigned Reading #31

The Method of Comparables

- Based on the law of one price (i.e., two identical assets should sell at the same price).
- Values an asset based on multiples of comparable (similar) assets.
- Is a relative valuation method, so the stock is evaluated relative to a benchmark.

The Method of Forecasted Fundamentals

- Uses multiples that are derived from forecasted fundamentals.
- These fundamentals may be related to the company's earnings, growth, or financial strength.

Price Multiples

Price to Earnings

Advantages:

- Earnings are key drivers of stock value.
- The ratio is simple to calculate and widely used in the industry.
- According to empirical research, differences in P/E ratios are significantly related to long-term stock returns.

Disadvantages:

- Companies that make losses have negative EPS. Negative P/E ratios are useless as far as relative valuation is concerned.
- It can be difficult to separate recurring components of earnings from transient components.
- Management may use different accounting standards and assumptions to prepare financial statements, which reduces the comparability of P/E ratios across companies.

Versions of the P/E Ratio

- The trailing P/E ratio divides the current stock price by earnings over the most recent four quarters.
  - It is used when future earnings are expected to be volatile and cannot be forecasted accurately.
- The leading P/E ratio divides the current stock price by expected earnings over the next year.
  - It is used if a company's business has changed fundamentally in the recent past (e.g., due to an acquisition).

Issues to Consider in Calculating Trailing P/E

- Potential dilution of EPS.
  - This is not such a major problem as companies now report both basic and diluted EPS.
- Transitory, non-recurring components of earnings that are company specific.
  - Analysts aim to estimate underlying or persistent earnings (that exclude non-recurring components). Financial statement footnotes and the MD&A section are important sources of information in this exercise.
- Transitory components of earnings related to business or industry cycle.
  - In order to eliminate the effects of business cycles on P/E ratios, analysts usually calculate normalized earnings.
- Differences in accounting methods.

Calculating Underlying or Persistent Earnings

- There are no prescribed rules for calculating underlying earnings.
- Analysts should not rely on company-reported core or continuing earnings.
- Analysts should compute the adjusted P/E ratio based on their own judgment regarding how the company's underlying earnings should be calculated, and the same basis should then be applied for all stocks under review.
- Non-recurring components of earnings cannot easily be identified by just looking at the income statement. The financial statement footnotes and the MD&A section can be important sources of information in this regard.
- Earnings may also be segregated into their cash flow and accrual component. A higher P/E should be assigned to the cash flow component when calculating P/Es.

Calculating Normalized Earnings

- Under the method of historical average EPS, normalized EPS is calculated as average EPS over the most recent full cycle.
  - This method does not account for changes in a company's size over the period.
- Under the method of average return on equity, normalized EPS is calculated as current book value per share times the average return on equity over the most recent full cycle.
  - This method does account for changes in a company's size.
- Other methods (that are particularly useful when a cyclical company reports a loss) include (1) multiplying total assets by estimated long-run return on assets, and (2) multiplying shareholders' equity by estimated long-run return on equity.

The Earnings Yield

- Earnings may sometimes be zero or negative, which makes the P/E ratio useless.
- In such cases, analysts use the reciprocal of the P/E ratio to rank investments. The earnings-to-price ratio is known as the earnings yield.
- Securities may be ranked based on earnings yield from highest to lowest i.e., from cheapest to most costly in terms of the amount of earnings per unit of price.

P/E based on the method of forecasted fundamentals

$$\text{Leading P/E} = \frac{P_0}{E_1} = \frac{D_1/E_1}{r-g} = \frac{(1-b)}{r-g}$$

$$\text{Trailing P/E} = \frac{P_0}{E_0} = \frac{D_0(1+g)/E_0}{r-g} = \frac{(1-b)(1+g)}{r-g}$$

P/Es based on cross-sectional regression

P/E ratios may also be calculated based on cross-sectional regression. However, such a model has the following limitations:

- It is only applicable for a specific stock for a specific time period.
- The relationships between P/E and fundamentals may change over time.
- The regression may suffer from multicollinearity.

The P/E-to-Growth (PEG) Ratio

The impact of earnings growth on the P/E ratio is captured by the P/E-to-growth (PEG) ratio. This ratio is calculated as the stock's P/E divided by the expected earnings growth rate in percent. All else being equal, investors prefer stocks with *lower* PEGs over stocks with higher PEGs. The PEG ratio has the following drawbacks:

- It incorrectly assumes a linear relationship between P/E and growth.
- It does not account for the different risks in different stocks.
- It does not account for differences in the duration of growth.

Price-to-Book Value

$$\text{P/B ratio} = \frac{\text{Market price per share}}{\text{Book value per share}}$$

Book value of equity = Common shareholders' equity = Shareholders' equity − Total value of equity claims that are senior to common stock

Book value of equity = Total assets − Total liabilities − Preferred stock

Advantages

- Book value usually remains positive even when the company reports negative earnings.
- Book value is typically more stable than reported earnings.
- For financial sector companies that have significant holdings of liquid assets, P/B is more meaningful as book values reflect recent market values.
- P/B is useful in valuing a company that is expected to go out of business.
- Studies suggest that differences in P/B ratios over time are related to differences in long-term average returns on stocks.

Disadvantages

- Book values ignore non-tangible factors such as the quality of a company's human capital and brand image.
- P/B can lead to misleading valuations if significantly different levels of assets are being used by the companies being studied.
- Accounting differences can impair the comparability of P/B ratios across companies.
- Inflation and changes in technology may result in significant differences between accounting book values and actual fair values of a company's assets.
- Share repurchases or issuances may distort historical comparisons.

Analysts usually make the following adjustments to book value in order to increase its comparability with other companies:

- They use tangible book value per share, which is calculated as common shareholders' equity less certain intangible assets (goodwill).
- They adjust reported financials to eliminate the effects of differences in accounting standards.
- They adjust the balance sheet for off-balance sheet items.
- They adjust certain balance sheet (historical) values to reflect current fair values.

P/B based on the method of forecasted fundamentals

$$\frac{P_0}{B_0} = \frac{ROE - g}{r - g}$$

Price to Sales

$$P/S \text{ ratio} = \frac{\text{Market price per share}}{\text{Sales per share}}$$

Advantages

- Sales are less prone to manipulation by management than earnings and book values.
- Sales are positive even when EPS is negative.
- The P/S ratio is usually more stable than the P/E ratio.
- Price-to-sales is considered an appropriate measure for valuing mature, cyclical, and loss-making companies.
- Studies have shown that differences in price-to-sales ratios are related to differences in long-term average returns on stocks.

Disadvantages

- Sales reveal no information about the operating profitability of a company.
- Using the P/S ratio does not reflect the differences in cost structure and operating efficiency between companies.
- Revenue recognition practices may allow management to distort revenue figures.

P/S ratio based on the method of forecasted fundamentals

$$\frac{P_0}{S_0} = \frac{(E_0/S_0)(1-b)(1+g)}{r-g}$$

Price to Cash Flow

$$P/CF\ ratio = \frac{Market\ price\ per\ share}{Free\ cash\ flow\ per\ share}$$

Advantages

- Cash flows are less susceptible to management manipulation than earnings.
- P/CF is more stable than the P/E ratio.
- Using the price to cash flow ratio gets around the problem related to differences in accounting methods used by companies.
- Differences in price to cash flow ratio over time are related to differences in long-term average returns on stocks.

Disadvantages

-
- When "EPS plus non-cash charges" is used as the definition for cash flow, non-cash revenue, and changes in working capital items are ignored.
- FCFE is more appropriate for valuing a company than operating cash flow. However, FCFE has the following drawbacks:
  - For many businesses it is more volatile than operating cash flow.
  - It is more frequently negative than operating cash flow.
- Companies may inflate certain cash flow measures (e.g., CFO).

Justified P/CF Multiple Based on Fundamentals

The justified P/CF multiple based on fundamentals can be determined by first computing the intrinsic value of the stock using a discounted cash flow model and then dividing the intrinsic value estimate by the chosen definition of cash flow.

For example, the constant growth FCFE model is given as:

$$V_0 = \frac{FCFE_0(1+g)}{(r-g)}$$

We could divide both sides of this equation by our desired definition of cash flow to obtain the justified P/CF multiple for a stock.

- The justified P/CF multiple is positively related to the growth rate of cash flows (g).
- The justified P/CF multiple is inversely related to stock's required rate of return (r).

Price-to-Dividends and Dividend Yield

> Dividend yield = Dividend per share / Price per share

Advantages

- The dividend yield is a component of total return.
- The dividend yield component of total return is less risky than the capital gains component.

Disadvantages

- The dividend yield is only one of the (two) components of total return. Ignoring the capital appreciation component in valuation is risky.
- Dividends paid now "displace" earnings in future periods. A higher dividend yield usually implies a lower earnings growth rate going forward.
- The argument that dividends are relatively safe (less risky) assumes that the market prices reflect differences in relative risk between the two components of total return.
- Trailing dividend yield is calculated by dividing the annualized amount of the most recent dividend by the current market price per share.
- Leading dividend yield is calculated by dividing next year's forecasted dividend per share by the current market price per share.

Dividend yield using the method based on forecasted fundamentals

$$\frac{D_0}{P_0} = \frac{r-g}{1+g}$$

- The dividend yield is positively related to the required rate of return on equity (r).
- The dividend yield is negatively related to the expected rate of growth in dividends (g). This implies that investing in a low-dividend-yield stock reflects a growth rather than a value strategy.

Enterprise Value Multiples

Enterprise Value to EBITDA

> Enterprise value = Market value of common equity + Market value of preferred stock
> + Market value of debt + Minority interest
> − Value of cash and short-term investments

Advantages

- The EV/EBITDA multiple is appropriate for comparing companies with different levels of financial leverage.
- Unlike net income, EBITDA controls for differences in depreciation and amortization among companies and therefore, is more appropriate for valuing capital-intensive businesses.
- EBITDA is often positive when EPS is negative.

Drawbacks

- EBITDA ignores the effects of differences in revenue recognition policies on cash flow from operations.
- EBITDA may overstate CFO if working capital is growing.
- Free cash flow to the firm (FCFF) can have a stronger link to company value than EBITDA.

Other enterprise value multiples, such as EV/FCFF and EV/Sales are also frequently used.

Alternative Definitions of Cash Flow for EV Multiples

EPS-plus non-cash charges (CF)

- Calculated as EPS + Depreciation + Amortization.
- Ignores non-cash revenue and changes in working capital items.

Cash flow from operations (CFO)

- May require adjustments for non-recurring components of cash flow.
- Adjustments may be required when comparing companies that use different accounting standards.

Free cash flow to equity (FCFE)

- Calculated as CFO – FCInv + Net borrowing
- Theoretically, it is the most suitable definition for free cash flow.
- However, it may be more volatile than CFO and may also be more frequently negative than CFO.

EBITDA

- Calculated by adding depreciation and amortization to EBIT.
- Since it represents a flow available to both equity holders and bond holders, it is more suited for calculating the value of the company; not the value of equity.

Valuation Based on Forecasted Fundamentals

All other things remaining the same, the justified EV/EBITDA multiple based on fundamentals is:

- Positively related to the expected growth rate of FCFF.
- Positively related to the return on invested capital, ROIC (expected profitability).
  - ROIC is calculated as operating profit after tax divided by total invested capital.
- Negatively related to the WACC.

Momentum Valuation Indicators

Unexpected earnings is the difference between a company's reported earnings and its expected earnings.

$$UEt = EPS_t - E(EPS_t)$$

- **Standardized unexpected earnings** is calculated by dividing a company's unexpected earnings by the standard deviation of past unexpected earnings over a period of time.

$$SUE_t = \frac{EPS_t - E(EPS_t)}{\sigma[EPS_t - E(EPS_t)]}$$

- **Relative-strength indicators** compare a stock's performance during a particular period, either with its own past performance, or with the performance of a group of comparable stocks.

Valuation Indicators: Issues in Practice

Average Multiples: The Harmonic Mean

The P/E for a portfolio or an index is most accurately calculated through the harmonic mean and the weighted harmonic mean.

$$\text{Simple harmonic mean: } X_H = \frac{n}{\sum_{i=1}^{n}(1/X_i)}$$

$$\text{Weighted harmonic mean} = X_{WH} = \frac{1}{\sum_{i=1}^{n}(w_i/X_i)}$$

- The simple harmonic mean inherently gives a lower weight to higher P/Es and a higher weight to lower P/Es.
- Using the median (as opposed to the mean) mitigates the effect of outliers.
- The harmonic mean may also be used to reduce the impact of outliers. However, while the harmonic mean mitigates the impact of large outliers, it may actually aggravate the impact of small outliers.
- For an equal-weighted index, simple harmonic mean, and weighted harmonic mean are equal.

Using Multiple Valuation Indicators

- When back-testing, analysts should be wary of look-ahead bias.
- Stock screens usually define criteria (based on valuation indicators) for including stocks in an investor's portfolio and provide an efficient way to narrow a search for investments.

RESIDUAL INCOME VALUATION
Cross-Reference to CFA Institute Assigned Reading #32

Residual Income

Residual income, or economic profit, recognizes the cost of equity capital. It is calculated by deducting a charge for equity capital from net income.

$$\text{Residual income} = \text{Net income} - \text{Equity charge}$$

$$\text{Equity charge} = \text{Cost of equity capital} \times \text{Equity capital}$$

- Companies with positive RI create value as they generate more income than their cost of obtaining capital.
- Companies with negative RI effectively destroy value as they do not generate sufficient income to cover their cost of capital.
- Companies with higher (lower) residual income should be associated with higher (lower) valuations.

Economic Value Added (EVA)

EVA measures the value added for shareholders by the management of a company during a given year.

$$\text{EVA} = [\text{EBIT}\,(1 - \text{Tax rate})] - (\text{C\%} \times \text{TC})$$

$$\text{EVA} = \text{NOPAT} - \$\text{WACC}$$

Market Value Added (MVA)

Market value added (MVA) measures the value created by management for the company's investors by generating economic profits over the life of the company.

$$\text{MVA} = \text{Market value of the company} - \text{Book value of invested capital}$$

$$\text{Market value of company} = \text{Market value of debt} + \text{Market value of equity}$$

The Residual Income Model

The residual income (RI) model breaks the intrinsic value of a stock into the following two components:

- Current book value of equity
- Present value of expected future residual income

The intrinsic value of a stock can be calculated as:

$$V_0 = B_0 + \sum_{t=1}^{\infty} \frac{RI_t}{(1+r)^t} = B_0 + \sum_{t=1}^{\infty} \frac{E_t - rB_{t-1}}{(1+r)^t}$$

The general residual income model may also be expressed as:

$$V_0 = B_0 + \sum_{t=1}^{\infty} \frac{(ROE_t - r)B_{t-1}}{(1+r)^t}$$

The intrinsic value of a stock under the residual income model can be expressed as:

$$V_0 = B_0 + \frac{ROE - r}{r - g} B_0$$

Under this constant-growth residual income model, the intrinsic value of a stock equals the sum of:

- Its current book value (B_0); and
- The present value of its expected stream of residual income [(ROE − r) × B_0/(r − g)]. This term represents the additional value created as a result of the company's ability to generate returns in excess of its cost of equity.

Also note that:

- If the return on equity (ROE) equals the required return on equity (r), the intrinsic value of the stock would equal its book value.
- If the return on equity (ROE) is greater than the required return on equity (r), the present value of the expected stream of residual income will be positive, the intrinsic value of the stock will be greater than its book value, and the justified P/B ratio will be greater than 1.
- If the return on equity (ROE) is less than the required return on equity (r), the present value of the expected stream of residual income will be negative, the intrinsic value of the stock will be lower than its book value, and the justified P/B ratio will be less than 1.

Therefore, a stock's justified P/B ratio is directly related to the company's expected future residual income.

Tobin's q

$$Tobin's\ q = \frac{Market\ value\ of\ debt\ and\ equity}{Replacement\ cost\ of\ total\ assets}$$

Tobin's q is different from the P/B in the following respects:

- It uses the market value of equity and debt (rather than just equity) in the numerator and uses total assets (rather than equity) in the denominator.
- Assets are valued at replacement cost (as opposed to book or accounting values).

All else equal, the greater the productivity of a firm's assets, the higher the Tobin's q.

Single-Stage Residual Income Model

The single-stage residual income model makes the following simplifying assumptions:

- The company earns a constant return on equity.
- The earnings growth rate is constant at a level that is lower than the required return on equity.

$$V_0 = B_0 + \frac{ROE - r}{r - g} B_0$$

- If the return on equity (ROE) equals the required return on equity (r), the intrinsic value of the stock would equal its book value.
- If the return on equity (ROE) is greater than the required return on equity (r), the intrinsic value of the stock would be greater than its book value.
- If the return on equity (ROE) is less than the required return on equity (r), the intrinsic value of the stock would be less than its book value.

The single-stage RI model assumes that the return on equity will remain in excess of the required rate of return on equity (resulting in positive RI) for an indefinite period of time. This assumption is a bit unrealistic as residual income will likely fall to zero at some point in time.

Multistage Residual Income Valuation

In the multistage residual income model, the intrinsic value of a stock has three components:

$$V_0 = B_0 + (\text{PV of future RI over the short-term}) + (\text{PV of continuing RI})$$

$$V_0 = B_0 + \sum_{t=1}^{T} \frac{(ROE_t - r)B_{t-1}}{(1+r)^t} + \frac{P_T - B_T}{(1+r)^T}$$

Analysts may make any one of the following assumptions regarding continuing residual income:

- It continues indefinitely at a positive level.
- It is zero from the terminal year forward.
- It declines to zero as ROE reverts to the cost of equity over time.
- It reflects the reversion of ROE to some mean level.

The more sustainable a company's competitive advantage and the brighter the industry's prospects, the higher the persistence factor.

$$V_0 = B_0 + \sum_{t=1}^{T-1} \frac{(E_t - rB_{t-1})}{(1+r)^t} + \frac{E_T - rB_{T-1}}{(1+r-\omega)(1+r)^{T-1}}$$

Implied Growth Rate

$$g = r - \left[\frac{(ROE - r) \times B_0}{V_0 - B_0} \right]$$

Advantages and Disadvantages of the Residual Income Model

Advantages

- Unlike DDM and FCF valuation models, the terminal value estimate (which has a significant amount of uncertainty associated with it) does not constitute a significant proportion of intrinsic value in the RI model. Most of the value under the RI model comes from current book value, which leads to earlier recognition of value relative to other valuation models.
- It uses accounting data which is easily available.
- It is applicable to companies that do not pay any dividends or have negative free cash flows.
- It is applicable to companies with uncertain cash flows.
- It focuses on economic profitability.

Disadvantages

- It is based on accounting data which can be manipulated by management.
- Accounting data must be adjusted to be used in the model.
- It assumes that the clean-surplus relation holds (i.e., ending book value of equity equals beginning book value plus earnings less dividends).
- It assumes that interest expense appropriately reflects the cost of debt capital.

Scenarios when the residual income model is appropriate

- The company does not have a history of paying dividends, or dividends cannot be predicted with certainty.
- The company's free cash flows are expected to remain negative for the foreseeable future.
- The estimates of terminal value using alternative valuation models entail a great amount of uncertainty.

Scenarios when the residual income model is not appropriate

- There are significant violations of the clean surplus relation.
- It is difficult to predict the main determinants of residual income (i.e., book value and ROE).

Important Considerations in RI Valuation

- Analysts should ensure that the clean-surplus relation holds. The clean-surplus relation may be violated if items are charged directly to equity without going through the income statement. If the clean-surplus relation does not hold, forecasted value of ROE obtained through the RI model will not be accurate.
- The book values of many balance sheet items may be significantly different from their fair values. If this is the case, analysts need to make adjustments to these items to reflect fair value.
- The balance sheet may contain intangible assets. These items require close attention as they can have a significant effect on book value.
- The book value of common equity should be adjusted for off-balance sheet items and amortization of certain intangible assets.
- Non-recurring items should be excluded when forecasting residual income.
- Analysts need to consider the reliability of earnings estimates, and whether "poor quality" accounting rules result in delayed recognition of value changes.

PRIVATE COMPANY VALUATION
Cross-Reference to CFA Institute Assigned Reading #33

Private versus Public Company Valuation

Company-Specific Factors

- Private companies are typically in an earlier stage of their life cycle compared to public companies, which generally tend to be more mature.
- Private companies are usually smaller in size than public companies, which is why they are more risky investments.
- Owners of private companies are usually also involved in the management of the company. In public companies, there is a distinction between owners and management, which gives rise to agency problems.
- Public companies are usually able to attract better quality management than private companies.
- Public companies are required by regulatory authorities to publish their financial statements regularly. This is not a requirement for private firms, which increases the level of risk for investors as they do not have access to credible financial information regarding the company. Higher risk results in lower valuations.
- Managers in public companies constantly face pressure to maintain or increase the company's stock price, which makes them focus on short-term goals. Managers of private companies do not face such pressures and therefore, pursue profitable long-term strategies even if they may have a negative short-term impact.
- Private companies are usually more concerned about taxes than public companies.

Stock-Specific Factors

- Private company shares are usually less liquid than public company shares.
- Control of private companies is generally concentrated in the hands of a few shareholders, who may pursue activities that benefit a few shareholders at the cost of others.
- Private companies may restrict shareholders from selling their stakes in the company, which further reduces the marketability of their equity interests.

Reasons for Performing Valuations

- Transaction-related valuations refer to valuations for:
  - Private financing
  - Initial public offering (IPO)
  - Acquisition
  - Bankruptcy
  - Share-based payment (compensation)
- Compliance-related valuations may be required by law and primarily focus on financial reporting and tax reporting.
- Litigation-related valuations arise from shareholder disputes, damage claims, etc.

Definitions of Value

Fair market value (FMV): The price that similarly informed buyers and sellers would agree to trade an asset where the trade must be an arm's length transaction and neither the buyer nor seller is under any external pressure to trade.

- Fair market value is mostly used for tax reporting purposes.

Market value: The estimated amount for which a property should exchange on the date of valuation between a willing buyer and willing seller in an arm's length transaction after proper marketing wherein the parties had each acted knowledgeably, prudently, and without compulsion.

- Market value is frequently used in appraisals of real estate and tangible assets when they are used as collateral for borrowings.

Fair value (financial reporting): Under IFRS, fair value is defined as "the price that would be received for an asset or paid to transfer a liability in a current transaction between two marketplace participants in the reference market for the asset or liability." Under U.S. GAAP, fair value is defined as "the price that would be received to sell an asset or paid to transfer a liability in an orderly transaction between market participants at the measurement date."

- This value is used in financial reporting and is very similar to the fair market value.

Fair value (litigation): The definition of fair value in a legal setting is generally similar to the definitions of fair value for financial reporting.

Investment value: The value of an asset to a particular buyer based on her investment requirements and expectations.

- Investment value is important in acquisitions of private companies.

Intrinsic value: The "true" or "real" value of an asset based on its risk-return expectations absent short-term mispricings.

- Intrinsic value is often used in investment analysis.

Private Company Valuation Approaches

- The income approach values a private company based on the present value of its expected future income.
- The market approach values a private company based on price multiples derived from sales of comparable companies.
- The asset-based approach values a private company based on the value of its underlying net assets.

Factors to Consider when Deciding on a Valuation Approach

Nature of operations and life cycle stage: **Generally speaking:**

- A company in the earliest stages of development should be valued using the asset-based approach as future cash flows might be too unpredictable and there is no guarantee that the company will be able to operate as a going concern for the foreseeable future.
- A company that has successfully negotiated the early development stage and is witnessing high growth should be valued using the income approach (based on discounted expected future cash flows).
- A stable, relatively mature company should be valued using the market approach.

Company size: **Generally speaking:**

- Use of multiples from larger public companies is not appropriate for smaller, relatively mature private firms with limited growth prospects.
- Use of multiples from large public companies is not appropriate for smaller private firms that entail significantly more risk.

Finally, note that non-operating assets (e.g., excess cash and investments) which are not part of the firm's core business should be accounted for in the valuation of an entity regardless of the valuation approach or method used.

Earnings Normalization Issues in Private Companies

Analysts may sometimes need to make significant adjustments to a private company's earnings due to the following reasons:

- There is concentration of control which may lead to significant discretionary and tax-motivated expenses being recognized on the income statement.
- Personal expenses may be included as company expenses.
- The effects of significant related-party transactions (which may be recorded at inflated or deflated prices) must be accounted for.
- The company's profitability may suffer if excessive compensation is being paid out to senior managers (owners).
- Revenues and expenses related to company-owned real estate should be removed from the company's income statement, and a market estimate for rent should be recognized instead. The property should be treated as a non-operating asset.
- In estimating normalized earnings for strategic buyers, the effects of synergies should be incorporated.

Cash Flow Estimation in Private Companies

Calculating free cash flow for private companies is a challenging process given the uncertainty of future cash flows. Further, company projections may be biased as they are usually prepared by managers who are also owners.

- Analysts may develop a number of scenarios to forecast cash flows and discount future cash flows in each scenario using an appropriate risk-adjusted discount rate. They can then calculate the value of the company as the weighted-average of the value in each scenario.
- Alternatively, they may forecast future cash flows in a single scenario considering all the associated risks and discount them at an appropriate risk-adjusted discount rate to calculate the value of the firm.

- Use of FCFF is preferred over FCFE when the company's capital structure is expected to change going forward as the WACC is less sensitive to leverage changes than the cost of equity capital.

Income Approach Methods of Private Company Valuation

- The free cash flow method calculates the value of a firm as the present value of future free cash flows expected to be generated by the firm discounted at an appropriate risk-adjusted discount rate.
- The capitalized cash flow method calculates firm value by dividing a single representative estimate of economic benefits by a capitalization rate, where the capitalization rate is calculated as an appropriate discount rate minus a growth rate.
- The excess earnings method calculates firm value by adding the value of the firm's intangible assets to the value of working capital and fixed assets. The value of intangible assets is calculated by capitalizing future earnings of the firm in excess of the estimated return requirements associated with working capital and fixed assets.

Challenges in Determining the Required Rate of Return

- A size premium must be added to the discount rate in valuing small private firms. Size premiums based on public company data can capture premiums for distress which may not be relevant for private companies.
- The use of the CAPM may not be appropriate for estimating the cost of equity for private firms (especially if they have slim chances of going public or being acquired by a public company).
- If the build-up approach is used, an industry risk premium must be included in the model. This premium may be difficult to determine.
- It may be more difficult for private companies to raise debt capital than for public companies. This makes them more reliant on equity financing, which results in a larger WACC. Further, the cost of debt is higher for private companies due to their smaller size and higher operating risk.
- When acquiring a private firm, the acquirer should use the target's capital structure and cost of capital to determine the WACC applicable to the target's cash flows.
- A premium for projection risk (the risk that arises due to uncertainty involved in projecting future cash flows of private firms) and managerial inexperience may be added to the required rate of return.

Market Approach Methods of Private Company Valuation

- The guideline public company method calculates the value of a private company based on price multiples from trading data of comparable public companies. The price multiple is adjusted to reflect the differences in the relative risk and growth prospects between the companies. Factors that require consideration include:
  - Type of transaction
  - Industry factors
  - Form of consideration
  - Reasonableness
- The guideline transaction method calculates the value of a private company based on price multiples obtained from past acquisitions of entire public or private companies. The multiples used must consider the following factors:
  - Synergies
  - Contingent consideration

  - Non-cash consideration
  - Availability of transactions
  - Changes between the transaction date and valuation date
- The prior transaction method calculates the value of a private company based on actual transactions in the stock of the subject private company.

Asset-Based Approach

This approach values a private company based on the fair value of its underlying net assets. This method is not appropriate for valuing going concerns and is only suitable for valuing:

- Small firms that are in the early stages of their life cycle.
- Firms with minimal profits, with no prospects for doing better in the future.
- Firms whose assets and liabilities are based on market values (e.g., banks).
- Investment companies where the value of underlying assets is determined using the market or income approaches (e.g., REITs).
- Firms with natural resources whose assets can be valued using data from comparable sales.

Valuation Discounts and Premiums

Discount for Lack of Control (DLOC)

A discount for lack of control is applied to the pro rate share of the value of an equity interest in a business to reflect the absence of all or some of the powers on control.

$$DLOC = 1 - \left[\frac{1}{1 + \text{Control Premium}} \right]$$

The application of DLOC varies with the method and basis used to value the equity interest:

- The guideline public company method values a company from a non-controlling perspective and therefore, a DLOC must not be applied.
- The guideline transaction method values a company from a control perspective and therefore, a DLOC should be applied.
- The application of DLOC in the capitalized cash flow or the free cash flow method depends on the type of cash flows used.
  - Generally speaking, the CCM and FCF models use cash flows and discount rates that are estimated on a controlling interest basis so a DLOC is applied to the results of the model.
  - However, if control cash flows are not used and/or the discount rate does not reflect an optimal capital structure, a DLOC must not be applied.

Discount for Lack of Marketability (DLOM)

A discount for lack of marketability is applied to the value of an ownership interest to reflect the relative absence of marketability. The DLOM is affected by the following variables:

- Prospects for liquidity
- Contractual arrangements affecting marketability

- Restrictions on transferability
- Pool of potential buyers
- Risk or volatility
- Size and timing of distributions
- Uncertainty of value
- Concentration of ownership

The DLOM may be estimated based on:

- Private sales of restricted stock in public companies relatively to their freely traded stock price.
- Private sales of a company's stock prior to an IPO.
- The pricing of put options.

The relationship between DLOC and DLOM is not additive, so you should compound when both exist. For example, if the DLOC is 5% and the DLOM is 3%, the total discount is not 8%, but:

$$1 - [(1 - 0.05)(1 - 0.03)] = 7.85\%$$

Important:

- If publicly traded shares are used as the basis for price multiples, control premiums should be added when measuring the total value of a private company.
- A DLOM may not need to be applied when there is a high likelihood of a liquidity event in the near future.

THE TERM STRUCTURE AND INTEREST RATE DYNAMICS
Cross-Reference to CFA Institute Assigned Reading #34

A forward rate is an interest rate that is determined today for a loan that will be initiated in the future. We denote the x-year forward rate y years from today as $_xf_y$. Here, a loan with a term of x years will be initiated y years from today.

- For example, the three-year forward rate two years from today will be denoted as $_3f_2$.

The Forward Pricing Model

The forward pricing model describes the valuation of forward contracts. It is based on the no-arbitrage argument.

> Forward pricing model: $P(T^* + T) = P(T^*)F(T^*,T)$

Determining Forward Rates from Spot Rates

$$(1+ _ys_0)^y (1+ _xf_y)^x = (1+ _{x+y}s_0)^{x+y}$$

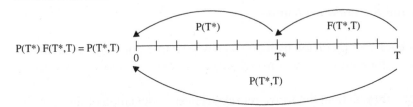

Forward Pricing Model

$$P(T^*) F(T^*,T) = P(T^*,T)$$

- Forward rates can be extrapolated from spot rates.
- A forward rate can be looked upon as a type of breakeven interest rate.
- A forward rate can also be looked upon as the rate that can be locked in by extending maturity by one year.
- The x-year spot rate today can be expressed as a geometric mean of the 1-year spot rate today, and a series of 1-year forward rates (where the number of 1-year forward rates equals x−1).

Other Important Relationships between Spot and Forward Rates

- If the yield curve is upward-sloping, then the x-year forward rate y years from today, $_xf_y$, will be greater than the long-term spot rate, $_{x+y}s_0$
  - Example: If $_3s_0 > _2s_0 > _1s_0$ then $_2f_1 > _3s_0$
- For an upward-sloping yield curve, the forward rate rises as y (the initiation date) increases.
  - Example: If $_3s_0 > _2s_0 > _1s_0$ then $_1f_2 > _3s_0$

- If the yield curve is downward sloping, then the x-year forward rate y years from today, $_xf_y$, will be lower than the long-term spot rate, $_{x+y}s_0$
  - Example: If $_3s_0 > {}_2s_0 > {}_1s_0$ then $_2f_1 < {}_3s_0$
- For a downward-sloping yield curve, the forward rate declines as y increases.
  - Example: If $_3s_0 > {}_2s_0 > {}_2s_0$ then $_1f_2 < {}_1f_1$
- If the yield curve is flat, all one-year forward rates are equal to the spot rate.

Yield to Maturity in Relation to Spot Rates and Expected and Realized Returns on Bonds

- The yield to maturity (YTM) is calculated as the internal rate of return on a bond's cash flows.
- It only equals the expected rate of return on a bond if (1) the bond is held until maturity, (2) all coupon and principal payments are made in full when due, and (3) all coupons are reinvested at the original YTM. This last condition typically does not hold.
- The YTM is a poor estimate of the expected return on a bond if (1) interest rates are volatile, (2) the yield curve has a steep slope, (3) there is significant risk of default, and (4) the bond contains embedded options.
- Even if we make the assumption that actual future spot rates will turn out to be the same as forward rates (that are based on current spot rates), the expected return on a bond still will not equal its YTM. This is because the YTM implicitly assumes that the yield curve is flat (the same discount rate is applied to each cash flow regardless of its maturity).
- The realized rate of return is the actual return earned by a bond investor over the holding period. It is based on (1) actual reinvestment rates and (2) the yield curve at the end of the holding period.

Yield Curve Movements and the Forward Curve

- If future spot rates evolve as predicted by today's forward curve, forward rates remain unchanged; and since forward rates remain unchanged, so does the forward contract price.
- A change in the forward rate (and the forward price) reflects a deviation of the spot curve from that predicted by today's forward curve.
- If a trader expects that the future spot rate will be lower than what is predicted by the prevailing forward rate, he would buy the forward contract because he expects its value to increase.
- If a trader expects that the future spot rate will be greater than what is predicted by the prevailing forward rate, he would sell the forward contract because he expects its value to decrease.

Active Bond Portfolio Management

- The return on bonds of varying maturities over a one-year period is always the one-year rate (the risk-free rate over the one-year period), if spot rates evolve (at the end of the first year) as implied by the current forward curve.
- If a portfolio manager's projected spot curve is above (below) the forward curve and his or her expectation turns out to be true, the return will be less (more) than the one-period risk-free interest rate because the market would have overpriced (underpriced) the forward contract.

Riding the Yield Curve

If the yield curve is upward-sloping, and if a trader is confident that the yield curve will not change its level and shape over her investment horizon, she would buy bonds with a maturity greater than her investment horizon (instead of bonds with maturities that exactly match her investment horizon) to enhance her total return.

THE SWAP RATE CURVE

The yield curve of swap fixed rates is known as the swap rate curve or swap curve. Since it is based on par swaps (the present values of the fixed- and floating-rate legs are equal at swap initiation), the swap curve is a type of par curve.

The swap market is a highly liquid market for two main reasons:

- Swap arrangements offer significant flexibility and customization in contract design.
- Swaps provide a very efficient way to hedge interest rate risk.

The Swap Spread

- The swap spread is defined as the difference between the swap fixed rate on a swap and the rate of the "on-the-run" government security with the same maturity/tenor as the swap.
- The swap spread can be used to measure credit risk and liquidity risk. The higher the swap spread, the higher the compensation demanded by investors for accepting credit and/or liquidity risk. Note, however, that if the bond entails no default risk, then the swap spread could indicate liquidity risk, or it could suggest that the bond is mispriced.
- A more accurate measure (than the swap spread) of credit and liquidity risk is the zero-spread (or z-spread). The z-spread is the constant spread that would be added to the implied spot curve such that the present value of the cash flows of a bond, when discounted at relevant spot rates plus the z-spread, equals its current market price.

Spreads as a Price Quote Convention

- The swap spread represents the difference between the swap rate and the government bond yield (of the same maturity).
  - The swap rate does reflect some counterparty credit risk, while the U.S. Treasuries are considered free from default risk, so the swap rate is typically greater than the corresponding Treasury note rate.
- The TED spread (Treasuries vs. Eurodollars) is calculated as the difference between LIBOR and the yield on a T-bill with the same maturity.
  - The TED spread indicates the perceived level of credit risk in the overall economy.
  - The TED spread can also be thought of as a measure of counterparty credit risk in swap contracts.
- The LIBOR-OIS spread is calculated as the difference between LIBOR and the overnight indexed swap (OIS) rate.
  - The LIBOR–OIS spread is an indicator of the risk and liquidity of money-market securities.
- The I-spread is calculated as the difference between the yield on a corporate bond and the swap rate on a swap with the same tenor as the bond.

TRADITIONAL THEORIES OF THE TERM STRUCTURE OF INTEREST RATES

Unbiased Expectations Theory

The unbiased expectations theory or pure expectations theory states that the forward rate is an unbiased predictor of future spot rates. This implies that bonds of **any** maturity are perfect substitutes for each other. The unbiased expectations theory assumes that investors are risk-neutral. The argument against this theory is that investors tend to be risk-averse.

Local Expectations Theory

The local expectations theory is similar but narrower than the unbiased expectations theory. Instead of asserting that every maturity strategy has the same expected return over a given investment horizon, this theory states that the return over a short-term investment horizon that starts today will be the same (i.e., the risk-free rate) regardless of maturity of the chosen security as long as forward rates are actually realized.

The local expectations theory is economically appealing, but it is often observed that short-term returns on longer-maturity bonds exceed those on shorter-maturity bonds.

Liquidity Preference Theory

The liquidity preference theory accounts for the fact that investors in long-term securities require some compensation for taking higher interest rate risk. This theory asserts that the longer the term to maturity, the greater the price sensitivity (duration) of a bond to changes in interest rates, and the greater the compensation (risk premium) required by investors.

Segmented Markets Theory

The segmented markets theory asserts that the yield for each maturity along the yield curve is determined independently, solely by the supply and demand of funds for the particular maturity, which means that yields do not reflect expected spot rates or liquidity premiums.

The Preferred Habitat Theory

The preferred habitat theory does not assert that yields at different maturities are determined independently of each other. In this theory, both market expectations and the institutional factors emphasized in the segmented markets theory influence the term structure of interest rates.

MODERN TERM STRUCTURE MODELS

Equilibrium Term Structure Models

- Equilibrium term structure models look to describe the dynamics of the term structure using fundamental economic variables that affect interest rates.
- They can be structured as one-factor or multifactor models.
- They make assumptions about the behavior of factors. For example, the model must make an assumption whether the short-term interest rate should be modeled as mean-reverting, or whether it should be modeled to exhibit jumps.
- They typically require estimation of less parameters than arbitrage-free term structure models (described later), but this comes at the cost of less precision in modeling the observed yield curve.

- They typically make an assumption regarding the term premium, i.e., the additional return required by lenders to invest in long-term securities. Arbitrage-free models do not make a term premium assumption.

The Cox-Ingersoll-Ross (CIR) Model

- The CIR model uses one factor, i.e., the short-term rate to determine the entire term structure of interest rates.
- The model has (1) a deterministic component and (2) a stochastic (or random) component.
    - The deterministic component is also called the drift term.
        - Within this deterministic component, the interest rate is modeled as mean-reverting (towards a level b).
        - Another parameter (a) represents the speed at which interest rates revert to the mean. The higher the value of this parameter, the quicker the mean reversion.
    - The stochastic term models risk (volatility).
        - This term makes volatility proportional to the short-term rate, i.e., interest rate volatility increases with the level of interest rates.
        - It also precludes the possibility of negative interest rates.

The Vasicek Model

- The Vasicek model also assumes that interest rates are mean-reverting.
- The model also has the same drift term as the CIR model.
- However, the stochastic component assumes that interest rate volatility is constant.
- The main disadvantage of the model is that it is theoretically possible for interest rates to be negative.

The yield curve estimated with the Vasicek or CIR model may not match the observed yield curve. However, if model parameters are believed to be correct, these models can be used to identify mispricings.

Arbitrage-Free Models

- Arbitrage-free models start with market prices of a reference set of financial instruments. Under the assumption that these instruments are correctly priced, a random process with a drift term and volatility factor is used to generate the yield curve.
- The advantage of arbitrage-free models is the ability to calibrate the model to market data. They exhibit greater accuracy in modeling the market yield curve.
- Arbitrage-free models are also known as partial equilibrium models because they do not attempt to explain the yield curve; instead they take the yield curve as given.

The Ho-Lee Model

- The Ho-Lee model uses the relative valuation concepts of the Black-Scholes-Merton option-pricing model.
- The time-dependent drift term of the model is inferred from market prices, so the model can accurately generate the current term structure.

- This exercise is typically performed via a binomial lattice-based model, which makes use of risk-neutral probabilities.
- The advantage of the model lies in its simplicity, and it can be used to illustrate most of the salient features of arbitrage-free interest rate models.
- Interest rate volatility can be modeled as a function of time in the model.
- The downside is that negative interest rates are theoretically possible.

YIELD CURVE FACTOR MODELS

- The sensitivity of a bond's price to changes in the shape of the yield curve is known as shaping risk.
- Studies that have made use of yield curve factor models have found that yield curve movements are historically well described by three independent movements—level, steepness, and curvature.
    - The level movement refers to upward or downward (parallel) shifts in the yield curve.
    - The steepness movement refers to changes in the slope of the yield curve. These movements are also known as yield curve twists.
    - The curvature movement refers to movements in the three segments of the yield curve. These movements are also known as butterfly shifts.

Managing Yield Curve Risks

Yield curve risk refers to the risk to portfolio value from unanticipated changes in the yield curve. It can be identified and managed using:

- Key rate duration, which measures the change in the value of a portfolio in response to a small change in the yield for a specific maturity.
- A measure based on the factor model, which uses three types of movements—level, steepness, and curvature, to explain changes in the yield curve.

The Maturity Structure of Yield Curve Volatilities

- Interest rate volatility is important for at least two reasons:
    1. Changes in the price of a bond results depends on (1) its duration and convexity, i.e., the impact per basis point change in the YTM **and** (2) the magnitude of the change in the YTM, i.e., yield volatility. Therefore, controlling the impact of interest rate volatility on a bond's price volatility is an important part of risk management.
    2. Most fixed-income instruments and derivatives contain embedded options, whose values depend on the level of interest rate volatility.
- The term structure of interest rate volatilities is a representation of the yield volatility of a zero-coupon bond for a range of maturities. This volatility curve (also known as vol or volatility term structure) measures yield curve risk.
- Interest rate volatility varies across different maturities. Generally speaking, short-term rates tend to be more volatile than long-term rates.
- Interest rate volatility is typically expressed in terms of an annualized standard deviation. For example, if the monthly standard deviation of the 3-month T-bill is 10.15%, then its yield volatility will be expressed as 0.3516 or 35.16% [$= 0.1015 \div (1/12)^{0.5}$].

THE ARBITRAGE-FREE VALUATION FRAMEWORK
Cross-Reference to CFA Institute Assigned Reading #35

- The law of one price states that two securities or portfolios that will generate identical cash flows in the future, regardless of future events, should have the same price today (in the absence of transaction costs).
- An arbitrage opportunity can be defined as a transaction that involves no cash outlay and results in a risk-less profit. There are two types of arbitrage opportunities.
  - Value additivity, where the value of the whole equals the sum of the values of the parts.
  - Dominance, where one asset offers a greater return for the same level of risk.

Arbitrage-Free Valuation for Fixed-Income Securities

The arbitrage-free valuation approach uses the relevant spot rate (i.e., YTM on the appropriate zero-coupon bond) to discount each individual cash flow from a bond. The sum of the present values of cash flows from a bond, individually discounted at the relevant spot rate, should equal the price of the bond.

INTEREST RATE TREES AND ARBITRAGE-FREE VALUATION

For bonds that contain embedded options, the challenge in developing an arbitrage-free valuation framework is to account for the fact that their expected cash flows are interest rate dependent. An interest rate tree represents the possible future interest rates consistent with the assumed level of volatility. The interest rate tree serves two purposes in the valuation process: (1) it is used to generate cash flows that are dependent on interest rates and (2) it supplies the interest rates that are used to compute present values of cash flows.

The binomial interest rate tree framework assumes that the one-year interest rate can take on one of two possible values in the next period. These two possible interest rates in the next period must be consistent with three conditions:

1. The interest rate model that dictates how interest rates move.
2. The assumed level of interest rate volatility.
3. The current benchmark yield curve.

Backward induction is then used to compute the value of the bond at any given node.

PATH-WISE VALUATION

Path-wise valuation computes the present value of a bond for each possible interest rate path and then computes the average of those values. The resulting price of an option-free bond is the same as the price determined through backward induction. Path-wise valuation entails the following steps:

1. Specify a list of possible paths through a tree.
2. Determine the present value of the bond through each potential path.
3. Compute the average present value across all possible paths.

The number of interest rate paths in the binomial model can be computed using Pascal's Triangle.

MONTE CARLO METHOD

The Monte Carlo method is a method for simulating a sufficiently large number of potential interest rate paths in an effort to discover how a value of a fixed-income security is affected. It is often used when a security's cash flows are path dependent, i.e., when the cash flow to be received in a particular period depends not only on the current level of interest rates, but also on the path interest rates have taken to reach their current level.

FI

VALUATION AND ANALYSIS: BONDS WITH EMBEDDED OPTIONS
Cross-Reference to CFA Institute Assigned Reading #36

Callable Bonds

Callable bonds give the **issuer** the right to redeem (or call) all or part of the bond before maturity. This embedded option offers the issuer the ability to take advantage of (1) a decline in market interest rates and/or (2) an improvement in its creditworthiness.

- Callable bonds include different types of call features:
    - An American-style callable bond can be called by the issuer at any time starting with the first call date until maturity.
    - A European-style callable bond can only be called by the issuer at a single date at the end of the lockout period.
    - A Bermudan-style callable bond can be called by the issuer on specified dates following the lockout period.

Putable Bonds and Extendible Bonds

Putable bonds give **bondholders** the right to sell (or put) the bond back to the issuer at a pre-determined price on specified dates. The embedded put option offers bondholders protection against an increase in interest rates, i.e., if interest rates increase (decreasing the value of the straight bond) they can sell the putable bond back to the issuer at the pre-specified price, and then reinvest the principal at (higher) newer interest rates.

- As is the case with callable bonds, putable bonds also typically include lockout periods.
- Most of the time they tend to be European-style and are rarely Bermudan-style, but there are no American-style putable bonds.
- Putable and extendible bonds are equivalent, except that their underlying option-free bonds are different.

Bonds with Other Types of (Complex) Embedded Options

Sometimes the option embedded in a bond may be contingent upon some future event. For example, death-put bonds (which come with an estate put or survivor's option) can be redeemed at par by the heirs of the deceased bondholder. The important thing to note here is that the value of such bonds depends not only on interest rate movements, but also on the holder's life expectancy.

Sinking fund bonds (or sinkers) require the issuer to retire a certain proportion of the issue each year following the lockout period (thereby reducing credit risk). These bonds may also contain additional options, for example:

- Standard call options, which allow the issuer to redeem the entire issue at any point in time following the lockout period.
- Acceleration provisions, which allow the issuer to repurchase more than the mandatory amount of bonds.

- Delivery options, which allow the issuer to satisfy a sinking fund payment by delivering bonds to the trustee instead of cash. If the bonds are trading at less than par, then it is more cost-effective for the issuer to buy back bonds from investors to meet sinking fund requirements than to pay par to redeem them. The delivery options benefit the issuer when interest rates rise.
- A combination of a call option and a delivery option is effectively a long straddle, where the sinking fund benefits the issuer not only if interest rates decline, but also if they rise.

VALUATION OF CALLABLE AND PUTABLE BONDS

Value of callable bond = Value of straight bond − Value of embedded call option

Value of putable bond = Value of straight bond + Value of embedded put option

Effect of Interest Rate Volatility on the Value of Callable and Putable Bonds

All else remaining the same:

- The embedded call option increases in value with higher interest rate volatility. Therefore, the value of a callable bond decreases with higher volatility.
- The embedded put option also increases in value with higher interest rate volatility. Therefore, the value of a putable bond increases with higher volatility.

Effect of Level and Shape of the Yield Curve on the Value of Callable and Putable Bonds

Callable Bonds

All else remaining the same:

- As interest rates decrease, the value of a straight bond increases, and the value of the embedded call option in a callable bond also increases. Since the investor is effectively short on the embedded call option, the value of the callable bond increases less than that of the straight bond, limiting the upside for the investor.
- The value of the embedded call option increases as the yield curve goes from being upward sloping to being flat to downward sloping.
- If the yield curve is upward-sloping at the time of issue and if a callable bond is issued at par, it implies that the embedded call option is out-of-the-money.
- Typically, callable bonds are issued at a large premium. Embedded call options are in-the-money and would be exercised if arbitrage-free forward rates actually prevailed in the future.

Putable Bonds

All else remaining the same:

- As interest rates increase, the value of a straight bond decreases, but the value of the embedded put option in a putable bond increases. Since the investor is effectively long on the embedded call option, the value of the putable bond decreases less than that of the straight bond, offering the investor protection on the downside.
- The value of the embedded put option decreases as the yield curve goes from being upward sloping to being flat to downward sloping.

Valuation of Default-Free Callable and Putable Bonds in the Presence of Interest Rate Volatility

- To value a callable bond, at each node during the call period, the value of the bond must equal the **lower** of (1) the value if the bond is not called (using the backward induction methodology) and (2) the call price.
- To value a putable bond, at every node we use the **higher** of (1) the value determined through backward induction and (2) the put price in the analysis.

Valuing Risky Callable and Putable Bonds: The Option-Adjusted Spread

In order to value bonds with embedded options using an interest rate tree, the option-adjusted spread (OAS) is used instead of the z-spread. The OAS is the constant spread that, when added to all the one-year forward rates in the interest rate tree, makes the arbitrage-free value of the bond equal to its current market price.

- The OAS essentially removes option risk from the z-spread.
- If the OAS for a bond is lower than that for a bond with similar characteristics and credit quality, it suggests that the bond is relatively overpriced (rich).
- If the OAS for a bond is greater than that for a bond with similar characteristics and credit quality, it suggests that the bond is relatively underpriced (cheap).
- If the OAS for a bond is close to that of a bond with similar characteristics and credit quality, the bond looks fairly priced.
- For a given bond price, the lower the interest rate volatility assumed, the lower the option cost and therefore, the higher the OAS for the callable bond given the z-spread.

INTEREST RATE RISK OF BONDS WITH EMBEDDED OPTIONS

Effective Duration

For bonds with embedded options, cash flows can change if the embedded options (which are typically contingent on interest rates) are exercised. Therefore, effective (or option-adjusted) duration, which is a curve duration measure, is the appropriate duration measure for bonds with embedded options.

$$\text{Effective Duration} = \frac{[[(PV)]]_-) - [[(PV)]]_+)}{2 \times (\Delta \text{ Curve}) \times PV_0}$$

ΔCurve = the magnitude of the parallel shift in the benchmark yield curve (in decimal).
PV_- = Full price of the bond when the benchmark yield curve is shifted down by ΔCurve.
PV_+ = Full price of the bond when the benchmark yield curve is shifted up by ΔCurve.
PV_0 = Current full price of the bond (i.e., with no shift).

Effective Durations of Callable, Putable, and Straight Bonds

The effective duration of a callable bond cannot exceed that of the straight bond.

- When interest rates are high relative to the bond's coupon, the callable and straight bonds have very similar effective durations.

- When interest rates fall, the limit on the upside of the callable bond due to the presence of the call option reduces the effective duration of the callable bond relative to that of the straight bond.

The effective duration of a putable bond also cannot exceed that of the straight bond.

- When interest rates are low relative to the bond's coupon, the putable bond and straight bond have very similar effective durations.
- When interest rates rise, the price of the putable bond does not fall as much as that of a straight bond as the put price acts as a floor on its value. Therefore, its effective duration is lower than that of the straight bond.

When the embedded option (call or put) is deep in-the-money, the effective duration of the bond with an embedded option resembles that of the straight bond maturing on the upcoming exercise date, reflecting the fact that the bond is highly likely to be called or put on that date.

Also note that:

- The effective duration of an option-free bond changes very little in response to interest rate movements.
- For a putable bond, its effective duration falls when interest rates rise, as the put moves into the money and the bond's price-yield profile flattens out.
- For a callable bond its effective duration falls when interest rates fall, as the call moves into the money and the bond's price-yield profile flattens out.
- Effective duration is not as effective in capturing the interest rate sensitivity of callable and putable bonds as (1) the price response to up-movements (i.e., one-sided up-duration) and (2) the price response to down-movements (i.e., one-sided down-duration). This is especially true when the embedded option is near-the-money.

Key Rate Duration

Key rate durations (or partial durations) measure the sensitivity of a bond's price to changes in specific maturities on the benchmark yield curve. Key rate durations are used to identify the shaping risk for bonds, i.e., the bond's sensitivity to changes in the shape of the yield curve (steepening and flattening).

- For option-free bonds that are not trading at par, a change in any of the key rate durations has an impact on the price of the bond.
- For option-free bonds that are not trading at par, a change in the key/par rate corresponding to the bond's maturity (10 years) has the greatest impact on price.
- For option-free bonds trading at par, the par rate corresponding to the bond's maturity is the only one that affects its price.
- Key rate durations can sometimes be negative at maturity points that are shorter than the maturity of the bond, if the bond has a very low coupon rate or is a zero-coupon bond.

For option-free bonds, duration is (among other factors) a function of time to maturity. For bonds with embedded options, duration depends on time to maturity and on time to exercise.

Callable Bonds

- When the bond's coupon rate is significantly less than market interest rates, it is highly unlikely to be called. In such a case it is more likely to behave like a straight bond, and the par rate that will have the largest impact on its price will be the rate corresponding to its maturity.
- As the bond's coupon increases relative to the market rate, the likelihood of the bond being called also increases. As a result, the bond's effective duration decreases and gradually, the rate that has the largest impact on the bond's price moves from rate corresponding to its maturity to the rate corresponding to the next call date.

Putable Bonds

- When the bond's coupon rate is significantly higher than market interest rates, it is highly unlikely to be put. In such a case it is more likely to behave like a straight bond, and the par rate that will have the largest impact on its price will be the rate corresponding to its maturity.
- As the bond's coupon decreases relative to the market yield, the likelihood of the bond being put increases. As a result, the bond's effective duration decreases and gradually, the rate that has the largest impact on the bond's price moves from rate corresponding to its maturity to the rate corresponding to the next put date.

Effective Convexity

$$\text{Effective Convexity} = \frac{[(PV)]_- + [(PV)]_+ - 2[(PV)]_0}{(\Delta \text{Curve})^2 \times PV_0}$$

- Option-free bonds exhibit positive effective convexity. Their prices rise slightly more when interest rates fall than they fall when interest rates rise by the same magnitude.
- For callable bonds:
  - When interest rates are high, they behave like straight bonds.
  - When interest rates fall and the embedded call option is at or near the money, their effective convexity turns negative. This is because their price is effectively capped at the call price.
- For putable bonds:
  - When interest rates are low, they behave like straight bonds.
  - When interest rates increase and the embedded put option is at or near the money, their effective convexity remains positive. At this point, the upside from a decrease in interest rates is far greater than the downside from an increase in interest rates, as the put price effectively serves as a floor on the putable bond's value.
- Therefore, putable bonds have more upside potential than otherwise identical callable bonds when interest rates fall, while callable bonds have more downside potential than otherwise identical putable bonds when interest rates rise.

VALUATION AND ANALYSIS OF CAPPED AND FLOORED FLOATING-RATE BONDS

Valuation of a Capped Floater

Valuing a capped floater using a binomial interest rate tree is different from valuing an option-free bond in the following two ways:

- Since it is a floating-rate security, the coupon payment on the capped floater on the next payment date is based on the interest rate today. Basically, the coupon for the period is determined at the beginning of the period, but paid (in arrears) at the end of the period.
- Since the coupon rate is capped, the coupon at each node must be adjusted to reflect the coupon characteristics of the cap. The effective coupon rate for the upcoming period is the **lower** of (1) the current rate and (2) the cap rate.

> Value of capped floater = Value of uncapped floater – Value of embedded cap

- The higher the cap rate, the closer the instrument will trade to its par value (as the embedded interest rate call options carry a lower likelihood of exercise, and are therefore less valuable to the issuer).

Valuation of a Floored Floater

A floor provision in a floater prevents the effective coupon rate on the bond from declining below a specified minimum rate. Therefore, it offers investors protection against declining interest rates.

> Value of floored floater = Value of non-floored floater + Value of embedded floor

- The procedure valuing a floored floater through a binomial interest rate tree is similar to that of valuing a capped floater, except that at each node, the effective coupon rate for the upcoming period is the **higher** of (1) the current rate and (2) the floor rate.

Ratchet Bonds

Ratchet bonds are floating-rate bonds with both investor and issuer options.

- Just like conventional floaters, the coupon rate is periodically reset according to a formula based on a reference rate and credit spread.
- However, the bonds are structured to ensure that at any reset date, the effective coupon rate can only decline; it can never exceed the existing level. As a result, the coupon rate "ratchets down" over time.
- In order to compensate investors for this, the coupon rate on ratchet bonds at the time of issuance is set at a level much higher than that of a standard floater.
- This makes a ratchet bond similar to a conventional callable bond in that when a bond is called, the investor can only purchase a replacement bond carrying a lower (prevailing) coupon rate. A ratchet bond can be thought of as the life cycle of a callable bond, with one callable bond being replaced by another until the bond's eventual maturity is reached. The appeal for the issuer is that the call decision is on autopilot, and there are no transaction costs.

- Ratchet bonds also contain investor options. At any coupon reset date, the investor has the option to put the bonds back to the issuer at par. Note that this put is actually a "contingent put" as it can only be exercised if the coupon is actually reset.
- Generally speaking, the market price of ratchet bonds remains above par at time of reset unless there has been a deterioration in the credit quality of the issuer.

VALUATION AND ANALYSIS OF CONVERTIBLE BONDS

A convertible bond is a hybrid security that grants the holder the option to convert the security into a predetermined number of common shares of the issuer (so it is essentially a call option on the stock) during a pre-determined conversion period at a pre-determined conversion price.

Convertible bonds offer benefits to the issuer and the investor:

- Investors accept lower coupons on convertible bonds compared to otherwise identical non-convertible bonds because they can participate in the upside of the issuer's equity through the conversion mechanism.
- Issuers benefit from lower coupon rates and from no longer having to repay the debt (if the bonds are converted into equity).

However, note that:

- The issuer's current shareholders face dilution if these securities are converted.
- If the bond is not converted (if the share price remains below the conversion price) the issuer may have to refinance the debt at a higher cost.
- If conversion is not achieved, bondholders would have lost out on interest income relative to an otherwise identical non-convertible bond.

Important Terminology

- The share price at which the investor can convert the convertible bond into ordinary shares is known as the conversion price.
- The number of shares of common stock that the holder of a convertible bond receives from converting the bonds into shares is dictated by the conversion ratio.
- Until they convert their bonds into shares, holders of convertible bonds only receive coupon payments, while common shareholders receive dividend payments.
- Annual dividends below the threshold dividend level have no impact on the conversion price. However, if annual dividends exceed this level, the conversion price is adjusted downward for annual dividend payments to compensate convertible bond holders.
- Almost all convertible bonds are callable and some are also putable.
  - The issuer may call the bond (1) if interest rates have fallen, (2) if its credit rating has improved, or (3) if it believes that its share price will improve significantly in the future.
  - If a convertible bond is callable, the issuer can force conversion if the underlying share price rises beyond the conversion price, in order to avoid making interest payments.
  - The put option may be classified as a hard put (which can only be redeemed for cash) or a soft put (which may be redeemed for cash, common stock, subordinated notes, or a combination of the three).

Analysis of a Convertible Bond

The conversion (or parity) value of a convertible bond indicates the value of the bond if converted at the market price of the shares.

$$\text{Conversion value} = \text{Market price of common stock} \times \text{Conversion ratio}$$

The minimum value of a convertible bond equals the greater of (1) its conversion value (the value if the security is converted into shares immediately) or (2) its straight value (its value without the conversion option). It acts as a moving floor on the value of the security.

The price that an investor effectively pays for common stock if a convertible bond is purchased and then converted into common stock is known as the market conversion price or conversion parity price. It basically reflects the "break-even" price for the investor.

$$\text{Market conversion price} = \frac{\text{Market price of convertible security}}{\text{Conversion ratio}}$$

The market conversion premium per share is the excess amount that an investor pays for acquiring the company's shares by purchasing a convertible bond instead of purchasing them in the open market.

$$\text{Market conversion premium per share} = \text{Market conversion price} - \text{Current market price}$$

The market conversion premium per share can be viewed as the price of the conversion call option. However, there is a difference between (1) buying a stand-alone call option on the issuer's stock and (2) purchasing the call option on the issuer's stock embedded in a convertible bond. The buyer of the stand-alone call option knows the exact dollar amount of downside risk (the call premium), while the buyer of the convertible bond only knows that her maximum loss equals the difference between the price paid for the convertible bond and its straight value. The straight value at any future date is unknown.

The market conversion premium ratio equals the market conversion premium per share divided by the current market price of the company's common stock.

$$\text{Market conversion premium ratio} = \frac{\text{Market conversion premium per share}}{\text{Market price of common stock}}$$

The premium over straight value is sometimes used as a measure for downside risk in a convertible bond. This interpretation, however, is theoretically flawed because the straight value (which serves as a floor on the convertible's price) changes as interest rates/credit spreads change. All other factors remaining the same, the higher the premium over straight value, the less attractive the convertible bond.

$$\text{Premium over straight value} = \frac{\text{Market price of convertible bond}}{\text{Straight value}} - 1$$

The upside potential for a convertible security depends on the prospects for the underlying stock, which are evaluated using techniques for analyzing common stocks.

Valuation of a Convertible Bond

$$\text{Convertible security value} = \text{Straight value} + \text{Value of the call option on the stock}$$

$$
\begin{aligned}
\text{Convertible callable bond value} = {}& \text{Straight value} + \text{Value of the call option} \\
& \text{on the stock} \\
& - \text{Value of the call option on the bond}
\end{aligned}
$$

$$
\begin{aligned}
\text{Convertible callable and putable bond value} = {}& \text{Straight value} + \text{Value of the call} \\
& \text{option on the stock} \\
& - \text{Value of the call option on the bond} \\
& + \text{Value of the put option on the bond}
\end{aligned}
$$

Investment Characteristics of a Convertible Security

- If the price of the company's common stock is relatively low, such that the straight value of a convertible bond is significantly greater than the conversion value, the security will trade like a fixed-income security, with factors such as interest rates and credit spreads having a significant impact on its price. In such a situation, the security may be referred to as a fixed-income equivalent or a busted convertible. Further, the closer the security is to the end of the conversion period, the more the convertible bond will behave like a fixed-income security, as it becomes increasingly likely that the call option on the stock with expire out of the money.
- If the price of the company's common stock is relatively high, such that the conversion value is significantly greater than the straight value, the security will trade like an equity instrument, with its value heavily influenced by share price movements and relatively immune to interest rate movements. In this case, the security may be referred to as a common stock equivalent. Note that when the embedded call option on the stock is in the money, it is more likely to be exercised when the conversion value exceeds the redemption value of the bond.

- In between these two scenarios, the convertible will trade as a hybrid security with characteristics of both fixed-income and equity instruments.
  - When the underlying share price is below the conversion price and increases toward it, the return on the convertible bond increases significantly, but at a lower rate than the underlying share price. Once the share price exceeds the conversion price, the change in the convertible bond's price increases at the same rate as the underlying share price.
  - When underlying share price is above the conversion price and decreases toward it, the relative change in the convertible bond's price is less than the change in the share price because the convertible bond has a floor on its value.
- Finally, note that except in the case of busted convertibles, the primary driver of a convertible bond's value is the underlying share price. However, large movements in interest rates or the issuer's credit spread continue to affect the value of a convertible bond. For a convertible bond with a fixed coupon, all else being equal:
  - If interest rates rise (fall) significantly, its value would decrease (increase).
  - If the issuer's credit rating were to improve (decline), its value would increase (decrease).

CREDIT ANALYSIS MODELS
Cross-Reference to CFA Institute Assigned Reading #37

Default risk addresses the likelihood of an event of default. **Credit risk** is a broader term because it considers both the default probability and how much is expected to be lost if default occurs.

Expected exposure to default loss is the projected amount of money the investor could lose if an event of default occurs, before factoring in possible recovery.

Recovery rate is percentage of the loss recovered from a bond in default.

Loss given default (LGD) is the amount of loss if a default occurs.

Probability of default (POD) is the probability that a bond issuer will not meet its contractual obligations on schedule.

Actual (or historical) versus risk-neutral default probabilities:

- Actual default probabilities do not include the default risk premium associated with uncertainty over the timing of possible default loss.
- The observed spread over the yield on a risk-free bond in practice also includes liquidity and tax considerations in addition to credit risk.

Credit valuation adjustment (CVA) is the value of the credit risk in present value terms.

$$\text{Probability of Survival (POS)} = (100\% - \text{Hazard rate})^{\text{Number of years}}$$
$$\text{Expected loss} = \text{LGD} \times \text{POD}$$
$$\text{Value of default-free bond} - \text{CVA} = \text{Fair value of risky bond}$$

- The probability of default in credit risk models incorporates (1) the likely time of incidence of default events as well as (2) uncertainty over the timing of the events.
- Generally speaking, for a given price and credit spread, the assumed probability of default and the recovery rate are positively correlated.

Credit scores are a rating system used by lenders to evaluate the creditworthiness of retail borrowers (individuals and small businesses) and to establish terms of a lending contract.

- Factors considered in assigning credit scores include payment history, debt burden, length of credit history, types of credit used, and recent "hard" searches for credit.
- Race, color, national origin, sex, marital status, age, salary, occupation, employment history, home address, and child/family support obligations are not considered.

Credit ratings are used to evaluate bonds and asset-backed securities (ABS) issued by corporations and governments. Credit ratings reflect the probability of default and loss given default (via notching).

The ratings transition matrix is used to compute the expected change in the price of a bond.

> Change in bond price = −Modified Duration ×
>
> (New Credit Rating Credit Spread − Original Credit Rating Credit Spread)

Taking credit rating transitions into account typically reduces a bond's expected return. This is because transition probabilities are skewed towards downgrades rather than upgrades and changes in credit spreads are much larger for lower ratings than higher ratings.

Structural Models versus Reduced-Form Models

Structural Models

A company defaults on its debt if the value of its assets falls below the amount of its liabilities and the probability of this event has the features of an option.

- Probability of default is endogenous. It increases with:
  - Variance of the future asset value.
  - Greater time to maturity.
  - Greater financial leverage.
- Equity holders essentially hold a call option on company assets where the strike price is the face value of debt.
- Debt holders own company assets and have written a call option on those assets.
- The premium received for writing this call option can be viewed as the cost of attaining priority of claim on company assets in the event that their value falls below the face value of debt.

Advantages:

- Provide insight into the nature of credit risk.
- Can be used for internal risk management, for banks' internal credit risk measures, and for publicly-available credit ratings.

Disadvantages:

- BSM assumes that the assets on which options are written are actively traded.
- Can be burdensome to implement.

Reduced-Form Models

- Do not focus on why default occurs but aim to explain statistically when it might occur.
- Default time can be modeled using a Poisson stochastic process.
- The key parameter here is default intensity, which represents the probability of default over the next time increment.

Advantages:

- Default is an exogenous variable that occurs randomly.
- Only require information that is generally available in financial markets.

- Default intensity is estimated using regression analysis on company-specific variables and macroeconomic variables so the model can directly reflect the business cycle in the credit risk measure.
- Used to value risky debt securities and credit derivatives.

Disadvantages:

- Do not explain economic reasons for default.
- Assume that default comes as a surprise and can occur at any time.

Valuing Risky Bonds Using the Arbitrage-Free Valuation Framework

All other things remaining the same:

- Interest rate volatility has an impact on the values of (1) bonds with embedded options and (2) bonds with credit risk.
- An increase in assumed interest rate volatility results in lower expected exposures to default loss, reducing loss given default and the credit valuation adjustment. The result is a slightly higher fair value for the bond.
- If the fair value of a floating-rate note is below par, the discount margin must be higher than the quoted margin.
- A lower recovery rate assumption would result in a higher credit spread

Components of a Corporate Bond Yield

- The benchmark yield accounts for expected inflation, expected real rate of return, and any compensation for uncertainty regarding inflation (macroeconomic factors).
- The spread over the benchmark yield accounts for liquidity, taxation, expected loss from default, and uncertainty associated with the expected loss from default (microeconomic factors).

Term Structure of Credit Spreads

The credit curve shows the spread over a benchmark security for an issuer for outstanding fixed-income securities with shorter to longer maturities.

The term structure of credit spreads is driven by:

- Credit quality.
- Financial conditions.
- Market supply and demand conditions.
- Company-value model results.
  - An increase in the implied default probability will tend to steepen the credit spread curve.

An upward-sloping credit curve implies that investors seek greater compensation for assuming default risk over longer periods.

- Positively sloped credit spread curves may arise when a high-quality issuer with a strong competitive position in a stable industry has low leverage, strong cash flow, and a high profit margin.
- High-yield issuers in cyclical industries sometimes face a downward-sloping credit term structure because of issuer- or industry-specific reasons.
- Bonds with a high likelihood of default tend to trade close to their recovery rate than on a spread to benchmark rates. In such cases, the credit curve is "distorted" in that it does not truly reflect the relative risk and rewards of long-term versus short-term bonds of the same issuer.
- If a portfolio manager disagrees with the market's expectation of a high near-term default probability that declines over time, she could sell short-term protection in the credit default swap market and buy longer-term protection.

Credit Analysis for Securitized Debt

Important considerations:

Homogeneity versus Heterogeneity

- **Homogeneity** refers to individual debt obligations within the asset pool of a securitized instrument being similar in nature (i.e., common underwriting criteria for borrowers), which allows credit analysts to draw generalized conclusions about the nature of loans.
- **Heterogeneity** refers to underlying debt obligations having different underwriting criteria, thereby requiring scrutiny on a loan-by-loan basis.
- **Granularity** refers to the number of individual debt obligations within the asset pool of a securitized instrument.
   ○ When an asset pool is highly granular, credit analysts will likely base their analysis on summary statistics versus looking at loans on an individual basis.
- **Quality of origination and servicer.** Because investors are exposed to operational and counterparty risk, they must rely on the originator/servicer to establish and enforce eligibility criteria, maintain documentation, facilitate repayments, and manage delinquencies.
- **Structure of the transaction**
   ○ Investors need to endure the fact that the originator can separate itself from the risk of bankruptcy in the securitized instrument through a "true sale" of assets to the SPE.
   ○ Credit enhancements

CREDIT DEFAULT SWAPS
Cross-Reference to CFA Institute Assigned Reading #38

CREDIT DEFAULT SWAPS: BASIC DEFINITIONS AND CONCEPTS

A **credit default swap (CDS)** is a bilateral contract between two parties that transfers the credit risk embedded in a reference obligation from one party to another. It is essentially an insurance contract.

The reference obligation is the fixed-income security on which the protection is written (or whose credit risk is transferred). This is usually a bond, but can also be a loan in some cases.

The protection buyer makes a series of periodic payments (think of them as periodic insurance premium payments) to the protection seller during the term of the CDS. In return for this series of periodic premium payments (known as the CDS fee or CDS spread), the protection buyer obtains protection against default risk embedded in the reference obligation.

The protection seller earns the CDS spread over the term of the CDS in return for assuming the credit risk in the reference obligation. If a credit event occurs, the protection seller is obligated to compensate the protection buyer for credit losses by means of a specified settlement procedure.

CDS are somewhat similar to put options. Put options give the option holder the right to sell (put) the underlying to the put writer if the underlying performs poorly relative to the strike price. The option holder is therefore compensated for poor performance. Similarly, CDS give the protection buyer compensation if the underlying (loan, bond, or bond portfolio) performs poorly.

Types of CDS

The reference entity is the entity issuing the reference obligation in a **single-name CDS** (where the CDS is on one borrower). The reference obligation is a particular instrument issued by the reference entity that serves as the designated instrument covered by the CDS. The designated instrument is usually a senior unsecured obligation (which can be referred to as senior CDS), but this instrument is not the only instrument covered by the CDS. Any debt issued by the reference entity that is pari passu (i.e., ranked equivalently in the priority of claims), or higher relative to the reference obligation is covered by the CDS. The payoff to the CDS is determined by the cheapest-to-deliver obligation, which is the instrument that can be purchased and delivered at the lowest cost, but has the same seniority as the reference obligation.

An index CDS involves several reference entities (borrowers), which allows market participants to take positions on the credit of a portfolio of companies. Generally speaking, the higher (lower) the correlation of default among index constituents, the higher (lower) the cost of obtaining credit protection on the index CDS.

A tranche CDS also covers a portfolio of borrowers, but only to a pre-specified amount of losses (similar to how tranches of asset-backed securities only cover a particular amount of losses).

Important Features of CDS Markets and Instruments

- Like any swap contract, a CDS also specifies a notional principal, which represents the size of the contract.
- The periodic premium paid by the protection buyer in a CDS pays to the protection seller is known as the CDS spread. The CDS spread is a return over LIBOR required to protect against credit risk and is sometimes also referred to as the credit spread.
- In recent years, standard annual coupon rates (basically standard credit spreads) have been established on CDS contracts.
  - Any discrepancy between the standard rate and the actual required credit spread is accounted for via an upfront premium.
    - If the standard rate is too low (to capture the credit risk), the protection buyer will pay the seller the upfront premium.
    - If the standard rate is too high, the protection seller will pay the buyer an **upfront premium**.
- Regardless of which party makes the upfront payment, the value or price of the CDS can change over the contract term due to changes in the credit quality of the reference obligation.
- In the CDS world, since the protection buyer promises to make a series of future payments, she is known as the short and the protection seller is known as the long.
  - The protection buyer, or short, benefits when things go badly (i.e., if the credit quality of the underlying instrument declines and CDS spreads increase).
  - The protection seller, or long, benefits when things go well (i.e., if the credit quality of the underlying instrument improves and CDS spreads decrease).

Credit and Succession Events

A credit event defines default by the reference entity. It is what triggers a payment from the protection seller on a CDS to the protection buyer. There are three types of credit events:

- Bankruptcy
- Failure to pay
- Restructuring

Determination of whether there has been a credit event is made by a 15-member Determinations Committee (DC) within the ISDA. A supermajority vote of 12 members is required to declare a credit event.

The DC also plays a role in determining whether a succession event has occurred. A succession event occurs when there is a change in the corporate structure of the reference entity (e.g., divesture, spinoff, or merger) such that the ultimate obligor of the reference obligation becomes unclear.

Settlement Protocols

- In a **physical settlement**, upon declaration of a credit event, the protection buyer delivers the underlying debt instrument to the protection seller. The par value of bonds delivered to the seller must equal the notional amount of the CDS. In return, the protection seller pays the buyer the par value of the debt (which is equal to the CDS notional amount).

- In a **cash settlement**, the idea is that the protection seller should pay the protection buyer an amount of cash equal to the difference between the notional amount and the current value of the bonds. Determining this amount is not an easy task as opinions can vary about how much money has actually been lost (in a default, a portion of the par value is generally recovered).
  - The percentage of the par value that is recovered is known as the recovery rate. This represents the percentage received by the protection buyer relative to the amount owed.
  - The payout ratio (which determines the amount that the protection seller must pay the protection buyer) is an estimate of the expected credit loss. The payout amount equals the payout ratio multiplied by the notional amount.

> Payout ratio = 1 − Recovery rate
> Payout amount = Payout ratio × Notional

Note that actual recovery is a very long process, which can stretch way beyond the settlement date of the CDS. Therefore, to estimate an appropriate recovery rate, there is typically an auction for the defaulted bonds to determine their post-default market value. The protection seller then pays the protection buyer the difference between the par value (which is equal to the CDS notional amount) and the post-default market value of the bonds.

CDS Index Products

CDS indices allow participants to take a position on the credit risk of several companies simultaneously, just like equity indices allow investors to gain exposure to stocks of several companies at the same time. CDS indices are all equally weighted.

If an entity within an index defaults, it is removed from the index and settled as a single-name CDS (based on its pro-rata share in the index). The index continues to move forward with a smaller notional.

BASICS OF VALUATION AND PRICING

Basic Pricing Concepts

When we talk about pricing CDS, we are interested in determining the CDS spread or in the case of standardized CDS (with 1% or 5% coupon rates) determining the upfront premium.

> Expected loss = Loss given default × Probability of default

- In the context of valuing CDS, we work with hazard rates that reflect the probability that default will occur given that it has not already occurred.
- The probability of default is calculated as 1 minus the probability of survival.
- The loss given default is computed based on expected recovery rates.

The Protection Leg

The protection leg refers to the contingent payment that the protection seller may have to make to the protection buyer. In order to value the protection leg, we must compute the present value of the contingent obligation of the protection seller to the protection buyer. This is calculated as the difference between:

- The present value of the hypothetical value of the bond if it had no credit risk; and
- The present value of the expected payoff on the (risky) bond, after accounting for the probability, amount and timing of each payment. In order to compute this value:
  - First we compute the expected payoff of each payment on the bond by multiplying the payment adjusted for the expected recovery rate by the probability of survival.
  - Next, we discount the expected payoff of each payment at the appropriate discount rate.
  - Then we sum all these amounts to come up with the expected payoff on the bond.

The difference between these two figures represents credit exposure.

> Value of protection leg = Credit risk = Value of risk-free bond − Expected payoff on risky bond

The Premium Leg

The premium leg refers to the series of periodic payments that the protection buyer promises to make to the protection seller. When it comes to valuing the premium leg, things are complicated by the fact that once default occurs, regardless of exactly when it occurs during the term of the CDS, the protection buyer ceases to make payments to the protection seller. As a result, hazard rates must be applied.

The Upfront Payment

The difference in values of the protection leg and premium leg equals the amount of the upfront payment.

> Upfront payment = Present value of protection leg − Present value of premium leg

If this difference is positive (negative), the protection buyer (seller) makes the upfront payment to the protection seller (buyer). In order to understand this, note that:

- PV of protection leg represents the value of the contingent payment that the protection seller will make to the buyer.
- PV of premium leg represents the value of expected premium payments that the protection buyer will make to the seller.
- If the value of payments that the seller will make over the term of the CDS is greater, the seller will receive a premium upfront so that overall, both the positions hold equal value at CDS inception.

> Upfront premium % ≅ (Credit spread − Fixed coupon) × Duration of CDS

> Present value of credit spread = Upfront payment + Present value of fixed coupon

> Price of CDS per 100 par = 100 − Upfront premium %

The Credit Curve

The credit curve presents credit spreads on a company's debt for a range of maturities. The credit spread refers to the spread on top of LIBOR required by investors to hold the debt instrument. With the evolution and high degree of efficiency in the CDS market, the credit curve for a borrower is essentially determined by CDS rates on its obligations.

One of the factors that influences the credit curve is the hazard rate:

- A constant hazard rate will result in a relatively flat credit curve.
- Upward (downward) sloping credit curves imply a greater (lower) likelihood of default in later years.

Value Changes in CDS during Their Lives

Just like any other swap, the value of a CDS also fluctuates during its term. Some of the factors that cause changes in the value of a CDS are:

- Changes in the credit quality or perceived credit quality of the reference entity.
- Changes in duration of the CDS (duration shortens through time).
- Changes in the probability of default, expected loss given default and in the shape of the credit curve.

The change in value of a CDS for a given change in the credit spread can be approximated as:

$$\text{Profit for protection buyer} \cong \text{Change in spread in bps} \times \text{Duration} \times \text{Notional}$$

The percentage price change in the CDS can be computed as:

$$\% \text{ Change in CDS price} = \text{Change in spread in bps} \times \text{Duration}$$

Monetizing Gains and Losses

- The first method is to enter into a new offsetting CDS.
- A second way to monetize a gain/loss on a CDS position is to exercise or settle the CDS upon default via a cash or physical settlement (discussed earlier).
- A third (least common) method occurs if there is no default. The parties simply hold their positions until maturity. By then, the seller has captured all the premium payments without having to make any payments to the protection buyer.

Applications of CDS

- Manage credit exposures i.e., take on or lay off credit risk in response to changing expectations; and/or
- Take advantage of valuation disparities i.e., differences in the pricing of credit risk in the CDS market relative to another market (e.g., that of the underlying bonds).

FI

Managing Credit Exposures

A party takes a position on a naked credit default swap when it has no underlying exposure to the reference entity.

- In entering a naked CDS as the protection buyer, the investor is taking a position that the entity's credit quality will deteriorate (credit spreads will increase).
- In entering a naked CDS as the protection seller, the investor is taking a position that the entity's credit quality will improve (credit spreads will decline).

In a long/short trade, the party takes a long position in one CDS and a short position in another CDS, where the two swaps are based on **different** reference entities. Such a trade represents a bet that the credit quality of one entity will improve relative to that of the other. The investor would sell protection on the entity whose credit quality it expects to improve (go long on the CDS), and purchase protection on the entity whose credit quality it expects to deteriorate (go short on the CDS).

A curve trade is a type of long/short trade. It involves buying a CDS of one maturity and selling a CDS with a different maturity, where both the CDS are on the **same** reference entity.

With an **upward-sloping** credit curve, a **steepening** (flattening) of the curve means that long-term credit risk has increased (decreased) relative to short-term credit risk.

- An investor who believes that long-term credit risk will increase relative to short-term credit risk (credit curve steepening) will purchase protection (or go short) on a long-term CDS and sell protection (or go long) on a short-term CDS.
  - A curve-steepening trade is bullish for the short run. It implies that the short-term outlook for the reference entity is better than the long-term outlook.
  - An investor who is bearish about a company's short term creditworthiness will enter into a curve-flattening trade.

The interpretation of the investor's position is the opposite if the credit curve is **currently downward-sloping** (which is rarely the case and generally results from short-term stress in financial markets). In this case, a **flattening** (not steepening) of the curve suggests that long-term credit-risk has increased relative to short-term credit risk.

Note that for a given (parallel) change in credit spreads across all maturities, longer-term CDS values will be more affected than shorter-term CDS values (due to their higher durations).

Valuation Differences and Basis Trading

A basis trade aims to profit from the difference in (1) the credit spread implied by the price/yield on a bond, and (2) the credit spread on a CDS on the same reference obligation with the same term to maturity.

Basis trades work on the assumption that any mispricing of credit risk across the bond and CDS markets is likely to be temporary and that credit spreads should converge once the disconnect has been recognized by participants.

In order to determine the profit potential of a basis trade, we must decompose the bond yield into the risk-free rate plus the funding spread plus the credit spread. The risk-free rate plus the funding spread equals LIBOR, so the credit spread equals the excess of the yield on the bond over LIBOR. This credit spread must then be compared to the credit spread on the CDS. If the credit spread on the bond is higher (lower) than in the CDS market, it is said to be a negative (positive) basis.

FI

STUDY SESSION 14: DERIVATIVES

PRICING AND VALUATION OF FORWARD COMMITMENTS
Cross-Reference to CFA Institute Assigned Reading #39

Introductory Definitions

A **forward commitment** is a derivative instrument in the form of a contract that provides the ability to lock in a price or rate at which one can buy or sell the underlying instrument at a specified future date, or exchange an agreed-upon amount of money at a specified series of dates.

A **forward** is a contract between two parties, where one (the long position) has the obligation to buy, and the other (the short position) an obligation to sell the underlying asset at a specified price (established at the inception of the contract) at a specified future date (also established at inception of the contract).

Price versus Value

The **price** of a forward/futures contract is the fixed price or rate at which the underlying transaction will occur at contract expiration. The forward/futures price is agreed upon at initiation of the contract. Pricing a forward/futures contract means determining this **forward/futures price**.

The **value** of a forward/futures contract is the amount that a counterparty would need to pay, or would expect to receive, to get out of, or terminate, an (already-assumed) forward/futures position.

Assumptions of Arbitrage

- Replicating instruments are identifiable and investable.
- Markets are frictionless.
- Short selling is allowed.
- Borrowing and lending are available at the risk-free rate.

Calculating the Forward Price Assuming No Carry Costs or Benefits

$$F_0(T) = S_0(1+r)^T$$

- An increase in the risk-free rate will lead to an increase in the forward price, and a decrease in the risk-free rate will lead to a decrease in the forward price. This relationship will generally hold as long as changes in interest rates do not influence the value of the underlying asset.
- The forward price is **not** influenced by the expected future spot price.

Valuing a Forward Contract at Initiation (t = 0) and Expiration (t = T)

Time	Long Position Value	Short Position Value
At initiation	Zero, as the contract is priced to prevent arbitrage	Zero, as the contract is priced to prevent arbitrage
At expiration	$S_T - F_0(T)$	$F_0(T) - S_T$

- At expiration, both forward and futures contracts are equivalent to a spot transaction in the underlying asset. This is known as **convergence**, implying that at contract expiration, the forward/futures price will be the same as the spot price [i.e., $F_T(T) = f_T(T) = S_T$].

Valuing a Forward Contract during Its Life (T = t)

$$V_t(T) = S_t - [F_0(T)/(1+r)^{T-t}]$$

$$V_t(T) = \text{PV of difference sin forward prices} = PV_{t,T}\left[F_t(T) - F_0(T)\right]$$

where $PV_{t,T}(\ )$ means the present value at time t of an amount paid in $T - t$ years (or at time T).

Futures versus Forward Contracts

As a result of the mark-to-market adjustment, the value of a futures contract at any point in time during its term is simply the difference between the current futures price and the futures price that was applied to make the last mark-to-market adjustment.

- The market value of a long position in a futures contract before marking to market is $v_t(T) = f_t(T) - f_{t_-}(T)$.
- The market value of a short position in a futures contract before marking to market is $v_t(T) = f_{t_-}(T) - f_t(T)$.
- The subscript $_{t_-}$ represents the point in time when the last mark-to-market adjustment was performed.

Calculating the Forward Price When the Underlying Has Cash Flows

$$F_0(T) = (S_0 - \gamma_0 + \theta_0)(1+r)^T$$

$$F_0(T) = S_0(1+r)^T - (\gamma_0 - \theta_0)(1+r)^T$$

With continuous compounding, the forward price is calculated as:

$$F_0(T) = S_0 e^{(r_c + \theta_c - \gamma_c)T}$$

Note that only carry costs and benefits incurred over the term of the forward contract are included in the preceding formulas.

- Carry costs, like the rate of interest, increase the burden of carrying the underlying instrument through time. Therefore, these costs are added in the forward pricing equation.
- Carry benefits decrease the burden of carrying the underlying instrument through time, so these benefits are subtracted in the forward pricing equation.

Valuing a Forward Contract When the Underlying Has Carry Benefits/Costs

$$V_t(T) = \text{PV of differences in forward prices} = PV_{t,T}\left[F_t(T) - F_0(T)\right]$$

Carry benefits and costs are accounted for in this equation in the computation of the two forward prices.

- If a dividend payment is announced between the forward's valuation and expiration dates, assuming that the news announcement does not change the price of the underlying, the **value** of the original forward will fall.
- The mark-to-market adjustment in futures markets results in the value of a futures contract after settlement equaling zero. Therefore, the values of otherwise identical forward and futures contracts will likely be different.

Interest Rate Forward and Futures Contracts

Forward Rate Agreements

A **forward rate agreement (FRA)** is a forward contract where the underlying is an interest rate on a deposit. It involves two counterparties: (1) the fixed payer/floating receiver (long position) and (2) the floating payer/fixed receiver (short position).

- A long FRA position can be replicated by holding a longer-term Eurodollar time deposit and at the same time shorting (or owing) on a shorter-term Eurodollar time deposit.

Think of the long position in an FRA as the party that has committed to take a hypothetical loan, and the short as the party that has committed to give out a hypothetical loan, at the fixed FRA rate.

FRA Payoffs

- If LIBOR at FRA expiration is *greater* than the FRA rate, the long benefits. Effectively, the long has access to a loan at lower-than-market interest rates, while the short is obligated to give out a loan at lower-than-market interest rates.
- Stated differently, the long benefits as the fixed payer and floating receiver.
- If LIBOR at FRA expiration is *lower* than the FRA rate, the short benefits. Effectively, the short position is able to invest her funds at higher-than-market interest rates, while the long is obligated to take a loan at higher-than-market interest rates.
- Stated differently, the short benefits as the fixed receiver and floating payer.

FRAs are settled on an **advanced set, advanced settled** basis. The interest rate effective on the underlying hypothetical loan is determined in advance (at the onset of the loan), and the contract is also settled in advance (at the onset of the loan).

$$\text{FRA payoff} = NP \times \frac{\left[(\text{Market LIBOR} - \text{FRA rate}) \times \text{No. of days in the loan term} / 360\right]}{1 + \left[\text{Market LIBOR} \times (\text{No. of days in the loan term} / 360)\right]}$$

Pricing a Forward Rate Agreement

The price of an FRA (forward price) represents the fixed interest rate at which the long position has the obligation to borrow funds, or the short position has the obligation to lend funds, for a specified period (term of the underlying hypothetical loan) starting at FRA expiration. Essentially, pricing an FRA is a simple exercise of determining the forward rate consistent with two (given) spot rates.

Valuing an FRA Prior to Expiration

The value of an FRA during its term (before expiration) is computed as the present value of the difference in the interest savings based on (1) the new (current) FRA rate and (2) the old (original/initial) FRA rate. To value an FRA at any time prior to expiration, we need to follow four steps:

- Calculate the new implied forward rate based on current spot rates.
- Calculate the interest savings based on this new or updated market forward rate.
- Discount these interest savings for a number of days equal to the number of days remaining until FRA expiration plus the number of days in the term of the underlying hypothetical loan.
- Make sure you use the appropriate discount rate.

Fixed-Income Forward and Futures Contracts

There are three unique factors that we need to account for when applying the carry arbitrage model to fixed-income forwards:

1. Clean versus dirty prices
2. Conversion factor adjustments
3. Cheapest-to-deliver (CTD) bond

Markets Where Accrued Interest Is Included in the Bond Price Quote

$$F_0(T) = \text{Future value of underlying adjusted for carry cash flows}$$
$$F_0(T) = (S_0 - \gamma_0 + \theta_0)(1+r)^T$$

Markets Where Accrued Interest Is Not Included in the Bond Price Quote

$$F_0(T) = QF_0(T) \times CF(T) \text{ and } QF_0(T) = 1/CF(T) \times F_0(T)$$
$$F_0(T) = [B_0(T+Y) + AI_0 - PVCI_{0,T}] \times (1+r)^T - AI_T$$
$$QF_0(T) = 1/CF(T) \times [B_0(T+Y) + AI_0 - PVCI_{0,T}] \times (1+r)^T - AI_T$$

Determining the Value of a Bond Forward Contract during Its Term

The value of a bond forward contract during its term is simply the present value of the difference in **quoted** forward/futures prices between (1) the original bond forward/futures contract and (2) an offsetting contract.

$$V_t(T) = \text{Present value of difference in forward prices} = PV_{t,T}\left[QF_t(T) - QF_0(T)\right]$$

Currency Forward Contracts

Pricing a Currency Forward Contract

$$F_{0,PC/BC} = S_{0,PC/BC} \times \frac{(1+r_{PC})^T}{(1+r_{BC})^T}$$

$$F_{0,PC/BC} = S_{0,PC/BC} \times e^{(r_{PC} - r_{BC}) \times T}$$

- If the forward rate is higher than the spot rate, it means that the price currency risk-free rate is higher than the base currency risk-free rate.
- If the forward rate is lower than the spot rate, it means that the price currency risk-free rate is lower than the base currency risk-free rate.

Valuing a Currency Forward Contract

$$V_t(T) = (F_{t,PC/BC} - F_{0,PC/BC}) / (1+r_{PC})^{T-t}$$

Note that the price currency risk-free rate is used in the denominator.

Swap Contracts

Plain-Vanilla Interest Rate Swaps

$$\text{Net fixed rate payment}_t = [\text{Swap fixed rate} - (\text{LIBOR}_{t-1} + \text{Spread})] * (\text{No. of days}/360) * \text{Notional principal}$$

- At the initiation of the swap, the **swap fixed rate** is set at a level at which the present value of the floating-rate payments (based on the current term structure of interest rates) equals the present value of fixed-rate payments so that there is zero value to either party. This swap fixed rate therefore represents the **price** of the swap.
- Over the term of the swap, as there are changes in the term structure of interest rates, the **value** of the swap will fluctuate.
- If interest rates increase after swap initiation, the present value of floating-rate payments (based on the new term structure) will exceed the present value of fixed-rate payments (based on the swap fixed rate).
- The swap will have a positive value for the fixed-rate payer (floating-rate receiver).
- The swap will be an asset to the fixed-rate payer and a liability for the floating-rate payer.
- If interest rates decrease after swap initiation, the present value of floating-rate payments will be lower than the present value of fixed-rate payments.
- The swap will have a positive value for the floating-rate payer (fixed-rate receiver).
- In this case, the swap will be an asset to the floating-rate payer and a liability for the fixed-rate payer.

Plain-Vanilla Interest Rate Swaps as a Combination of Bonds

Taking a position as a fixed-rate payer (floating-rate receiver) on a plain-vanilla interest rate swap is equivalent to issuing a fixed-rate bond (on which fixed payments must be made) and using the proceeds to purchase a floating-rate bond (on which floating payments will be received). In other words, the fixed-rate payer can be viewed as being long on a floating-rate bond and short on a fixed-rate bond.

- If interest rates increase, the fixed-rate payer benefits, as there is a positive difference between her (floating-rate) receipts and (fixed-rate) payments.
- In terms of the positions on bonds, the value of the fixed-rate bond decreases as interest rates increase, but the value of the floating-rate bond remains at par. Since the fixed-rate payer is long on the floating-rate bond and short on the fixed-rate bond, she benefits from the increase in interest rates.
- If interest rates decrease, the fixed-rate payer loses out, as there is a negative difference between (floating-rate) receipts and (fixed-rate) payments.
- In terms of the positions on bonds, the value of the fixed-rate bond increases as interest rates decrease, but the value of the floating-rate bond remains at par. Since the fixed-rate payer is long on the floating-rate bond and short on the fixed-rate bond, she loses out as a result of the decrease in interest rates.

Pricing a Plain-Vanilla Interest Rate Swap: Determining the Swap Fixed Rate

$$\text{Swap fixed rate} = \left[\frac{1 - B_0(N)}{B_0(1) + B_0(2) + B_0(3) + \ldots + B_0(N)} \right] \times 100$$

Valuing a Plain-Vanilla Interest Rate Swap

$$V = NA * (PSFR_0 - PSFR_t) * \text{Sum of PV factors of remaining coupon payments as of } t = t$$

where PSFR is the periodic swap fixed rate.

Currency Swap Contracts

Pricing a Currency Swap

- The fixed rates on a currency swap are still the fixed rates on plain-vanilla interest rate swaps in the respective countries.
- However, we must adjust the notional principal in the foreign currency by dividing the notional principal in the domestic currency by the current spot rate (expressed as DC/FC).

For fixed-for-floating currency swaps:

- The rate on the fixed side is just the fixed rate on a plain-vanilla interest rate swap in the given currency.
- The payments on the floating side will have the same present value as the payments on the fixed side as long as the foreign notional principal is adjusted.

For floating-for-floating currency swaps:

- We do not need to determine the price (swap fixed rate), as both sides pay a floating rate.
- However, we do still need to adjust the foreign notional principal to ensure that the present values of payments on both sides of the swap are equal.

Valuing a Currency Swap

In order to value a currency swap, we need to account for fluctuations in exchange rates, which apply to (1) settlement payments during the tenor of the swap **and** (2) exchange of notional amounts at expiration of the swap.

$$
\begin{aligned}
V = NA_{PC} * (&PSFR_{PC} * \text{Sum of PV factors of remaining coupon payments}_t \\
&+ \text{PV factor for return of notional amount}_t) \\
-S_{t,PC/BC} * NA_{BC} * (&PSFR_{BC} * \text{Sum of PV factors of remaining coupon payments}_t \\
&+ \text{PV factor for return of notional amount}_t)
\end{aligned}
$$

Equity Swap Contracts

Pricing Equity Swaps

- The price of a "pay a fixed rate and receive return on equity" swap refers to the fixed swap rate that will give the swap a zero value at inception.
- For a "pay a floating rate and receive return on equity" swap there is no fixed rate that we need to solve for. The market value of the swap at initiation equals zero.
- For a "pay the return on one equity instrument and receive the return on another equity instrument" swap there is no fixed rate that we need to solve for. The market value of the swap at initiation equals zero.

Valuing Equity Swaps

The value of a **pay-fixed, receive-return-on-equity** swap at any point in time is calculated as the difference between the value of the (hypothetical) equity portfolio and the present value of remaining fixed-rate payments:

$$
\left[(1 + \text{Return on equity}) * \text{Notional amount}\right] - \text{PV of the remaining fixed} - \text{Rate payments}
$$

The value of a **pay-floating, receive-return-on-equity** swap at any point in time is calculated as the difference between the value of the (hypothetical) equity portfolio and the par value of the bond (assuming that we are determining the value of the swap on a settlement date):

$$
\left[(1 + \text{Return on equity}) * \text{Notional amount}\right] - \text{PV}\left(\text{Next coupon payment} + \text{Parvalue}\right)
$$

The value of a **pay-return-on-one-equity-instrument, receive-return-on-another-equity-instrument** swap is calculated as the difference between the values of the two (hypothetical) equity portfolios:

$$
\left[(1 + \text{Return on Index 2}) * \text{Notional amount}\right] - \left[(1 + \text{Return on Index 1}) * \text{Notional amount}\right]
$$

VALUATION OF CONTINGENT CLAIMS
Cross-Reference to CFA Institute Assigned Reading #40

A **contingent claim** is a derivative that gives the owner the right, but not the obligation to a payoff based on an underlying asset, rate, or other derivative.

The One-Period Binomial Model

Assumptions

- The underlying is the only uncertain factor that affects the price of the option.
- Time moves in discrete (not continuous) increments.
- Given the current price of the underlying asset, over the next period the price can move to one of two possible new prices.
- There are no costs or benefits from owning the underlying.

Hedge Ratio for Calls

$$h = \frac{c^+ - c^-\ -}{S^+ - S^-\ -}$$

Value of a Call Option

$$c = \frac{\pi c^+ + (1 - \pi)c^-}{(1 + r)}$$

where:

$$\pi = \frac{(1 + r - d)}{(u - d)}$$

Hedge Ratio for Puts

$$h = \frac{p^+ - p^-\ -}{S^+ - S^-\ -}$$

Value of a Put Option

$$c = \frac{\pi c^+ + (1 - \pi)c^-}{(1 + r)}$$

where:

$$\pi = \frac{(1 + r - d)}{(u - d)}$$

One-Period Binomial Arbitrage Opportunity

If the price of the option is greater than the value computed from the model, the option is overpriced. To exploit this opportunity we would sell the option and buy h units of the underlying stock for each option sold.

If the price of the option is lower than the value computed from the model, the option is underpriced. To exploit this opportunity we would buy the option and sell h units of the underlying stock for each option purchased.

No-Arbitrage Approach over One Period

Single-Period Call Valuation Equation

$$c = hS + PV(-hS^- + c^-) \text{ or } c = hS + PV(-hS^+ + c^+)$$

- Note that h is (mathematically) **positive** for call options.
- This means that in order to hedge a short position on a call, we must go long on the underlying stock, and vice versa.
- If the stock price increases, the stock position will benefit, but the short call position loses out, and vice versa.

Single-Period Put Valuation Equation

$$p = hS + PV(-hS^- + p^-) \text{ or } p = hS + PV(-hS^+ + p^+)$$

- The hedge ratio for puts is **negative**.
- This means that in order to hedge a long position on a put, we would actually go long on the underlying as well. If the price of the underlying falls, the put benefits, while the long underlying position loses out.
- Since h is negative for puts, a put is equivalent to a short position in the underlying and lending out the proceeds of the short sale. Specifically, a long position on a put can be interpreted as lending that has been partially financed with a short position in shares.

Writing Options

- A written call is equivalent to selling the stock short and investing the proceeds.
- A written put is equivalent to buying the stock with borrowed funds.

The Expectations Approach over One Period

$$c = PV_r\left[E(c_1)\right]$$
$$p = PV_r\left[E(p_1)\right]$$

The price of a call or put option, under this approach, is calculated directly from expected terminal option payoffs.

The no-arbitrage approach and the expectations approach can be used to value options in a single-period setting.

The Two-Period Binomial Model

The two-period binomial model makes use of a **recombining** two-period binomial tree. Option values are determined through **backward induction**.

Two important concepts related to the two-period binomial option valuation model are **dynamic replication** and **self-financing**. When applied to call options:

- **Dynamic replication** means that the portfolio of stock and borrowing dynamically replicates the value of the call through the binomial lattice.
- **Self-financing** means that if additional funds are required to purchase more shares to maintain the hedge, the amount of borrowed funds will automatically increase.

The Expectations Approach in a Two-Period Setting

$$c = PV\left[\pi^2 c^{++} + 2\pi(1-\pi)c^{+-} + (1-\pi)^2 c^{--}\right]$$
$$p = PV\left[\pi^2 p^{++} + 2\pi(1-\pi)p^{+-} + (1-\pi)^2 p^{--}\right]$$

Very important: Under this approach, the value of the option is computed based **solely** on possible terminal values.

American-Style Options

American-Style Options and Early Exercise

- An American-style call option on non-dividend-paying stock will never be exercised early, because the minimum value of the option will exceed its exercise value.
- There may be cases where early exercise of an American-style call option on a dividend-paying stock is optimal.
- Early exercise of American-style put options on both dividend-paying and non-dividend-paying stocks may be warranted in certain cases.

No-Arbitrage versus Expectations Approach in a Multi-Period Setting

- Generally speaking, European-style options **can** be valued based on the expectations approach. Under this approach, option value is determined as the present value of the expected future option payouts, where the discount rate is the risk-free rate and the expectation is based on the risk-neutral probability measure.
- Both American-style options and European-style options can be valued based on the no-arbitrage approach, which provides clear interpretations of the component terms.
- Option value is determined by working backward through the binomial tree to arrive at the correct current value.
- For American-style options, early exercise may influence option values and hedge ratios as one works backward through the binomial tree. This is the case for American calls on dividend-paying stocks and American puts. Therefore, these options cannot be valued using the expectations approach. They can be valued using only the no-arbitrage approach.
- American calls on non-dividend-paying stock can be valued using the expectations approach because there is no reason to exercise them early.

Interest Rate Options

In order to value interest rate options, we need to work with arbitrage-free interest rate trees.

- The arbitrage-free interest rate tree is given.
- The risk-neutral probability of an up/down move at each node is 50%.

The one-period forward rates used to discount the expected payoffs at each node in the binomial lattice are different. This is because interest rates are allowed to vary in this model.

The underlying instrument for an interest rate option is the one-year spot rate.

- A call option would be in-the-money when the current spot rate is above the exercise rate.
- A put option would be in-the-money when the current spot rate is below the exercise rate.

The Black-Scholes-Merton (BSM) Option Valuation Model

Key Assumptions

- The underlying follows a statistical process called **geometric Brownian motion (GBM)**, which implies that returns follow the lognormal distribution. This basically means that the continuously compounded return is normally distributed.
- Prices are continuous, meaning that the price of the underlying instrument does not jump from one value to another, but moves smoothly from value to value.
- The underlying instrument is liquid, meaning that it can be easily bought and sold.
- Continuous trading is available, meaning that one can trade at every instant.
- Short selling of the underlying instrument with full use of the proceeds is permitted.
- Markets are frictionless, meaning that there are no transaction costs, regulatory constraints, or taxes.
- There are no arbitrage opportunities in the market.
- Options are European, so they cannot be exercised prior to expiration.
- The continuously compounded risk-free interest rate is known and constant. Further, borrowing and lending are allowed at the risk-free rate.
- The volatility of the return on the underlying is known and constant.
- If the underlying instrument pays a yield, it is expressed as a continuous, constant yield at an annualized rate.

The BSM Model for Non-Dividend-Paying Stock

$$c = SN(d_1) - e^{-rT}XN(d_2)$$
$$p = e^{-rT}XN(-d_2) - SN(-d_1)$$

Interpreting the BSM Model: Approach 1

The BSM model can be described as the present value of the expected option payoff at expiration.

$$c = PV_r\left[E(c_T)\right] \text{ where } E(c_T) = Se^{rT}N(d_1) - XN(d_2)$$
$$p = PV_r\left[E(p_T)\right] \text{ where } E(p_T) = XN(-d_2) - Se^{rT}N(-d_1)$$

- The discount factor in this context is simply e^{-rT}.
- The expectation is based on risk-neutral probabilities (not actual probabilities), and the discount factor is based on the risk-free rate, not on the required rate of return (which includes a premium for risk).

Interpreting the BSM Model: Approach 2

The BSM model can be described as having two components: (1) a stock component and (2) a bond component.

- For call options, the stock component is $SN(d_1)$ and the bond component is $e^{-rT}XN(d_2)$.
  - The value of the call equals the stock component minus the bond component.
- For put options, the stock component is $SN(-d_1)$ and the bond component is $e^{-rT}XN(-d_2)$.
  - The value of the put equals the bond component minus the stock component.

Interpreting the BSM Model: Approach 3

Finally, the BSM model can be viewed as a dynamically managed portfolio of the stock and zero-coupon bonds.

In the analysis that follows, the cost of the replicating portfolio is expressed as $n_S S + n_B B$, where:

- n_S denotes the number of shares of the underlying in the portfolio.
- n_B denotes the number of zero-coupon bonds in the portfolio.
- S is the current price of the stock.
- $e^{-rT}X$ is the current price (the present value) of the bond.

For call options:

- n_S equals $N(d_1)$, which is greater than 0. This means that we are buying the underlying.
- n_B equals $-N(d_2)$, which is less than 0. This means that we are selling/shorting the bond, or borrowing.
- Effectively, in taking a position on a call option, we are simply buying stock with borrowed money. Therefore, a call option can be viewed as a leveraged position in the stock.

For put options:

- n_S equals $-N(-d_1)$, which is less than 0. This means that we are shorting the stock.
- n_B equals $N(-d_2)$, which is greater than 0. This means that we are buying the bond, or lending.
- Effectively, in taking a position on a put option, we are simply buying bonds with the proceeds of shorting the stock.

The positon of the **writer** of a put option can be viewed as an extremely leveraged position on the stock, where the amount borrowed actually exceeds the total cost of the underlying (hence the positive cash flow at position initiation).

BSM and Binomial Option Valuation Model Comparison

Option Valuation Model Terms	Call Option		Put Option	
	Underlying	Financing	Underlying	Financing
Binomial Model	hS	$PV(-hS^- + c^-)$	hS	$PV(-hS^- + p^-)$
BSM Model	$N(d_1)S$	$-N(d_2)e^{-rT}X$	$-N(-d_1)S$	$N(-d_2)e^{-rT}X$

- The hedge ratio in the binomial model, h, is comparable to $N(d_1)$ in the BSM model.
- For call options, $-N(d_2)$ implies borrowing money or short selling $N(d_2)$ shares of a zero-coupon bond trading at $e^{-rT}X$.
- For put options, $N(-d_2)$ implies lending money or buying $N(-d_2)$ shares of a zero-coupon bond trading at $e^{-rT}X$.
- If the value of the underlying, S, increases, then the value of $N(d_1)$ also increases.
- Therefore, the replicating strategy for calls requires continually buying shares in a rising market and selling shares in a falling market.
- Since market prices do not move continuously, hedges tend to be imperfect. Further, volatility cannot be known in advance. As a result, options are typically more expensive than predicted by the BSM model.

Also note that:

- $N(d_2)$ represents the risk-neutral probability that the call option expires in-the-money.
- $1 - N(d_2) = N(-d_2)$ represents the risk-neutral probability that the put expires in-the-money.

BSM Model When the Underlying Offers Carry Benefits

Carry benefits include dividends for stock options, foreign interest rates for currency options, and coupon payments for bond options.

$$c = Se^{-\gamma T}N(d_1) - e^{-rT}XN(d_2)$$
$$p = e^{-rT}XN(-d_2) - Se^{-\gamma T}N(-d_1)$$

Interpreting the BSM Model with Carry Benefits: Approach 1

The carry-benefit-adjusted BSM model can be described as the present value of the expected option payoff at expiration.

- $c = PV_r[E(c_T)]$ where $E(c_T) = Se^{(r-\gamma)T}N(d_1) - XN(d_2)$
- $p = PV_r[E(p_T)]$ where $E(p_T) = XN(-d_2) - Se^{(r-\gamma)T}N(-d_1)$.
- The discount factor is e^{-rT}.

Note that carry benefits basically lower the expected future value of the underlying.

Interpreting the BSM Model with Carry Benefits: Approach 2

The carry-benefit-adjusted BSM model can also be described as having two components: (1) a stock component and (2) a bond component.

- For call options, the stock component is $Se^{-\gamma T}N(d_1)$ and the bond component is $e^{-rT}XN(d_2)$.
  - The value of the call equals the stock component minus the bond component.
- For put options, the stock component is $Se^{-\gamma T}N(-d_1)$ and the bond component is $e^{-rT}XN(-d_2)$.
  - The value of the put equals the bond component minus the stock component.
- Note that d_1 and d_2 are both also reduced by carry benefits. The reduction in d_2, and hence $N(d_2)$, indicates a lower risk-neutral probability of the call being in-the-money.
- An increase in carry benefits will lower the value of a call option and increase the value of a put.

Interpreting the BSM Model with Carry Benefits: Approach 2

The dividend-yield-adjusted BSM model can be interpreted as a dynamically managed portfolio of the stock and zero-coupon bonds.

- For call options $n_S = e^{-\gamma T}N(d_1)$, which is greater than 0, while $n_B = -N(d_2)$, which is less than 0.
- For put options, $n_S = -e^{-\gamma T}N(-d_1)$, which is less than 0, while $n_B = N(-d_2)$, which is greater than 0.

Dividends lower the values of d_1 and d_2, and therefore of $N(d_1)$ and $N(d_2)$.

- This means that dividends lower the number of shares that must be bought in the call replicating portfolio, and reduce the number of shares that must be sold short in the put replicating portfolio.
- Further, higher dividends lower the number of bonds to sell short in the call replicating portfolio, and the number of bonds to purchase in the put replicating portfolio.

Foreign Exchange Options

Note: We work with foreign exchange quotes expressed as DC/FC.

- For foreign exchange options, the carry benefit, γ, is the continuously compounded foreign risk-free interest rate, r^f.
- The underlying and the exercise price must be quoted in the same currency unit (DC/FC).
- Volatility here refers to the volatility of the log return of the spot exchange rate.

The BSM model for currencies also has two components: a foreign exchange component and a bond component.

- For call options, the foreign exchange component is $Se^{-r^fT}N(d_1)$ and the bond component is $e^{-rT}XN(d_2)$, where r is the domestic risk-free rate.
  - The value of a call option is simply the foreign exchange component minus the bond component.
- For put options, the foreign exchange component is $Se^{-r^fT}N(-d_1)$ and the bond component is $e^{-rT}XN(-d_2)$.
  - The value of a put option is simply the bond component minus the foreign exchange component.

Black Option Valuation Model

The **Black model** is applicable to options on underlying instruments that are costless to carry, such as options on futures (e.g., equity index futures) and forward contracts (e.g., interest-rate-based options, such as caps, floors, and swaptions).

European Options on Futures

Assumptions:

- The futures price follows geometric Brownian motion (GBM).
- Margin requirements and marking to market are ignored.

Under the Black model, European-style options on futures are valued as:

$$c = e^{-rT}\left[F_0(T)N(d_1) - XN(d_2)\right]$$
$$p = e^{-rT}\left[XN(-d_2) - F_0(T)N(-d_1)\right]$$

Interpreting the Black Model: Approach 1

The Black model has two components, a futures component and a bond component.

- For call options, the futures component is $F_0(T)e^{-rT}N(d_1)$ and the bond component is again $e^{-rT}XN(d_2)$.
  - The call price is simply the futures component minus the bond component.
- For put options, the futures component is $F_0(T)e^{-rT}N(-d_1)$ and the bond component is again $e^{-rT}XN(-d_2)$.
  - The put price is simply the bond component minus the futures component.

Interpreting the Black Model: Approach 2

The Black model simply computes the present value of the difference between the futures price and the exercise price, where the futures price and exercise price are adjusted by the N(d) functions.

- For call options, the futures price is adjusted by $N(d_1)$ and the exercise price is adjusted by $-N(d_2)$.
- For put options, the futures price is adjusted by $-N(-d_1)$ and the exercise price is adjusted by $+N(-d_2)$.

Interest Rate Options

The underlying for an interest rate option is a forward rate agreement (FRA) that expires on the option expiration date. In turn, the underlying of the FRA is a term deposit.

For example, consider an interest rate call option on three-month Libor that expires in six months.

- The underlying on this option is an FRA on three-month Libor that expires in six months.
- The underlying of the FRA is a three-month Libor deposit that is made after six months and matures nine months from option initiation.

For interest rate options:

- Interest rates are typically set in advance, but interest payments are made in arrears (referred to as "advanced set, settled in arrears").
- Interest rates are quoted on an annualized basis, so if the underlying implied deposit is for less than a year, they must be unannualized.
- An interest rate call option gives the call buyer the right to a certain cash payment when the underlying interest rate exceeds the exercise rate.
- An interest rate put option gives the put buyer the right to a certain cash payment when the underlying interest rate is below the exercise rate.

The interest rate option valuation model described next is known as the **standard market model**.

Notation

- t_{j-1} denotes the time to option expiration.
- t_{j-1} also denotes the time to FRA expiration.
- The term of the deposit underlying the FRA is denoted by t_m. This term starts at option/FRA expiration (t_{j-1}) and lasts until t_j ($= t_{j-1} + t_m$).
- Interest accrual on the underlying begins at the option expiration (t_{j-1}).
- $FRA(0, t_{j-1}, t_m)$ denotes the fixed rate on an FRA at $t = 0$ that expires at t_{j-1}, where the underlying deposit matures at time t_j ($= t_{j-1} + t_m$), with all times expressed on an annual basis.
  - For example, $FRA(0, 0.5, 0.25) = 1.50\%$ denotes the 1.5% fixed rate on a forward rate agreement that expires in six months with underlying deposit maturing nine months from today. This means that the settlement amount on the FRA will be paid nine months from today.
- We assume the FRA is 30/360 day count.
- R_X denotes the exercise rate on the option (expressed on an annual basis).
- σ denotes volatility of the interest rate.

Under the standard market model, the prices of interest rate call and put options can be expressed as:

$$c = (AP)\, e^{-r(t_{j-1}+t_m)}\left[FRA(0,t_{j-1},t_m)N(d_1) - R_X N(d_2) \right]$$

$$p = (AP)\, e^{-r(t_{j-1}+t_m)}\left[R_X N(-d_2) - FRA(0,t_{j-1},t_m)N(-d_1) \right]$$

where:
AP = Accrual period in years

$$d_1 = \frac{\ln\left[FRA(0,t_{j-1},t_m)/FRA(0,t_{j-1},t_m)R_X R_X \right] + (\sigma^2/\sigma^2 22)t_{j-1}}{\sigma\sqrt{t_{j-1}}}$$

$$d_2 = d_1 - \sigma\sqrt{t_{j-1}}$$

Note the following:

- The formulas here give the value of the option for a notional amount of 1. We would have to multiply this cost of the option by the notional amount to obtain the full cost of the option.
- The FRA rate, $FRA(0,t_{j-1},t_m)$, and the strike rate, R_X, are both stated on an annual basis. The option premium that we obtain after applying the preceding formulas must be adjusted for the accrual period.
- Other (more subtle) differences between the standard market model and the Black model are:
  - The discount factor, $e^{-r(t_{j-1}+t_m)}$, does not apply to the option expiration, t_{j-1}. Instead, it is applied to the maturity of the deposit underlying the FRA. This is because settlement occurs in arrears.
  - The underlying is not a futures price, but a forward interest rate.
  - The exercise price is also an interest rate, not a price.
  - The time to the option expiration, t_{j-1}, is used in the calculation of d_1 and d_2.

Analysis

The standard market model can be described as simply the present value of the expected option payoff at expiration.

- The standard market model for calls can be expressed as $c = PV[E(c_{tj})]$ where $E(c_{tj}) = (AP)[FRA(0,t_{j-1},t_m)N(d_1) - R_X N(d_2)]$.
- The standard market model for puts can be expressed as $p = PV[E(p_{tj})]$, where $E(p_{tj}) = (AP)[R_X N(-d_2) - FRA(0,t_{j-1},t_m)N(-d_1)]$.
- The present value term in this context is simply $e^{-rt_j} = e^{-r(t_{j-1}+t_m)}$. Note that we discount from time t_j, the time when the deposit underlying the FRA matures.

Using Interest Options to Create Other Derivative Instruments

- If the exercise rate equals the current FRA rate, then a long position on an interest rate call option combined with a short position on an interest rate put option is equivalent to a receive-floating, pay-fixed FRA; a short position on an interest rate call option combined with a long position on an interest rate put option is equivalent to a receive-fixed, pay-floating FRA.

- Floating-rate payments can be hedged with positions on interest rate caps. Floating-rate receipts can be hedged with positions on interest rate floors.
- Taking a long position on an interest rate cap and a short position on an interest rate floor with the same exercise rate is equal to a receive-floating, pay-fixed interest rate swap. Taking a long position on an interest rate floor and a short position on an interest rate cap with the same exercise rate is equal to a receive-fixed, pay-floating interest rate swap.
- If the exercise rate is set equal to the swap rate, then the value of the cap must be equal to the value of the floor.

Swaptions

A **swaption** gives the holder the right, but not the obligation, to enter a swap at the predetermined swap rate (the exercise rate). It basically is an option to enter a swap.

- A **payer swaption** is an option to enter a swap as the pay-fixed, receive-floating side.
- A **receiver swaption** is an option to enter a swap as the receive-fixed, pay-floating side.

The holder of a payer swaption hopes that the market swap fixed rate increases before expiration of the swaption, whereas the holder of a receiver swaption hopes that the market swap fixed rate decreases.

The Black model can be used to value swaptions:

$$\text{Payer swaption} = (AP)PVA\left[R_{FIX}N(d_1) - R_X N(d_2)\right]$$
$$\text{Receiver swaption} = (AP)PVA\left[R_X N(-d_2) - R_{FIX}N(-d_1)\right]$$

Note the following:

- Swap payments are advanced set, settled in arrears.
- The actual premium would need to be scaled by the notional amount.
- Compared to the traditional Black model, the swaption model just described requires adjustments for (1) the accrual period (AP) and (2) the present value of an annuity (PVA).
- Other, more subtle differences between the Black model and the swaption model are as follows:
  - The payoff is not a single payment but a series of payments, and the PVA incorporates the option-related discount factor. There is no explicit discount factor in the formulas here.
  - Rather than the underlying being a futures price, the underlying is the fixed rate on a forward interest rate swap.
  - The exercise price is expressed as an interest rate.
  - Both the forward swap rate and the exercise rate should be expressed in decimal form and not as percentages.

Interpreting the Black Model Applied to Swaptions: Approach 1

The swaption model can be described as simply the present value of the expected option payoff at expiration:

- Payer swaption = $PV[E(PAY_{SWN,T})]$ where $E(PAY_{SWN,T}) = e^{rT}PAY_{SWN}$.
- Receiver swaption = $PV[E(REC_{SWN,T})]$ where $E(REC_{SWN,T}) = e^{rT}REC_{SWN}$.
- The present value term in this context is simply e^{-rT}.

Interpreting the Black Model Applied to Swaptions: Approach 2

The swaption model can be described as having two components, a swap component and a bond component.

- For payer swaptions, the swap component is $(AP)PVA(R_{FIX})N(d_1)$ and the bond component is $(AP)PVA(R_X)N(d_2)$.
  - The value of a payer swaption is simply the swap component minus the bond component.
- For receiver swaptions, the swap component is $(AP)PVA(R_{FIX})N(-d_1)$ and the bond component is $(AP)PVA(R_X)N(-d_2)$.
  - The value of a receiver swaption is simply the bond component minus the swap component.

Equivalence of Swaps to Other Derivative Instruments

- Being long an interest rate cap and short an interest rate floor with the same exercise rate is comparable to taking a receive-floating, pay-fixed position on an interest rate swap. Being short an interest rate cap and long an interest rate floor with the same exercise rate is comparable to taking a pay-floating, receive-fixed position on an interest rate swap.
  - In terms of swaptions, the position is equal to being long a payer swaption and short a receiver swaption, or being long a receiver swaption and short a payer swaption, with the same exercise rate.
  - Note that if the exercise rate is selected such that the receiver and payer swaptions have the same value, then the exercise rate is equal to the at-market forward swap rate.
- Being long a callable fixed-rate bond can be viewed as being long a straight fixed-rate bond and short a receiver swaption.
- The **issuer** of a callable bond can effectively convert its position into a straight bond by selling a receiver swaption.

Option Greeks and Implied Volatility

Delta

Option delta measures the change in the value of an option given a small change in the value of the underlying stock, holding everything else constant.

- While it is a measure of the magnitude of change in the value of an option given a change in the underlying, delta does not measure the probability of the change in value.
- Delta equals the slope of the prior-to-expiration curve.

$$\text{Call option delta} = e^{-\delta T}N(d_1)$$
$$\text{Put option delta} = -e^{-\delta T}N(-d_1)$$

- Call option values and underlying prices are positively related, so for a call option, delta is always positive.
  - It will increase toward 1.0 as the underlying price moves up, and decrease toward 0 as the underlying price moves down.

- Put option values and underlying prices are negatively related, so for a put option, delta is always negative.
  - It will decrease toward –1.0 as the underlying price moves down, and increase toward 0 as the underlying price moves up.

Option delta is also influenced by time to expiration.

- If the underlying price remains unchanged, as a call option moves toward expiration:
  - Delta will move toward 1.0 if the call is in-the-money.
  - Delta will move toward 0 if the call is out-of-the-money.
- If the underlying price remains unchanged, as the put option moves toward expiration:
  - Delta will move toward –1.0 if the put is in-the-money.
  - Delta will move toward 0 if the put is out-of-the-money.

Applications of Delta

Delta Hedging

The optimal number of hedging units:

$$N_H = -\frac{\text{Portfolio delta}}{\text{Delta}_H}$$

Estimating the Value of an Option

$$\text{For calls: } \hat{c} - c \cong \text{Delta}_c(\hat{S} - S)$$
$$\text{For puts: } \hat{p} - p \cong \text{Delta}_p(\hat{S} - S)$$

- For very small changes in stock value, the delta-based approximation is quite accurate.
- However, for large changes in stock value, delta-based estimates understate actual call values. Importantly, this is the case for large increases **and** decreases in the price of the stock.
- The implication here is that delta-based estimation is not perfect, and it gets more and more inaccurate as the stock moves away from its initial value.

Gamma

Option gamma is defined as the change in an option's delta given a small change in the value of the underlying stock, holding everything else constant. Option gamma measures the curvature in the option price–stock price relationship.

- The gamma of a long or short position in one share of stock is zero. Delta stays at +1.0 for a long position on a stock, and at –1.0 for a short position.
- The gammas for call and put options are the same and can be expressed as:
  - $\text{Gamma}_c = \text{Gamma}_p = \frac{e^{-\delta T}}{S\sigma\sqrt{T}}n(d_1)$
- Gamma is always nonnegative.
- As the stock price changes and as time to expiration changes, gamma is also changing.

Gamma measures how sensitive delta is to changes in the price of the underlying stock. Stated differently, gamma measures the nonlinearity risk or the risk that remains once the portfolio is delta neutral.

- When gamma is large, delta is very sensitive to changes in the value of the underlying stock and cannot provide a good approximation of how much the value of the option would change given a change in the price of the underlying stock.
- When gamma is small, delta is not as sensitive to changes in the value of the underlying stock and can provide a reasonably good approximation of how much the value of the option would change given a change in the price of the underlying stock.
- Gamma is largest when there is great uncertainty regarding whether the option will expire in-the-money or out-of-the-money.
  - This implies that gamma will tend to be large when an option is at-the-money and close to expiration.
  - This also means that a delta hedge would work poorly when an option is at-the-money and close to expiration. On the other hand, when an option is deep-in-the-money or deep-out-of-the-money, gamma approaches zero, as changes in the price of the underlying do not have a significant impact on delta.

Applications of Gamma

Gamma-Neutral Portfolios

A gamma-neutral portfolio implies that gamma is zero. If we want to alter the gamma and delta exposures of our portfolio, our first step would be to bring gamma to an acceptable level using options as the hedging instruments and then alter the overall portfolio's delta by buying or selling stock.

Estimating the Value of an Option

$$\text{For calls}: \hat{c} - c \approx \text{Delta}_c (\hat{S} - S) + \frac{\text{Gamma}_c}{2}(\hat{S} - S)^2$$

$$\text{For puts}: \hat{p} - p \approx \text{Delta}_p (\hat{S} - S) + \frac{\text{Gamma}_p}{2}(\hat{S} - S)^2$$

- For very small changes in the stock, the delta approximation and the delta-plus-gamma approximations for call values are fairly accurate.
- For large changes in the value of the stock, the delta-plus-gamma-based estimate is a more accurate approximation of the value of the call than the estimate based on delta alone. This is the case for large up **and** down moves in the stock.
- When the stock moves up by a large amount, the delta-plus-gamma-based estimate overestimates the price of the call. When the stock moves down by a large amount, the delta-plus-gamma-based estimate underestimates the price of the call.

Theta

Option theta is defined as the change in the value of an option for a given small change in calendar time, holding everything else constant. Theta effectively measures the decline in an option's time value as it approaches expiration (also known as **time decay**). At expiration, of course, an option is worth only its exercise value (time value = 0).

- Stocks do not have an expiration date, so stock theta is zero. Therefore, like gamma, portfolio theta cannot be adjusted by undertaking stock trades.
- Theta is fundamentally different from delta and gamma in the sense that the passage of time does not involve any uncertainty. Time decay will always occur for options.
- Theta is negative for both calls and puts. Further, the rate at which option values decline accelerates as time to expiration decreases.

Vega

Vega measures the sensitivity of the value of an option to changes in volatility of the underlying stock. Volatility refers to the standard deviation of the continuously compounded return on the underlying stock.

- The vega of a call option is the same as the vega of an otherwise identical put option.
- Vega is positive for both calls and puts.
  - All other things remaining the same, an increase in volatility increases option values.
- Unlike other Greeks, vega is based on a parameter (future volatility) that is not observable in the market.
- Of all the Greeks, option values are most sensitive to volatility changes.
- Vega is highest when options are near-the-money or at-the-money and close to expiration.
- Volatility is typically hedged using other options. However, note that volatility itself tends to be quite volatile. As a result, it is sometimes treated as a separate asset class or separate risk factor.
- If volatility approaches 0, option values approach their lower bounds.

Rho

Rho measures the sensitivity of the price of an option to small changes in the risk-free rate, holding everything else constant.

Both call and put options on most assets are not very sensitive to changes in the risk-free rate. Generally speaking:

- The rho of call options is positive. Call option values increase in response to an increase in the risk-free rate.
- The rho of put options is negative. Put option values decrease in response to an increase in the risk-free rate.

Note that when interest rates are zero, call and put option values are the same for at-the-money options.

Implied Volatility

Given option prices in the marketplace and values for all other inputs in the model (the value of the underlying, the exercise price, the expiration date, the risk-free rate, and dividends paid by the underlying), the BSM model is often inverted and used to infer future volatility. This inferred volatility is known as implied volatility (the volatility built into, or implied by, current market prices of options).

Implied volatility enables us to understand the collective opinions of investors on the volatility of the underlying and the demand for options. If the demand for options increases, options prices would rise, and so would implied volatility.

Note that:

- While the BSM model assumes that volatility is constant, in practice it is quite common to observe different implied volatilities for otherwise identical calls and puts.
- Implied volatility also varies across time to expiration as well as across exercise prices.
    - The implied volatility with respect to time to expiration is known as the term structure of volatility.
    - The implied volatility with respect to the exercise price is known as the volatility smile or volatility skew.
    - A three-dimensional plot of the implied volatility with respect to both time to expiration and exercise price is known as the volatility surface.
        - If BSM assumptions were true, we would expect the volatility surface to be flat.
- Implied volatility is also not constant through calendar time. An increase in implied volatility indicates an increased market price of risk.
- For example, an increase in the implied volatility of a put indicates a higher cost of attaining downside protection, or that the market price of hedging is increasing.

Volatility indexes (e.g., the VIX) measure the collective opinions of investors on the volatility of the broader market. Investors can trade futures and options on these indexes in an effort to manage their vega exposures.

- The CBOE Volatility Index (VIX) is quoted as a percentage and represents the approximate implied volatility of the S&P 500 over the next 30 days.
- It is often referred to as "the fear index" because it is a gauge of market uncertainty.
    - An increase in the VIX indicates greater investor uncertainty.
- Historically, the VIX has spiked up in times of market crises, indicating great fear/ uncertainty in the equity market. Since implied volatility reflects (1) beliefs regarding future volatility and (2) demand for risk-mitigating products like options, a higher reading of the VIX during a crisis reflects both higher expected future volatility and higher demand for buying rather than writing options.

DR

In some markets, options are quoted in terms of volatility. Quoted volatility allows traders to make effective comparisons across options with different exercise prices and expiration dates in a common unit of measure.

For example, consider two call options on the same stock. Option A has a longer term to expiration, but a higher exercise price, whereas Option B has a lower exercise price but a shorter term to expiration. Based on this information alone, it is difficult to tell which option should be priced higher. But if Option A had a higher implied volatility, we would be able to conclude that, after taking into account the effects of exercise price and term to expiration, Option A is the more expensive one.

DERIVATIVES STRATEGIES
Cross-Reference to CFA Institute Assigned Reading #41

Interest Rate Swaps versus Interest Rate Futures

Using Interest Rate Swaps and Interest Rate Futures to Manage a Fixed-Income Portfolio

Description	Interest Rate Swap	Interest Rate Futures (Underlying Is a Bond)
Increase overall portfolio duration (outlook: falling interest rates).	Receive fixed (pay LIBOR) with swap duration higher than portfolio duration.	Buy contracts to add positive duration to the portfolio.
Decrease overall portfolio duration (outlook: rising interest rates).	Pay fixed (receive LIBOR) with swap duration lower than portfolio duration.	Sell contracts to add negative duration to the portfolio.
Trade location and counterparty risk.	Private contract in the over-the-counter market. There is counterparty risk.	Exchange-traded and guaranteed by a clearinghouse. There is zero counterparty risk.

Currency Swaps and Currency Futures/Forwards

A currency swap is different from an interest rate swap in three ways: (1) The interest rates are associated with different currencies, (2) periodic settlement payments may not be netted, and (3) the notional amount may be exchanged at swap initiation and expiration. Currency swaps enable a company to effectively determine its preferred funding currency and preferred payment currency.

A company may also use currency futures or forward contracts to manage currency risk.

> Number of currency futures contracts = Foreign currency required / Futures contract size denominated in foreign currency

Note: You will need to round your answer up or down, as you cannot trade fractional contracts.

Equity Swaps and Equity Futures

- If the portfolio manager wants to *increase* equity exposure, she would choose to *receive* the total return on an equity index and pay another return, such as another equity index or LIBOR.
- If the portfolio manager wants to *decrease* equity exposure, she would choose to *pay* the total return on an equity index and receive another return, such as another equity index or LIBOR.

The portfolio manager could also use stock index futures to manage the risk of her portfolio.

> Number of currency futures contracts = Size of equity portfolio to be hedged / (Futures multiplier * Stock index value)

If the existing portfolio has a beta less than 1.0, then fewer S&P 500 index futures contracts would be required to hedge the position. A portfolio with a beta greater than 1.0 would require more contracts.

Position Equivalencies

Synthetics Relating to Stock Options

- Synthetic long asset = Long call and short put
- Synthetic short asset = Long put and short call
- Synthetic put = Short stock and long call
- Synthetic call = Long stock and long put

Note that we assume that the exercise prices of the calls and puts are equal to the current underlying stock price.

Regarding options on currencies, always pay careful attention to the quoting convention used. Also note that given a set exercise price, the right to deliver euros in exchange for yen is exactly the same as the right to buy yen in exchange for euros. Stated differently, given the exercise price, a put option on one currency is equivalent to a call option on the other currency in the exchange rate quote.

Synthetics Relating to Futures Contracts

- Synthetic risk-free rate (synthetic cash) = Long stock and short futures
- Synthetic stock = Risk-free rate and long futures

Covered Calls

A covered call strategy occurs when an investor who already owns the underlying stock sells a call option on that stock.

> Covered call = Long underlying stock + Sell (short) a call on the stock

Motivations for Writing a Covered Call

- Income generation
- Improving on the market
- Target price realization

> Total premium income = Premium per option sold * Number of options per contract * Number of contracts

The investor keeps this premium income no matter what happens to the underlying until the expiration date. Even if the stock declines to nearly zero, the loss is less with the covered call compared to holding the underlying asset alone, because the option writer always gets to keep the option premium. However, it is important to note that the investor gives up the upside potential of the underlying stock beyond the exercise price of the call option.

- Maximum gain = $(X - S_0) + c_0$
- Maximum loss = $S_0 - c_0$
- Breakeven price = $S_0 - c_0$
- Expiration value of option = $S_T - \text{Max}[(S_T - X), 0]$
- Profit or loss at expiration = $S_T - \text{Max}[(S_T - X), 0] + c_0 - S_0$

Protective Puts

A protective put strategy occurs when an investor who already owns the underlying stock buys a put option on that stock.

> Protective put = Long underlying stock + Buy (long) a put on the stock

The primary motivation for purchasing a protective put is to mitigate losses when the underlying stock falls in value, so that the downside of the return distribution is eliminated. Using a deep out-of-the-money put (one with a relatively low exercise price) reduces the cost of the downside protection.

The occasional purchase of a protective put to deal with a temporary situation can be a sensible risk-reducing activity. However, continually purchasing puts to protect against a possible stock price decline is an expensive strategy that would wipe out most of the long-term gain on an otherwise good investment.

- Maximum gain = Theoretically unlimited
- Maximum loss = $(S_0 - X) + p_0$
- Breakeven point = $S_0 + p_0$
- Expiration value = $\text{Max}(S_T, X)$
- Profit at expiration = $\text{Max}(S_T, X) - S_0 - p_0$

Equivalence to Long Asset/Short Forward Position

Delta measures how the price of an option changes in response to changes in the price of the underlying.

- Call deltas range from 0 to 1.0, and put deltas range from 0 to −1.0.
- At-the-money calls have a delta of approximately 0.5, whereas at-the-money puts have a delta of approximately −0.5.
- A long position in the underlying asset has a delta of 1.0, whereas a short position has a delta of −1.0.
- Long positions in forwards/futures also have a delta of 1.0, whereas short positions in forwards/futures have a delta of −1.0.

Cash-Secured Puts

- In a cash-secured put, instead of buying a put, an investor writes a put and simultaneously deposits an amount equal to the exercise price in an escrow (third-party) account.
- This position provides a guarantee to the option buyer that the put writer (seller) would be able to purchase the stock if the buyer chose to exercise.
- This strategy is appropriate for someone who is bullish on a stock or who wants to acquire shares at a particular price.

- The cash in a cash-secured put is similar to the stock part of a covered call. It covers/secures the holder of the position in case the option holder exercises her option.

Collars

A **collar** (also known as **fence** or **hedge wrapper**, and as a **risk reversal** when it comes to foreign exchange transactions) combines an existing long position in the underlying stock with a long put (with an exercise price that is lower than the current stock price) and a short call (with an exercise price that is higher than the current stock price). The cost of the put is largely and often precisely offset by the income from writing the call.

> Collar = Long underlying stock + Buy (long) a put + Sell (short) a call

A collar sacrifices the upside on the stock position in exchange for protection on the downside. The resulting narrow distribution of possible investment outcomes reduces risk, with the cost of limited return potential.

- Maximum gain = $X_H - S_0 - p_0 + c_0$
- Maximum loss = $(S_0 - X_L) + p_0 - c_0$
- Breakeven point = $S_0 + p_0 - c_0$

Note that when an existing long position on the stock is combined with a same-strike collar, the risk is completely eliminated.

Spreads

Bull Spread

A bull spread is the simultaneous purchase of a call (or put) with a lower strike price and the sale of a call (or put) with a higher strike price.

> Bull spread = Long a call (or put) at a lower exercise price (X_L) + Sell a call (or put) with a higher exercise price (X_H)

The motivation for entering a bull spread is to take advantage of an expected directional price increase in the underlying stock, with part of the upside profit potential given up in exchange for a lower cost of the position. Just like the collar, the bull spread removes the lower and upper tails of the return distribution, leaving only the price uncertainty between the exercise prices. The stock price must rise above the lower strike price for the bull spread to be profitable.

If a spread requires a net cash outflow, this is generally known as a **debit spread** with the result of a net long position. Conversely, if a spread generates a net cash inflow, this is generally known as a **credit spread** with the result of a net short position.

The following formulas apply to bull spreads that use call options:

- Net premium = $c_L - c_H$
- Maximum gain = $X_H - X_L -$ Net premium

- Maximum loss = $c_L - c_H$, where neither of the calls is in-the-money, so the loss is limited to the net premium paid.
- Breakeven point = Occurs in the region where the lower call is in-the-money. The share price must rise enough above the lower exercise price to cover the net premium = $X_H + (c_L - c_H)$.

Bear Spreads

A bear spread is the simultaneous purchase of a put (or call) with a higher strike price and the sale of a put (or call) with a lower strike price.

$$\text{Bear spread} = \text{Long a call(or put)at a higher exercise price}(X_H) + \text{Sell a call}$$
$$\text{(or put)with a lower exercise price}(X_L)$$

The motivation for entering a bear spread is to take advantage of an expected directional price decrease in the underlying stock, with part of the profit potential given up in exchange for a lower cost of the position. Just like the collar and bull spread, the bear spread removes the lower and upper tails of the return distribution, leaving only the price uncertainty between the exercise prices. The stock price must fall below the higher strike price for the bear spread to be profitable.

The following formulas apply to bear spreads that use put options:

- Net premium = $p_H - p_L$
- Maximum gain = $X_H - X_L -$ Net premium
- Maximum loss = $p_H - p_L$, where neither of the puts is in-the-money, so the loss is limited to the net premium paid.
- Breakeven point = Occurs in the region where the higher put is in-the-money. The share price must fall enough below the higher exercise price to cover the net premium = $X_L + (p_H - p_L)$.

Note the following:

- Bull spreads can also be done with puts, and bear spreads can also be done with calls. If this is the case, the result is a credit spread with an initial cash inflow.
- While spread strategies are primarily a directional play on the underlying spot price, they can also be used to take advantage of changes in the level of volatility.
- Spreads are similar to collars in that the tails of the return distribution are taken out of play, leaving the investor exposed only to price uncertainty between the option exercise prices.

Calendar Spreads

Calendar Spread Positions

	Stock Price Expected to Increase	Stock Price Expected to Decrease
Change in stock price is imminent.	Short calendar spread using calls	Short calendar spread using puts
Change in stock price is not imminent.	Long calendar spread using calls	Long calendar spread using puts

Straddles

A straddle is called a **combination strategy** because it combines both a call and a put. A straddle involves the simultaneous purchase of a put and a call with the same strike price and expiration date.

> Long straddle = Long a put and long a call with the same strike price and expiration

The motivation for entering a long straddle is to take advantage of an expected increase in volatility of the underlying stock. The straddle is *not* a directional bet on the stock's movement. When volatility of the underlying stock is expected to remain low or decrease, then the appropriate strategy would be to short the straddle by selling both the put and the call.

- Maximum gain = Theoretically unlimited as the share price increases and the call becomes deeper in-the-money
- Maximum loss = Net premium
- Breakeven points = There are two breakeven points because only one of the options can be in-the-money at any point in time.
- Higher breakeven point = X + Net premium
- Lower breakeven point = X – Net premium

    %change in underlying price required to break even = Net premium paid / S_0

$\sigma_{annual} = \sigma_{daily} *$ Square root (# trading days in the year / Days until option expires)

- If the breakeven volatility is lower than the historical volatility, engaging in the long straddle is expected to be profitable.
- If the breakeven volatility is higher than the historical volatility, engaging in the long straddle is not expected to be profitable.

Investment Objectives and Strategy Selection

Direction and Volatility with Options

	Direction		
Volatility	**Bearish**	**Neutral/No Bias**	**Bullish**
High	Buy puts	Buy straddle	Buy calls
Average	Write calls and buy puts	Spreads	Buy calls and write puts
Low	Write calls	Write straddle	Write puts

AI

PRIVATE REAL ESTATE INVESTMENTS
Cross-Reference to CFA Institute Assigned Reading #42

Real Estate Investment: Basic Forms

Real estate investments can be classified into different forms on the basis of:

- Whether the investment is being made in the private or public market.
  - Investments in private markets can be made either directly or indirectly.
  - Investments in public markets are usually made *indirectly* through ownership of securities that serve as claims on the underlying assets.
- Whether the investment is structured as equity or debt.
  - An equity investor has an ownership interest in real estate or in securities of an entity that owns real estate.
  - A debt investor is a lender who owns a mortgage loan or mortgage securities.

Table 1: Examples of the Basic Forms of Real Estate Investment

	Equity	Debt
Private	Direct investments in real estate. This can be through sole ownership, joint venture, real estate limited partnerships, or other forms of commingled funds.	Mortgages
Publicly traded	Shares of real estate operating companies and shares of REITs.	Mortgage-backed securities (Residential and commercial)

Each form of real estate investment has its own risks, expected returns, regulations, legal structures, and market structures:

- Private real estate investments are indivisible and therefore, tend to involve larger amounts.
- Public real estate investments allow the ownership or claim on the property to be divided, which makes them more liquid than private real estate investments, and also allows investors to diversify by purchasing ownership interests across several properties.
- Private equity investment in real estate requires the owner to manage the property herself or to hire a property manager. REOCs and REITs have professional teams to manage their real estate investments, so investors in publicly traded real estate investments do not require real estate management expertise.
- Equity investors usually require a higher rate of return than debt investors as they take on greater risk. Their claim on the interim cash flows and proceeds from sale of real estate property is subordinate to that of debt holders. However, debt investors usually do not participate in any upside in the value of the underlying real estate.
- The return to equity investors in real estate has two components: an income stream (e.g., rental income) and a capital appreciation component.

Real Estate Characteristics

- Heterogeneity and fixed location
- High unit value
- Management intensive
- High transaction costs
- Depreciation
- Need for debt capital
- Illiquidity
- Difficulties in price determination

Real Estate Classifications

Real estate investments may be classified as residential or non-residential properties. Another potential classification is single-family residential, commercial, farmland, and timber.

Benefits of Real Estate Equity Investments

- Real estate investments can generate current income by letting, leasing, or renting the property.
- Real estate prices may increase over time, so capital appreciation can contribute to an investor's total return.
- Real estate values usually rise in an inflationary environment, so real estate investments serve as an inflation hedge.
- Investments in real estate provide diversification benefits to investors.
- Investors in real estate may receive favorable tax treatment.

Risks Factors

- Business conditions: Changes in economic factors such as GDP growth, employment, household income, interest rates, and inflation rates affect both (1) real estate values and (2) rental income.
- Long lead time for new developments: Real estate projects take a long time to be completed and market conditions can change significantly during their development.
- Cost and availability of capital: Scarcity of capital and high financing costs lead to lower real estate values.
- Unexpected inflation: If the real estate market is relatively weak, high vacancy rates and low rents could mean that real estate values may not keep up with inflation.
- Demographics: The demand for real estate is also affected by factors such as the size and age distribution of the population in the local market, the distribution of socio-economic groups, and the rate of new household formation.
- Lack of liquidity: Real estate investments tend to have poor liquidity due to (1) the large outlays required and (2) the time taken and costs incurred to sell.
- Environmental: Poor environmental conditions (e.g., contaminants related to a prior owner or an adjacent property owner) can have an adverse impact on the value of a property.
- Availability of information: There is a risk of overpaying for a property if the owner makes the investment decision based on insufficient or inaccurate information.

- Management: Management risk reflects the ability of both asset managers and property managers to make the right decisions regarding the operation of the property.
- Leverage: A small decrease in NOI can have a significant negative impact on the cash flow available to equity investors after meeting debt servicing obligations.
- Other risk factors: Other risk factors include unobserved physical defects in the property, natural disasters, and acts of terrorism.

Investment Characteristics of Commercial Property Types

Office

The demand for office buildings is influenced by employment growth, especially in industries that are heavy users of office space. Lease lengths are generally influenced by (1) the desirability of the property, (2) the financial strength of the tenant and (3) other terms in the lease such as future rent changes and whether there is an option to extend the lease.

An important consideration in office leases is whether it is the owner or the tenant who bears the risk of operating expenses (e.g., utilities) increasing in the future.

Industrial and Warehouse

The demand for industrial and warehouse properties is heavily influenced by the strength of the overall economy, prospects for growth, and import and export activity. Leases for industrial and warehouse properties may be structured as net leases, gross leases or leases with expense reimbursements.

Retail

The demand for retail space is primarily influenced by consumers' willingness to spend, which in turn is influenced by the strength of the overall economy, job growth, population growth, and savings rates.

Lease terms for retail space are influenced by the quality of the property as well as by the size and importance of the tenant.

Multifamily

The demand for multifamily space depends on demographic factors such as population growth, relevant age segment for renters, and propensity to rent. Demand also depends on the cost of ownership relative to the cost of renting i.e., the ratio of home prices to rents. If home prices rise, people will lean towards renting, and vice versa. Home prices are also influenced by the level of interest rates. Higher mortgage rates make purchases more expensive to finance so people shift towards renting.

Appraisals and Value

Since real estate properties are traded relatively infrequently and are unique, appraisals (estimates of value) are important for performance measurement and evaluation. In most cases, appraisals aim to estimate the market value of a property, which can be defined as the amount a *typical* investor would be willing to pay for the property.

Highest and Best Use

The highest and best use of a vacant site refers to the use that would result in the highest implied value for a property, irrespective of what it is currently being used for. Implied value equals the value of the property after construction less costs to construct the building.

- Value after construction refers to what the property would sell for once it is constructed and leased.
- The cost to construct the building includes profit to the developer for handling construction and getting the property leased.

The value of a piece of land should be based on its highest and best use even if there is an existing building on the site. If there is an existing building that is not the highest and best use, then the value of the building will be lower, not the value of the land.

THE INCOME APPROACH TO VALUATION

The **direct capitalization method** and **discounted cash flow method** are two income approaches used to estimate the value of commercial (income-producing) property. Both these methods focus on **net operating income (NOI)** as a measure of income and a proxy for cash flow.

Net Operating Income

> Rental income at full occupancy
> \+ Other income (such as parking)
> = Potential gross income (PGI)
> – Vacancy and collection loss
> = Effective gross income (EGI)
> – Operating expenses (OE)
> **= Net operating income (NOI)**

- Operating expenses include items such as property taxes, insurance, maintenance, utilities, repairs, and insurance.
- NOI is a before-tax unleveraged measure of income. It is calculated before deducting financing costs and federal income taxes on income generated from the property.
- Sometimes leases may be structured such that tenants are responsible for paying operating expenses. In such cases, those operating expenses are not deducted from income when calculating NOI. In case they have been deducted, the additional income received from the tenants as expense reimbursements would be included in the calculation of NOI.

The Direct Capitalization Method

Under this method, the value of a property is estimated by capitalizing its current NOI at a rate referred to as the **capitalization rate** (or **cap rate**).

The cap rate is applied to first-year NOI, while the discount rate is applied to current and future NOI. Generally, **when income and value are growing constantly at the same rate,** the relationship between the cap rate and discount rate can be expressed as:

$$\text{Cap rate} = \text{Discount rate} - \text{Growth rate}$$

The term going-in cap rate is sometimes used to clarify that the cap rate is based on the first year of ownership.

$$Value = \frac{NOI_1}{Cap\ rate}$$

An estimate of the appropriate cap rate for a property can be obtained from the selling price of similar or comparable properties.

$$Cap\ rate = \frac{NOI_1}{Sale\ price\ of\ comparable\ property}$$

Other Forms of the Income Approach: Gross Income Multiplier

$$Gross\ income\ multiplier = \frac{Selling\ price}{Gross\ income}$$

$$Value\ of\ subject\ property = Gross\ income\ multiplier \times Gross\ income\ of\ subject\ property$$

A drawback of this approach is that it does not explicitly consider vacancy rates and operating expenses.

The Discounted Cash Flow Method (DCF)

Under this method, the value of a property is estimated by projecting income beyond the first year and then discounting the income stream (using an appropriate discount rate).

The investor's total return (discount rate) comes from (1) the return on first-year income (cap rate) and (2) growth in income and value over time (growth rate). If NOI for the property is expected to grow at a constant rate, then the value of the property can be calculated as:

$$Value = \frac{NOI_1}{(r - g)}$$

If NOI is expected to remain constant (growth rate = 0) like a perpetuity, then the cap rate and discount rate will be the same.

The Terminal Capitalization Rate

If the growth rate in NOI is not expected to remain constant, investors forecast (1) NOI for each year during a specific holding period and (2) a terminal value (estimated sale price) at the end of the holding period (instead of projecting NOI into infinity). The sum of the present values of these amounts (discounted at the required rate of return) is used as an estimate of the value of the property.

The direct capitalization method is used to estimate terminal value at the end of the holding period.

$$\text{Terminal value} = \frac{\text{NOI for the first year of ownership for the next investor}}{\text{Terminal cap rate}}$$

The terminal cap rate (also called residual cap rate) is selected at the time of valuation and refers to the cap rate that is applied to expected income for the first year after the anticipated sale of the property.

- The terminal cap rate is usually higher than the going-in cap rate as it is applied to an income stream that is more uncertain. Other reasons for a higher terminal cap rate include higher expected future interest rates (discount rates) or lower growth in NOI.
- The terminal cap rate can be lower than the going-in cap rate if investors expect interest rates to be lower and/or growth in NOI to be higher in the future.

Adopting to Different Lease Structures

- The term and reversion approach splits total value into two components (1) term rent and (2) reversion. The value of each component is appraised separately by applying different capitalization rates.
- The layer method assumes that one component of income is the current contract rent, which will continue indefinitely (like a perpetuity), and then adds a second component which comes from the value of the incremental rent expected to be received after the rent review.

General Steps to a DCF Analysis

- Project income from existing leases
- Make assumptions about lease renewals
- Make assumptions about operating expenses
- Make assumptions about capital expenditures
- Make assumptions about absorption of any vacant space
- Estimate resale value (reversion)
- Select discount rate to find PV of cash flows

Direct Capitalization Method versus Discounted Cash Flow Method

- Under the direct capitalization approach, a capitalization rate or income multiplier is applied to first-year NOI. Any growth in NOI is *implicit* in the capitalization rate. The higher the expected growth, the lower the capitalization rate, and the higher the value of the property.
- Under the DCF approach, the future income pattern, including the effects of growth, is *explicitly* considered. Further, DCF valuation can incorporate other cash flows that might occur in the future and are not reflected in NOI, such as capital expenditures.

Advantages and Disadvantages of the Income Approach

- The advantage of using income approach, such as DCF analysis, is that it considers **all** the cash flows that investors are concerned with. Further, it is not dependent on current transactions from comparable sales as long as an appropriate discount rate is selected.

- The disadvantage of the income approach is that it requires detailed information and assumptions regarding the growth rate of NOI, and detailed lease-by-lease analysis. Further, selecting an appropriate discount rate and terminal cap rate is critical to the valuation because slight changes in these assumptions have a significant impact on the property's estimated value.

THE COST APPROACH

The cost approach is based on the view that a buyer would not pay more for a property than it would cost to purchase the land and construct a comparable building on it. This approach is generally used to value unique properties or those with a specialized use for which it is relatively difficult to obtain market comparables. Under the cost approach, the value of a property is estimated as the sum of:

- The value of the land, which is usually determined using the sales comparison approach; and
- The value of the building, which is based on adjusted replacement cost.

Replacement cost refers to the cost of constructing the building today using current construction costs and standards. This replacement cost is then *adjusted* for different types of depreciation (loss in value) to arrive at adjusted or depreciated replacement cost.

The different types of depreciation include:

- Physical deterioration: This refers to the physical wear and tear of the property as it ages over time.
  - Curable physical deterioration refers to a problem whose fixing/repairing will add at least as much to the value of the building as it costs to repair. The cost of fixing curable items is deducted from replacement cost.
  - Incurable physical deterioration refers to a problem whose cost of repair would exceed the increase in value resulting from the repair, making it unfeasible to fix the problem. Since the costs of repairing such deterioration are not actually borne (since the problem is not repaired) analysts account for the affect of the property's age on its value through a depreciation charge. This depreciation charge is based on the effective age of the property relative to its economic life. The loss from incurable physical deterioration (depreciation) is estimated by applying this ratio to replacement cost *after* deducting the cost of curable physical deterioration.
- Functional obsolescence: This refers to the loss in the value of a building because its current design is not ideally suited for its intended use.
- External obsolescence: This refers to the loss in the value of a building due to external factors, such as the location of the property or economic conditions.
  - Locational obsolescence occurs when the location of the building is no longer optimal for its intended use.
  - Economic obsolescence occurs when it is not feasible to construct a new building under current economic conditions. This can happen when rent levels are not high enough to generate a value for a newly constructed property that is at least equal to development costs (including profit to the developer).

Advantages and Disadvantages of the Cost Approach

- The cost approach can be used to determine the upper limit on the value of a property as an investor would never pay more for a property than it costs to purchase the land and construct a comparable building.
- The main disadvantage of this approach is that it is difficult to estimate depreciation for a property that is older and/or has much obsolescence. Therefore, the cost approach is most appropriate for newer properties that have a relatively modern design in a stable market.

THE SALES COMPARISON APPROACH

The sales comparison approach is based on the view that the value of a property depends on what investors are paying for similar properties in the current market. Since it is impossible to find a comparable property that (1) is exactly the same as the subject property in all respects and (2) is sold on the same date as the date of appraisal of the subject property, adjustments must be made for differences between the subject property and comparable properties relating to size, age, location, property condition and market conditions at the time of sale. The idea is to determine what comparable properties would have sold for if they were like the subject property.

The quality of the value estimate from the sales comparison approach depends on the number of recent transactions involving comparable properties. Application of this approach is relatively easy when the market is active, but difficult when the market is weak. Even in an active market, it might be difficult to find comparable sales for some properties (e.g., regional malls and special purpose properties).

Further, the sales comparison approach assumes that purchasers behave rationally (i.e., the prices they pay reflect current market values). However, this may not always be the case as the investment value of a property to a particular investor may exceed its market value. Further, in times of exuberance when real estate markets are in a "bubble," the sales comparison approach can lead to inflated valuations, especially when considered in light of values in more "normal" market conditions.

The sales comparison approach is generally used to value single-family homes for which income is not relevant and there is availability of sales data for reasonable comparisons.

Due Diligence in Private Equity Real Estate Investment

Due diligence usually includes the following:

- Review of the lease and history of rental payments.
- Review of operating expenses by obtaining copies of bills (e.g., utility bills).
- Review of cash flow statements of the previous owner.
- An environmental inspection to ensure that there are no contaminant materials on the site.
- A physical/engineering inspection to ensure that there are no structural issues with the property and to check the condition of the building systems, structures, foundation, and adequacy of utilities.

- Review of ownership history to ensure that there are no issues related to the seller's ability to transfer free and clear title that is not subject to any previously unidentified liens.
- Review of service and maintenance agreements.
- A property survey to ensure that any physical improvements are within boundary lines and to identify any easements that may affect value.
- Verification that the property is compliant with zoning, environmental regulations, parking ratios, etc.
- Verification of payment of property taxes, insurance, special assessments, etc.

While due diligence can be costly, it lowers the risk of unidentified legal and physical problems.

PRIVATE EQUITY REAL ESTATE INVESTMENT INDICES

Appraisal-Based Indices

These indices rely on appraisals of value (rather than prices from actual transactions) to estimate changes in the value because real estate transactions involving a specific property occur relatively infrequently. Appraisal-based indices combine valuation information from individual properties to provide a measure of market movements.

The return for all the properties is calculated as:

$$\text{Return} = \frac{\text{NOI} - \text{Capital expenditures} + (\text{Ending market value} - \text{Beginning market value})}{\text{Beginning market value}}$$

- Beginning and ending market values are based on appraisals of the properties.
- The return computed from the formula is the holding period return or the single-period IRR.

The returns on all the properties in the index are then value-weighted to get the index return.

Appraisal-based indices allow investors to compare the performance of real estate relative to other asset classes such as stocks and bonds. Further, the quarterly returns can be used to measure risk (standard deviation). Investors may also use appraisal-based indices to benchmark returns on their real estate portfolios.

One of the disadvantages associated with appraisal-based indices is the appraisal lag as appraised values tend to lag transaction prices when there are sudden shifts in the market.

Transaction-Based Indices

These indices are based on actual transactions rather than appraised values.

- A repeat sales index relies on the repeat sales of the same property. The idea is that if a specific property is sold twice in a given period, its change in value between the two sale dates indicates how market conditions have changed over time. Regression analysis is then used to allocate the change in value to each quarter.

- A hedonic index requires only one sale (instead of repeat sales of the same property). In order to account for the fact that different properties are being sold each quarter, it includes (independent) variables in the regression that control for differences in the characteristics of each property, such as size, age, quality of construction, and location. The unexplained variation in the regression reflects the impact of changes in overall market conditions on values.

Transaction-based indices are considered better than appraisal-based indices. However, the need to use statistical techniques to estimate the index can lead to random elements in the observations (noise).

Private Market Real Estate Debt

The amount of debt an investor can obtain to finance the purchase of commercial real estate is usually limited by (1) the loan-to-value-ratio (LTV ratio) or (2) the debt service coverage ratio (DSCR), depending on which measure results in a lower loan amount.

$$\text{LTV ratio} = \frac{\text{Loan amount}}{\text{Appraised value}}$$

$$\text{DSCR} = \frac{\text{NOI}}{\text{Debt service}}$$

Debt service (also referred to as the loan payment) includes both interest payments and principal payments (if required).

When investors use debt to finance the purchase of a property, they often calculate the equity dividend rate to measure how much cash flow they are getting as a percentage of their equity investment. This is also referred to as the cash-on-cash return.

$$\text{Equity dividend rate} = \frac{\text{First year cash flow}}{\text{Equity investment}}$$

PUBLICLY TRADED REAL ESTATE SECURITIES
Cross-Reference to CFA Institute Assigned Reading #43

Investment Characteristics of REITs

Exemption from income taxes: REITs are typically exempt from income taxes at the corporate/trust level if (1) a specified majority of their income and assets relate to income-producing property and (2) they distribute all their potentially taxable income to shareholders.

High income distributions: Due to the fact that REITs must distribute virtually all their income to shareholders in order to qualify for income tax exemption, they typically offer higher dividend yields than most publicly traded equities.

Relatively low volatility of reported income: Due to the fact that they must generate most of the earnings from income-producing property (rental income) to qualify for income tax exemption, REITs typically use conservative, rental-property focused business models, which result in relatively stable revenue streams (except in the case of hotel REITs).

More frequent secondary equity offerings compared with industrial companies: Due to the distribution requirement, REITs are not able to retain earnings to finance growth. Therefore, they rely on new equity issues to finance property acquisitions.

Advantages of Publicly Traded Equity Real Estate Securities

- Greater liquidity
- Lower investment requirements
- Limited liability
- Access to superior quality properties and a range of properties
- Active professional management
- Diversification
- Protection

Advantages of Investing in REITs as Opposed to Publicly Traded REOCs

- Exemption from taxes
- Earnings predictability
- High income payout ratios and yields

Advantage of Investing in REOCs as Opposed to REITs

- Operating flexibility

Disadvantages of Publicly Traded Equity Real Estate Securities

- Taxation
- Control
- Costs
- Stock market determined pricing
- Structural conflicts
- Moderate income growth potential
- Potential for forced equity issuance at disadvantaged pricing

Considerations in Analysis and Due Diligence of Equity REITs

- Remaining lease term
- Inflation protection
- Market rent analysis
- Cost of re-leasing space
- Tenant concentration
- Availability of new competitive supply
- Balance sheet/leverage analysis
- Management

Characteristics of REIT Property Subtypes

REIT Type	Economic Value Determinants	Investment Characteristics
Retail	• Growth in national GDP • Retail sales growth • Job creation	• Stable revenue stream over the medium term
Office	• Growth in national GDP • Job creation	• Long lease terms • Stable year-to-year income
Residential	• Growth in national GDP • Population growth • Job creation	• Short term one-year leases • Relatively stable demand • Typically structured as gross leases
Health care	• Growth in national GDP • Population growth	• REITs lease facilities to health care providers. • Typically structured as net leases
Industrial	• Growth in national GDP • Retail sales growth • Population growth	• Less cyclical than some other REIT types • Typically structured as long-term net leases • Can be preleased
Hotel	• Growth in national GDP • Job creation • New space supply relative to demand.	• REITs lease facilities to taxable subsidiaries • Volatile income
Storage	• Growth in national GDP • Population growth • Job creation	• Space is leased under gross leases and on a monthly basis

Principal Risks	Due Diligence Considerations
• Trends in consumer spending	• Rental rates and sales per square foot
• Changes in office market vacancy and rental rates • Dislocations between supply and demand • Office industry cycle	• New space under construction • Quality of office space • Site location and access to public transport • Business conditions
• Competition • Tenant inducements • Regional economic strength and weakness • Effects of inflation on operating costs • Taxes and maintenance cost	• Demographics and income trends • Age and competitive appeal • Cost and availability • Rent controls • Fuel and energy costs
• Demographics • Government funding • Construction cycles • Financial conditions of operators • Tenant litigation • Dislocations between supply and demand	• Operating trends • Government funding trends • Litigation settlements • Insurance costs • Development of competing facilities
• Shifts in the composition of local and national industrial bases and trade.	• Tenants' requirements • Obsolescence of existing space • Need for new types of space • Access to transportation links • Trends in local supply and demand
• Changes in business and leisure travel • Dislocations between supply and demand	• Occupancy, room rates, and profit margins relative to industry averages • Revenue per available room (RevPAR) • Trends in forward bookings • Maintenance expenditures • New construction in local markets • Financial leverage
• Ease of entry can lead to overbuilding	• Construction of competing facilities • Trends in housing sales • Local demographic trends • Business start-up activity • Seasonal trends in demand for storage facilities

AI

Economic Value Determinants of REITs

Table 1: Importance of Factors Affecting Economic Value for Various Property Types[1]

	National GDP Growth	Job Creation	Retail Sales Growth	Population Growth	New Space Supply vs. Demand
Retail	1	3	2	4	4
Office	1	2	5	4	3
Industrial	1	5	2	3	4
Multifamily	1	2	5	2	4
Storage	1	3	5	2	4
Health care	1	4	5	2	3
Hotels	1	2	5	4	3

Note 1: = most important, 5 = least important
Source: Based on data from the authors' research

The largest driver of economic value for all REIT types is growth in the overall economy or national GDP. Economic growth leads to the creation of more jobs, which leads to higher demand for office space. Economic growth also leads to more disposable income and higher demand for multifamily accommodation, hotel rooms, storage space, and retail space.

Principal Risks

Risks tend to be highest for REITs that concentrate on properties (1) where demand for rental space can fluctuate widely in the short term (especially hotels), and (2) in which dislocations between demand and supply are likely to happen (especially offices, hotels, and healthcare). Further, a REIT's risk profile is also determined by the quality and location of the properties it holds, and its leasing and financing status.

VALUATION: NET ASSET VALUE APPROACH

Analysts generally use **net asset value per share (NAVPS)** for valuing REITs and REOCs. NAVPS is the amount (on a per share basis) by which the current market value of a company's assets exceeds the current market value of its liabilities.

In cases where reliable appraisals are not available, analysts estimate the value of operating real estate by capitalizing net operating income (NOI). The cap rate is estimated based on recent comparable transactions.

$$\text{Capitalizaton rate} = \frac{\text{NOI of a comparable property}}{\text{Total value of comparable property}}$$

In order to compute expected **NOI for the coming year**, the following adjustments must be performed on current year actual NOI:

- **Non-cash rents** should be deducted from current period NOI.
- Current-year NOI must also be increased to reflect a full year's rent for properties acquired during the year.
- An expected growth rate may then be applied to estimate NOI for the coming year.

Once next year's expected NOI is capitalized at the appropriate cap rate to compute the value of the REIT's operating real estate, the value of other tangible assets (e.g., prepaid expenses, cash, accounts receivable, land for future development, etc.) is added, and the value of liabilities subtracted, to compute the REITs total net asset value. This total net asset value is then divided by the total number of shares outstanding to calculate NAVPS.

Important Considerations in a NAV-Based Approach to Valuing REITS

- NAV reflects the value of the REIT's assets to a private market buyer, which is usually different from the value that public equity investors ascribe to the business.
- NAV implicitly treats a company as an individual asset or as a static pool of assets. This treatment is not consistent with the going-concern assumption.
- NAV estimates can be quite subjective in times when property markets are illiquid and/or there are few comparable transactions.

VALUATION: RELATIVE VALUATION (PRICE MULTIPLE) APPROACH

Analysts commonly use (1) the price to funds from operations ratio, (2) the price to adjusted funds from operations ratio and (3) enterprise value to EBITDA ratio to value shares of REITs and REOCs.

Funds from operations (FFO) is calculated as:

Accounting net earnings
Add: Depreciation charges on real estate
Add: Deferred tax charges
Add (Less): Losses (gains) from sale of property and debt restructuring
Funds from operations

Adjusted funds from operations (AFFO) (also referred to as **funds available for distribution** or **cash available for distribution**) is considered a more accurate measure of current economic income. It is calculated as:

Funds from operations
Less: Non-cash rent
Less: Maintenance-type capital expenditures and leasing costs
Adjusted funds from operations

AFFO is preferred over FFO as it takes into account the capital expenditures necessary to maintain the economic income of a property portfolio. Practically however, FFO is more commonly used because AFFO is subject to more variation and error in estimation.

For a REIT, EBITDA can be computed as NOI minus general and administrative (G&A) expenses.

Factors Affecting Valuation Multiples

- Expectations for growth in FFO/AFFO
- Risk associated with the underlying real estate
- Risk associated with the company's capital structures and access to capital

P/FFO and P/AFFO Multiples: Advantages and Drawbacks

Advantages:

- Earnings multiples are widely accepted in evaluating shares across global stock markets and industries.
- They enable portfolio managers to put the valuation of REITs and REOCs into context with other investment alternatives.
- Estimates for FFO are readily available through market data providers.
- They can be used in conjunction with expected growth and leverage levels to deepen the relative analysis among REITs and REOCs.

Drawbacks:

- They may not capture the intrinsic value of all real estate assets (e.g., land parcels and empty buildings that are currently not producing any income) held by the REIT or REOC.
- P/FFO does not adjust for the impact of recurring capital expenditures needed to keep properties operating smoothly.
- New revenue recognition rules and increased levels of one-time gains and accounting charges in recent times have made P/FFO and P/AFFO more difficult to calculate and compare across companies.

VALUATION: DISCOUNTED CASH FLOW APPROACH

REITs and REOCs return a significant portion of their income to their investors in the form of dividends, which makes dividend discount models appropriate for valuing their shares.

Considerations when Forecasting Long-Term Growth Rates

- Internal growth potential resulting from rent increases over time.
- Impact of investment activities (e.g., acquisitions and new development) on the long-term growth rate.
- Impact of changes in capital structure on growth.
- Contribution of retaining and reinvesting a portion of free cash flow on the growth rate.

PRIVATE EQUITY VALUATION
Cross-Reference to CFA Institute Assigned Reading #44

Valuation Methodologies[1]

Valuation Technique	Brief Description	Application
Income approach: Discounted cash flows (DCF)	Value is obtained by discounting expected future cash at an appropriate cost of capital.	Generally applies across the broad spectrum of company stages. Given the emphasis on expected cash flows, this methodology provides the most relevant results when applied to companies with a sufficient operating history. Therefore, most applicable to companies operating from the expansion up to the maturity phase.
Relative values: Earnings multiples	Application of an earnings multiple to the earnings of a portfolio company. The earnings multiple is frequently obtained from the average of a group of public companies operating in a similar business and of a comparable size. Commonly used multiples include:Price/Earnings (P/E), Enterprise Value/EBITDA, Enterprise Value/Sales.	Generally applies to companies with a significant operating history and predictable stream of cash flows. May also apply with caution to companies operating at the expansion stage. Rarely applies to early stage or start-up companies.
Real option	The right to undertake a business decision (call or put option). Requires judgmental assumptions about key operational parameters.	Generally applies to situations in which the management or shareholders have significant flexibility in making radically different strategic decisions (i.e., option to undertake or abandon a high-risk, high-return project). Therefore, generally applies to some companies operating at the seed or start-up phase.
Replacement cost	Estimated cost to recreate the business as it stands as of the valuation date.	Generally applies to early (seed and start-up) stage companies or companies operating at the development stage and generating negative cash flows. Rarely applies to mature companies as it is difficult to estimate the cost to recreate a company with a long operating history. For example, it would be difficult to recreate a long established brand like Coca-Cola, whereas the replacement cost methodology may be used to estimate the brand value for a recently launched beverage (R&D expenses, marketing costs, etc.).

1 - Exhibit 2, pg 138, Vol 6, CFA Program Curriculum 2018

Important Considerations in Private Equity Valuation

- How the PE firm can improve the business's financing, operations, management, and marketing.
- Exogenous factors and drivers of business value.
- Valuation of control premium.
- Determination of discounts for lack of liquidity and marketability.
- Evaluation of country risk.

Value Creation in Private Equity

- PE companies have the expertise to re-engineer and reorganize investee companies.
- They are more capable of raising higher levels of debt as they have a reputation for having raised and successfully repaid high levels of debt in past transactions.
- They are better at aligning interest of management with their own and incentivizing management to focus more on long-term performance.

Aligning Management Interests with Those of the PE Firm

Private equity firms retain control over the management of investee companies through the following control mechanisms:

- Results-driven management pay packages.
- Contractual provisions (e.g., tag-along, drag-along rights) that enable management to participate in the upside in value from a successful exit from the portfolio company.
- Provisions that ensure that the PE firm attains control through board representation if the company experiences a major corporate event (e.g., takeover, restructuring, IPO, bankruptcy, or liquidation).
- Non-compete clauses that restrict founders of portfolio companies from launching competing companies for a predefined period of time.
- Clauses that entitle the PE firm to preference dividends, and guarantee the PE firm a multiple of its original investment in the company before other shareholders receive any returns.
- Clauses that make certain important matters (e.g., changes in business plan, acquisitions and divestures) subject to approval or veto by the PE firm.
- Mechanisms (known as earn-outs) that link the acquisition price paid by the PE firm to the portfolio company's future financial performance.

Contrasting Valuation in Venture Capital and Buyout Settings[2]

Buyout Investments	Venture Capital Investments
Steady and predictable cash flows	Low cash flow predictability, cash flow projections may not be realistic
Excellent market position (can be a niche player)	Lack of market history, new market and possibly unproven future market (early stage venture)
Significant asset base (may serve as basis for collateral lending)	Weak asset base
Strong and experienced management team	Newly formed management team with strong individual track record as entrepreneurs
Extensive use of leverage consisting of a large proportion of senior debt and significant layer of junior and/or mezzanine debt	Primarily equity funded. Use of leverage is rare and very limited
Risk is measurable (mature businesses, long operating history)	Assessment of risk is difficult because of new technologies, new markets, lack of operating history
Predictable exit (secondary buyout, sale to a strategic buyer, IPO)	Exit difficult to anticipate (IPO, trade sale, secondary venture sale)
Established products	Technological breakthrough but route to market yet to be proven
Potential for restructuring and cost reduction	Significant cash burn rate required to ensure company development and commercial viability
Low working capital requirement	Expanding capital requirement if in the growth phase
Buyout firm typically conducts full blown due diligence approach before investing in the target firm (financial, strategic, commercial, legal, tax, environmental)	Venture capital firm tends to conduct primarily a technology and commercial due diligence before investing; financial due diligence is limited as portfolio companies have no or very little operating history.
Buyout firm monitors cash flow management, strategic, and business planning	Venture capital firm monitors achievement of milestones defined in business plan and growth management

(Table continued on next page...)

2 - Exhibit 3, pg 149, Vol 5, CFA Program Curriculum 2018

Buyout Investments	Venture Capital Investments
• Returns of investment portfolios are generally characterized by lower variance across returns from underlying investments; bankruptcies are rare events	• Returns of investment portfolios are generally characterized by very high returns from a limited number of highly successful investments and a significant number of write-offs from low performing investments or failures
• Large buyout firms are generally significant players in capital markets	• Venture capital firms tend to be much less active in capital markets
• Most transactions are auctions, involving multiple potential acquirers	• Many transactions are "proprietary," being the result of relationships between venture capitalists and entrepreneurs
• Strong performing buyout firms tend to have a better ability to raise larger funds after they have successfully raised their first funds	• Venture capital firms tend to be less scalable relative to buyout firms; the increase in size of subsequent funds tend to be less significant
• Variable revenue to the general partner (GP) at buyout firms generally comprise the following three sources: carried interest, transaction fees, and monitoring fees.	• Carried interest (participation in profits) is generally the main source of variable revenue to the general partner at venture capital firms; transaction and monitoring fees are rare in practice

Private Equity Valuation Techniques

There are six techniques that are generally used to value private equity portfolio companies.

- The income approach (discounted cash flows) is generally applied to companies with sufficient operating history (typically expansion to mature stage companies).
- Relative valuation (using earnings multiples) is generally applied to companies with significant operating history and a predictable stream of cash flows.
- Real option valuation is applied in situations where management/shareholders have significant flexibility in decision-making. It is generally applied to companies in the seed or start-up phase.
- Replacement cost is applied to early-stage companies that are in the development stage and are currently generating negative cash flow. It rarely applies to mature companies.
- The venture capital method and the leveraged buyout model are discussed later in this reading.

Using Market Data in Private Company Valuation

- Valuation ratios (e.g., EV/EBITDA) for publicly traded comparable firms are used to value private companies.
- The WACC for public companies is used to estimate the discount rate when valuing private companies (in DCF approaches).
- The beta of public comparable companies is adjusted for financial and operating leverage to estimate beta for private companies.
- The terminal value of an investment in a private company is determined based on trading multiples in public markets.

Challenges in Private Equity Valuation

- Forecasting the company's future profitability and cash flows based on expectations of exogenous factors (e.g., interest rates, exchange rates, etc.) and value drivers for the business (sales margins, etc.).
- Incorporating ways through which the PE firm can enhance financing, operations, management and marketing of the portfolio company into those forecasts.
- Determining the appropriate (1) premium for control, (2) lack of liquidity discount (as investments in portfolio companies are typically not readily convertible into cash), and (3) lack of marketability discount (as investors usually face restrictions on the sale of shares).
- Estimating the country risk premium (when valuing companies in emerging markets).

Valuation Issues in Buyout Transactions

The LBO Model

In LBO transactions buyers use a significant amount of debt to finance their purchase of the target company. The LBO model is used to determine the impact of capital structure, purchase price, and various other factors on expected return for the private equity firm from the transaction. It has three main inputs:

- Forecasted cash flows of the target company.
- Expected returns for providers of various types of capital.
- The amount of financing available for the transaction.

Value creation comes from:

- Earnings growth from operational improvements.
- Multiple expansion depending on potential exit.
- Optimal financial leverage and debt repayment with operating cash flow before exit.

Exit value = Initial cost + Earnings growth + Multiple expansion + Debt reduction

Venture Capital Transactions

- Pre-money valuation (PRE) refers to the agreed value of the company prior to a round of financing.
- Post-money valuation (POST) refers to the value of the company after the round of financing.

$$POST = PRE + I$$

The proportionate ownership of the VC investor is calculated as: I / POST

Importance of Exit Routes

- Because private equity investments are not very liquid, it is extremely important for private equity investors to consider exit strategies before making an investment.
- The timing of exit also has an impact on firm value and therefore, is an important consideration.

Types of Exit

Initial Public Offerings (IPO)

An IPO is an appropriate exit route for large companies with excellent growth prospects.

Advantages:

- Generally results in highest valuation for the company.
- Increases liquidity of company shares.
- Gives the company access to large amounts of capital.
- Enables the company to attract higher-caliber managers.

Disadvantages:

- The process of taking the company public can be quite cumbersome.
- The company is left with less flexibility.
- It entails significant costs.

Secondary Market Sale

This involves a private sale of an ownership stake in the company to other financial or strategic investors.

Advantages:

- Typically results in highest valuation for the company outside of an IPO.
- Specialized PE firms can create additional value for the company.

Management Buyout (MBO)

This involves the purchase of the company by its management. Although this method results in the best alignment of interests, the company suffers from reduced flexibility due to significant financial leverage.

Liquidation

This involves an outright sale of the company's assets and results in the lowest value for the company.

Private Equity Fund Structures

One of the most common forms of private equity structures is the limited partnership.

- Limited partners (LPs) are the providers of funds that are invested in target companies. They are only liable for losses up to the amount of funds invested by them.
- General partners (GPs) manage the fund and are liable for all of the firm's debt.

Private Equity Fund Terms

Economic Terms

- Management fees
- Transaction fees
- Carried interest
- Ratchet
- Hurdle rate
- Target fund size
- Vintage year
- Term of the fund

Corporate Governance Terms

- Key man clause
- Disclosure and confidentiality
- Clawback provision
- Distribution waterfall
- Tag-along, drag-along rights
- No-fault divorce clause
- Removal for "cause"
- Investment restrictions
- Co-investment

Due Diligence Investigations by Potential Investors

Prior to investing in a private equity fund, prospective investors should conduct a thorough due diligence of the fund because:

- Their investments are locked in for the long term.
- Returns of the funds tend to persist over time.
- The difference in returns between well-performing funds and poor-performing funds is significant.

Determining a Private Equity Fund's Value

A fund's NAV can be determined in the following ways:

- At cost with significant adjustments for subsequent financing events or deterioration.
- At lower of cost or market value.
- By revaluing a portfolio company whenever a new financing round involving new investors takes place.
- At cost with no interim adjustment until exit.
- With a discount for restricted securities.
- Marked to market by reference to a peer group of public comparables and applying illiquidity discounts.

AI

Issues in Calculating a PE Fund's NAV

- If value is only adjusted when a new round of financing occurs, the NAV will be outdated if there is an extended period with no financing round.
- The value of investments in target companies cannot be calculated with certainty before exit as there is no market for them.
- Undrawn LP commitments represent liabilities of the LP, but they are not accounted for in the calculation of NAV.
- Market multiples that are used to value portfolio companies may be inflated during bubbles.
- Valuations are usually performed by GPs.

Differences between Private and Public firms

- Unlike public firms, whose shares are available for purchase to the general public, private equity investments are often only available to qualified investors.
- In public firms, the capital acquired from the sale of shares is almost immediately invested in the business. On the other hand, the capital committed by investors to private equity firms is drawn down in stages as it is invested in target companies.
- Private equity firms typically experience the J-curve effect in their earnings. This refers to the low or negative earnings in the early years of the private equity fund, followed by increased earnings in the later years.

Risks and Costs of Investing in Private Equity

Risks

- Illiquidity of investments
- Unquoted investments
- Competition for attractive investment opportunities
- Reliance on the management of investee companies (agency risk) Loss of capital
- Adverse impact of government regulations
- Taxation risk
- Valuation of investments
- Lack of investment capital
- Lack of diversification
- Market risk, i.e., adverse impact of changes in general market conditions (interest rate, currency exchange rates, etc.).

Costs

- Transaction fees
- Investment vehicle fund setup costs
- Administrative costs
- Audit costs
- Management and performance fees
- Dilution
- Placement fees

Evaluating Fund Performance

Internal Rate of Return (IRR)

- Gross IRR reflects cash flows between the private equity fund and its portfolio companies and is thus a relevant measure for evaluating the investment management team's performance.
- Net IRR reflects cash flows between the private equity fund and LPs and is thus a relevant measure for return to investors.

IRR should be interpreted with caution because investments in private equity are quite illiquid, while IRR assumes that interim cash flows are reinvested at the IRR.

Multiples

- PIC (Paid-in capital): Ratio of invested capital to committed capital.
- DPI (Distributed to paid-in): Ratio of cumulative distributions paid to LPs to cumulative invested capital.
- RVPI (Residual value to paid-in): Ratio of LPs' holdings held with the fund to cumulative invested capital.
- TVPI (Total value to paid-in): Sum of DPI and RVPI.

Qualitative Measures

- Analysis of investments realized since inception, evaluating all successes and failures.
- Analysis of unrealized investments, highlighting red flags and expected times to exit each investment.
- Cash flow forecasts at the portfolio company level as well as for the entire portfolio.
- Analysis of portfolio valuation, NAV, and audited financial statements.

The Basic Venture Capital Method (in Terms of NPV)

Step 1: Determine the post-money valuation.

$$\text{Post-money value} = \frac{\text{Exit value}}{(1+\text{Required rate of return})^{\text{Number of years to exists}}}$$

Step 2: Determine the pre-money valuation.

$$\text{Pre-money value} = \text{Post-money value} - \text{Investment}$$

Step 3: Calculate the ownership percentage of the VC investor.

$$\text{Ownership proportion of VC investor} = \frac{\text{Investment}}{\text{Post-money value}}$$

Step 4: Calculate the number of shares to be issued to the VC investor.

$$\text{Shares to be issued} = \frac{\text{Proportion of venture capitalist investment} \times \text{Shares held by company founders}}{\text{Proportion of investment of company founders}}$$

Step 5: Calculate the price of shares.

$$\text{Price per share} = \frac{\text{Amount of venture capital investment}}{\text{Number of shares issued to venture capital investment}}$$

Venture Capital Method (in Terms of the IRR)

The venture capital method can also be explained in terms of the IRR. Whether based on NPV or IRR, the venture capital method gives exactly the same answer. The IRR method involves the following steps.

Step 1: Calculate the future wealth required by the VC investor to achieve its desired IRR.

$$\text{Required wealth} = \text{Investment} \times (1 + \text{IRR})^{\text{Number of years to exit}}$$

Step 2: Calculate the ownership percentage of venture capital investor.

$$\text{Ownership proportion} = \text{Required wealth} / \text{Exit value}$$

Step 3: Calculate the number of shares to be issued to the venture capital investor.

$$\text{Shares to be issued} = \frac{\text{Proportion of venture capitalist investment} \times \text{Shares held by company founders}}{\text{Proportion of investment of company founders}}$$

Step 4: Calculate the price of shares.

$$\text{Price per share} = \frac{\text{Amount of venture capital investment}}{\text{Number of shares issued to venture capital investors}}$$

Step 5: Determine the post-money valuation.

$$\text{Post-money value} = \text{Investment} / \text{VC's ownership proportion}$$

Step 6: Determine the pre-money valuation.

$$\text{Pre-money valuation} = \text{Post-money valuation} - \text{Investment}$$

Venture Capital Method with Multiple Rounds of Financing

When there are 2 rounds of financing, the venture capital method requires the following steps:

Step 1: Define appropriate compound interest rates between each financing round.

Step 2: Determine the post-money valuation after the second round.

Step 3: Determine the pre-money valuation after the second round.

Step 4: Determine the post-money valuation after the first round.

Step 5: Determine the pre-money valuation after the first round.

Step 6: Determine the required ownership percentage for second round investors.

Step 7: Determine the required ownership percentage for first round investors. Note that this is not their final ownership percentage as their equity interest will be diluted in the second round.

Step 8: Determine the number of shares that must be issued to first round investors for them to attain their desired ownership percentage.

Step 9: Determine price per share in the first round.

Step 10: Determine the number of shares at the time of the second round.

Step 11: Determine the number of shares that must be issued to second round investors for them to attain their desired ownership percentage.

Step 12: Determine price per share in the second round

Accounting for Risks

Venture capitalists typically apply very high discount rates when evaluating target companies for the following reasons:

- VC firms must be compensated for the significant non-diversifiable risk inherent in portfolio companies.
- Estimates of terminal value do not necessarily reflect *expected earnings*. They reflect future earnings in some kind of *success scenario*.

These risks may be accounted for in the following two ways:

- By adjusting the discount rate.

$$\text{Adjusted discount rate} = \frac{1 + \text{Unadjusted discount rate}}{1 - \text{Probability of failure}} - 1$$

- By adjusting the terminal value using scenario analysis.

AI

COMMODITIES AND COMMODITY DERIVATIVES: AN INTRODUCTION
Cross-Reference to CFA Institute Assigned Reading #45

Studies have shown that commodities as an asset class have historically had:

- A low average return correlation with stocks and bonds
- Inflation-hedging qualities

COMMODITY SECTORS

Energy

Crude Oil

- Crude oil has natural storage space under the ground and will be extracted only if the marginal cost of extraction is less than the marginal benefit of selling it.
- It has limited use by itself. It must be extracted, transported, and refined into useful products.
- Weather has only a temporary impact on crude oil supply.
- Economic growth is an important factor that drives crude oil demand.
- Technology affects oil usage in three forms: the level of technology for extraction, the level of technology and efficiency in which oil is transformed into useful products, and the efficiency with which these products are used by the engines that burn them.
- Political instability can cause significant reductions in the supply of oil for two reasons: Oil cannot be extracted during these conflicts, and transportation routes become unreliable.

Natural Gas

- Transportation and storage costs tend to be higher for natural gas than for other commodities.
- Its supply is not directly driven by the demand for gas, but rather by oil demand.
- Key determinants of supply and demand include the weather, the technology in the electrical generation process, greenhouse gas emission concerns, and general economic conditions.
- Natural gas can be consumed soon after extraction from the ground.

Refined Products (e.g., Gasoline and Heating Oil)

- The supply of and demand for refined products depend on the weather, in terms of both major events like hurricanes and also extreme heat or cold that will increase demand.
- Supply conditions depend on technology to extract, store, and transport these products, while greenhouse gas emission concerns can lessen demand.
- The life cycle of refined products has a number of potential processing steps depending on the quality of crude oil input and the relative demand for the various products.

Energy Life Cycle

- Extraction takes between 50 and 100 days.
- Transportation takes between 1 and 10 days. Trains, ships, planes, trucks, and pipes are used to transport both crude oil and natural gas.
- Storage occurs over a few days to months. Oil and natural gas can be stored almost anywhere in the world.
- Trading occurs only with natural gas at this point because it is ready to be consumed at this stage.
- Refining takes between three and five days as crude oil is converted to gasoline, propane, and heating oil.
- Additional transportation and trading take between 5 and 20 days to move the refined products to their ultimate consumption destination.
- Refineries and pipelines are extremely expensive to build, but they are still not as expensive as the costs of oil exploration.

Grains (e.g., Corn, Wheat, and Soya Beans)

- Grains are global commodities.
- The supply of and demand for grains depend on weather, disease, pests, and technology and politics (genetic modification, biofuel substitution).
- Grain life cycles typically involve the following steps:
  - Planting
  - Growth
  - Pod, head, or ear formation
  - Harvest

Industrial (Base) Metals (e.g., Copper, Nickel, Lead, and Zinc)

- These commodities are used in industrial production.
- Their demand is directly affected by gross domestic product (GDP) growth.
- Most can be stored for several years, so supply is not generally influenced by weather.
- Demand, however, can be influenced by weather and seasonal factors.
- Other influences on price include politics, development decisions, and environmental concerns.

Precious Metals (e.g., Gold, Silver, and Platinum)

- Investors tend to buy precious metals as hedges against inflation.
- Precious metals also tend to perform well in times of national government deficits.
- Precious metals can be stored almost indefinitely. Demand mostly depends on inflation expectations, fund flows, and commercial production.
- Technology is very important on the demand side, especially for platinum as it used in a variety of production processes.
- While total supply of these metals is fixed, available supply depends on the willingness of mining firms to extract them.

Life Cycle for Industrial and Precious Metals

- Extraction
- Grinding

- Concentrating
- Roasting
- Smelting
- Converting
- Electro refining
- Storage and logistics

Note that:

- The life cycle of both precious and industrial metals is very flexible, as the ore, as well as the finished products, can be stored for long periods of time if stored properly.
- Realizing economies of scale is very important for smelter and processing plants to be viable in the long run.
- Firms in this industry will perform better during economic expansions because the increased demand helps cover their huge costs. During recessions, however, these firms are particularly susceptible to losses in cash flow because it is not easy for them to reduce or shut down operations.

Livestock (e.g., Cattle, Poultry, and Hogs)

- Both supply and demand depend on grain market activity and GDP. Expanding economies with significant grain production tend to have large livestock supplies. Livestock storage costs depend on grain prices necessary to keep the animals healthy and growing.
- Livestock prices may fall over the short term when grain prices are high, and may rise when grain prices are low.
- Weather and disease affect the health of any herd or flock and can significantly change prices.
- The time to maturity for livestock depends on the type of animal.
- Once slaughtered, there is high concern for spoilage, even as firms have developed efficient freezing systems.
- Improvements in technology have allowed the transportation of frozen meat globally, which has increased the global demand for the final product.

Cash Crops (e.g., Coffee and Sugar)

- Storage costs can be high because cash crops lose value as their freshness fades.
- Global economic growth influences demand and supply, as do weather, disease, and the popularity of consumption.
- The following steps are relevant for the coffee life cycle:
  - Planting
  - Harvesting
  - Removal of husk and fruit
  - Bagging
  - Transportation to buyers
  - Delivery to retailers

COMMODITY VALUATION AND MARKETS

- Commodity ownership is quite different from debt or equity ownership in that there are no cash flow promises made. Further, commodity ownership entails storage and transportation costs.
- Spot pricing is a function of macroeconomic and microeconomic variables.

- Different commodities have different inherent values depending on their economic use.
- Forward/futures pricing depends on (1) spot value, (2) expected supply and demand conditions, (3) price volatility, and (4) storage and transportation costs.
- While the spot price is typically greater than the forward/futures price (due to storage and transportation costs), this relationship may not hold in certain market conditions.

Commodity Market Participants

- Hedgers have natural spot positions in the commodity and use futures contracts to remove price uncertainty from a future trade.
- Speculators are investors who have strong opinions on future commodity prices. Speculators often take the opposite position from hedgers and can be long or short, depending on their expectations.
- Commodity traders and investors are typically grouped as informed investors, liquidity providers, or arbitrageurs.
  - Informed investors are hedgers or speculators who believe they possess superior knowledge about commodity prices.
  - Liquidity providers charge a premium for providing capital to the futures market and do so whenever producers or consumers experience a rush to buy or to sell.
  - Arbitrageurs generally have access to physical storage or transportation systems and are able to manage inventory to generate an arbitrage profit.
- Commodity futures exchanges provide financial services to international businesses and offer the support system to enable futures trading to operate efficiently. They provide clearinghouses to improve the integrity of the market, and they furnish an outlet for commodity price discovery.
- Commodity market analysts provide a valuable service to all investors by using fundamental and technical analysis on price information, volatility, and supply and demand conditions in futures markets.
- Regulators are government bodies that attempt to improve the quality of markets through development of rules and regulations.

Spot and Futures Pricing

- The **spot price** of a commodity is simply its market value designated for current delivery. Spot prices of commodities vary across regions, reflecting logistical constraints and supply and demand imbalances that prevent the movement of materials.
- The **futures price** of a commodity is the market value designated for future delivery. Futures prices tend to be more global and are used by producers, consumers, and governments in decision making.
- The **basis** of a commodity is the difference between the spot price and the futures price.
  - **Contango** occurs when the futures price exceeds the spot price.
  - **Backwardation** occurs when the spot price exceeds the futures price.
- Backwardation and contango are also used to describe the relationship between two futures contracts of the same commodity.
  - When the near-term futures price is higher than the longer-term futures price, the futures market is in backwardation.
  - When the near-term futures price is lower than the longer-term futures price, the futures market is in contango.
  - The price difference (whether in backwardation or in contango) is called the calendar spread.

FUTURES RETURNS

Insurance Theory (Theory of Normal Backwardation)

- Producers use commodity futures markets for insurance by locking in prices and thus making their revenues more predictable. Due to persistent selling by producers, which pushes prices down in the future, the futures market will be in backwardation normally.
- Another way to think about this is that the futures price must be lower than the current spot price to compensate the counterparty that takes on the price risk and provides price insurance to the commodity seller. As the futures contract nears maturity, the futures price will converge to the higher spot price (assuming no change in front prices) providing positive excess returns, or a risk premium, to the futures contract buyer.
- Academic and professional research does not typically offer support for this theory, however, as several studies show that backwardation in markets does not lead to statistically significant positive returns or that contango leads to negative returns.

Hedging Pressure Hypothesis

- Futures prices are determined by the quantity of hedgers on both the short side and the long side of futures contracts.
  - If consumers have greater demand for hedging than producers, the market will be in contango.
  - If producers have greater demand for hedging than consumers, the market will be in backwardation.
- One issue with this theory is that producers generally have greater exposure to commodity price risk than consumers do.
- A second issue is that both producers and consumers speculate on commodity prices, whether the speculation is intended or unintended, and measuring any asymmetry in hedging pressure between buyers and sellers of a commodity is very difficult.

Theory of Storage

- A commodity that is regularly stored should have a higher price in the future (i.e., contango) to account for those storage costs.
- A commodity that is consumed along a value chain and entails minimal storage should have a lower price in the future (i.e., backwardation).
- An available supply of a commodity offers a buffer to potential supply disruption. This convenience yield is inversely related to inventory size and general availability of the commodity.
- Therefore, futures prices can be written as:
  - Futures price = Spot price of the physical commodity + Direct storage costs (such as rent and insurance) – Convenience yield
- Limitations of this theory include the following:
  - Storage costs are not always easily available.
  - The convenience yield can be very volatile.
  - Defining inventory for certain commodities can be tricky.

COMPONENTS OF FUTURES RETURNS

The **price return** is the change in commodity futures prices, generally the front month contract.

Price return = (Current price – Previous price) / Previous price

The **roll return** is effectively the accounting difference (in percentage terms) between the near-term commodity futures contract price and the farther-term commodity futures contract price.

Roll return = [(Near-term futures contract closing price
    – Farther-term futures contract closing price) /
    Near-term futures contract closing price]
    × Percentage of the position in the futures contract being rolled

- Hedgers holding long positions in contango markets will sell the maturing contract for a lower price than what they will be paying for the new longer-term contract. Their roll return will be negative.
- Hedgers holding long positions in backwardation markets will sell the maturing contract for a higher price than what they will be paying for the new longer-term contract. Their roll return will be positive.

The **collateral return** is the yield (e.g., interest rate) for the bonds or cash used to maintain the investor's futures position(s). Note that for return calculations on indexed investments:

- The amount of cash considered in the calculation equals the notional value of the contracts.
- The yield on a risk-free government bond of similar term is used as the expected return.

Studies have shown that:

- Periods of either backwardation or contango do not persist indefinitely.
- Positive price returns are associated with negative roll returns as well as positive roll returns.
- Industrial metals, agriculture, livestock, precious metals, and soft commodities have statistically strong negative mean roll returns.
- Only energy has a reasonable statistical possibility of a positive mean roll return.
- Roll return can have an important impact on any single period return but overall has been relatively modest compared with price return.
- Roll return is very sector dependent.

COMMODITY SWAPS

Advantages of using commodity swaps instead of futures contracts:

- The daily settlement process can be avoided, as managing a significant number of futures contracts can be cumbersome.
- Swaps provide the opportunity for both a transfer of risk as well as additional ways to manage risk.

AI

- Swaps can be tailored to meet almost any investor need.
- Swaps offer greater flexibility because they are typically cash settled.

Types of Commodity Swaps

- In an **excess return swap**, two parties agree to exchange payments above a reference rate or price. An oil company might agree to exchange a constant premium for a payment equal to the difference between the current market price of oil and a specified price (fixed).
- A **total return swap** is an exchange of the return on a commodity index for a money market return plus a spread. This swap is typically used by institutional investors as a means to gain exposure to the commodity asset class.
- A **basis swap** is one in which the return on two commodities that are not highly correlated is exchanged. The basis swap typically involves commodities of two different liquidity levels, and the basis can be defined in almost any way as the difference between two commodity prices.
- A **variance swap** is similar to a fixed-for-floating interest rate swap, but the variance of a commodity is used as the reference point instead of an interest rate. Variance swaps are volatility bets in which one party believes the variance in one commodity will exceed the variance of the other one.
- A **volatility swap** is one in which actual volatility is swapped for expected volatility of one specific commodity.

COMMODITY INDEXES

Benefits of Commodity Indexes

Commodities indexes provide:

- A benchmark to evaluate diversified or concentrated commodity investments
- Inputs to make macroeconomic forecasts
- A reference value or return to price derivative securities

Key Characteristics of Commodity Indexes

- Breadth of coverage refers to the number of different commodities and sectors represented.
- Each index must have relative weightings assigned to each commodity or component of the index.
- The methodology for rolling the contracts as they mature will have an impact on returns.
- Rebalancing techniques and frequency of rebalancing may provide an opportunity to earn extra returns if there are strong positive or negative correlations between index components and the likelihood of the components to exhibit mean reversion.
- Rules-based indexes and selection-based indexes govern the manner in which the key characteristics are implemented.

Summary of Important Index Characteristics

- Value weighting tends to place more emphasis on energy companies' returns because they tend to have higher prices.

- The rolling method selected for each index is critical in that some indexes specifically choose commodities that trade in backwardation, which will give the appearance of higher returns because of the positive roll yield.
    - In fact, some indexes pursue a policy to maximize weights of commodities in backwardation and minimize weights of commodities in contango.
    - Many indexes try to avoid any weights in commodities trading in contango.
    - Some indexes include near-term contracts with only the highest liquidity to avoid any drag on returns.
- The rebalancing method will influence returns on an index mostly when frequent rebalancing hurts performance, especially when markets are trading with momentum or significant trends. Rebalancing influences index returns more significantly when prices are mean reverting. Timing is critical, as reversion to the mean creates more opportunities for the index to generate more return when commodities with rising prices are sold and when commodities with falling prices are purchased. If the rebalancing date matches the mean reversion, rebalancing can add significant returns to the index. Frequent rebalancing, however, can lead to opportunity costs as upward-trending commodities are sold before they reach their peaks and downward-trending commodities are bought before they reach their bottoms.
    - For indexes that rebalance monthly, returns will be higher when mean reversion occurs more frequently.
    - For indexes that rebalance annually, returns will be higher when mean reversion occurs less frequently or not at all.

AI

PM

THE PORTFOLIO MANAGEMENT PROCESS AND THE INVESTMENT POLICY STATEMENT
Cross-Reference to CFA Institute Assigned Reading #46

IMPORTANCE OF THE PORTFOLIO PERSPECTIVE

Risk can either be systematic (non-diversifiable) or unsystematic (diversifiable). Most equity pricing models assume that investors hold diversified portfolios and are only compensated for systematic risk. Therefore, instead of evaluating each investment in isolation, investment managers should take a portfolio perspective when evaluating an investment.

THE PORTFOLIO MANAGEMENT PROCESS

Planning

1. Identifying and Specifying the Investor's Objectives and Constraints
   - **Risk Objectives**
     - Risk may be measured in absolute or relative terms.
     - Risk measures include variance, standard deviation and value at risk (VAR).
     - Risk tolerance is a function of the investor's ability and willingness to take risk.
     - Generally speaking, a client with a longer time horizon, high expected income, and greater net worth has a greater ability to bear risk. A client's willingness to bear risk is based on more subjective factors including her psychological makeup, and level of understanding of financial markets.
   - **Return Objectives**
     - Return objectives may also be stated in absolute or relative terms.
     - The return an investor wishes to achieve is called her desired return, while the minimum level of return she needs to achieve is called her required return.
     - A portfolio manager should take the total return perspective.
     - The portfolio manager needs to ensure that the client's return objectives are realistic in light of her tolerance for risk.
   - **Investment Constraints**
     - Liquidity
     - Time
     - Tax concerns
     - Legal and regulatory factors
     - Unique circumstances
2. Creating the Investment Policy Statement
   An IPS includes the following:

   - An introduction that describes the client.
   - A statement of purpose.

- A statement of duties and responsibilities of all the parties involved.
- A statement of investment goals, objectives, and constraints.
- A schedule for review of investment performance as well as the IPS itself.
- Performance measures and benchmarks to be used in performance evaluation.
- Any considerations to be taken into account in developing the strategic asset allocation.
- Investment strategies and investment style.
- Guidelines for rebalancing the portfolio based on feedback.

An IPS serves the following purposes:

- It helps the investor decide on realistic investment goals after learning about financial markets and associated risks.
- It creates a standard according to which the portfolio manager's performance can be judged.
- It guides the actions of portfolio managers, who should refer to it from time to time to assess the suitability of particular investments for their clients' portfolios.

3. Forming Capital Market Expectations

In this step, the portfolio manager develops long-run risk-return forecasts for various asset classes.

4. Creating the Strategic Asset Allocation

Strategic asset allocation (SAA) refers to the allocation of funds across different asset classes. A portfolio's SAA is important because it is a portfolio's allocation across various asset classes (not its allocation across securities within those asset classes) that is the primary determinant of portfolio returns.

Execution

The execution of the strategy is as important as the planning as it also has a significant impact on portfolio returns. Poorly executed strategies can increase transaction costs hence reducing investment returns. Transaction costs can be both explicit (e.g., commissions, fees, taxes, etc.) and implicit (e.g., missed trade opportunity costs, market price impacts of large trades, etc.).

Feedback

- Monitoring and rebalancing: A portfolio manager must monitor changes in the capital market expectations and investor needs, and rebalance the portfolio accordingly.
- Performance evaluation: Investors should periodically evaluate the performance of the portfolio in light of their investment objectives.

ETHICAL RESPONSIBILITIES OF PORTFOLIO MANAGERS

Portfolio managers generally have more knowledge regarding capital markets compared to their clients. Their conduct affects the well-being of their clients and many other people. In order to maintain the trust of their clients, portfolio managers should hold themselves to the highest standards of competence and standards of conduct.

AN INTRODUCTION TO MULTIFACTOR MODELS
Cross-Reference to CFA Institute Assigned Reading #47

Multifactor models assert that there is more than just the one factor that can explain differences in expected returns across assets (i.e., they incorporate multiple sources of systematic risk).

ARBITRAGE PRICING THEORY

Arbitrage pricing theory (APT) describes the expected return of an asset (or portfolio) as a linear function of the risk of the asset (or portfolio) with respect to a set of factors that capture systematic risk. APT is an equilibrium pricing model that does not indicate the identity or even the number of risk factors.

Assumptions

1. Asset returns are described by a factor model.
2. There are many assets so investors can form well-diversified portfolios that have zero asset-specific risk.
3. No arbitrage opportunities exist among well-diversified portfolios.

APT Equation

$$E(R_p) = R_F + \lambda_1 \beta_{p,1} + \ldots + \lambda_K \beta_{p,K}$$

$E(R_p)$ = Expected return to portfolio p
R_F = Risk-free rate
λ_j = Expected reward for bearing the risk of factor j
$\beta_p j$ = Sensitivity of the portfolio to factor j
K = Number of factors

- The **factor risk premium** (or **factor price**), λ_j, represents the expected reward for bearing the risk of a portfolio with a sensitivity of 1 to factor j, and a sensitivity of 0 to all other factors. Such a portfolio is called a **pure factor portfolio** (or more simply, the **factor portfolio for factor** j.
- The sensitivity of the portfolio's return to factor j, $\beta_p j$, represents the increase in portfolio return in response to a one-unit increase in factor j, holding all other factors constant.
- The intercept term in the model is the risk-free rate. It represents the rate of return if the portfolio has 0 sensitivity to all risk factors (or 0 systematic risk).

The Carhart Model

The **Carhart four-factor model** (also known as the **four-factor model** and the **Carhart model**) is a commonly used multifactor model. It asserts that the excess return on a portfolio is a function of:

1. Its sensitivity to the market index (RMRF) that represents exposure to the market.
2. A market capitalization factor (SMB) that represents exposure to size.
3. A book-value-to-price factor (HML) that represents exposure to a value orientation.
4. A momentum factor (WML).

$$E(R_p) = R_F + \beta_{p,1} RMRF + \beta_{p,2} SMB + \beta_{p,3} HML + \beta_{p,4} WML$$

PM

TYPES OF MULTIFACTOR MODELS

- **Macroeconomic factor models** use surprises in macroeconomic variables that significantly explain returns as factors.
- **Fundamental factor models** use company- or stock-specific fundamentals (e.g., P/B ratio, P/E ratio, market capitalization, etc.) that explain cross-sectional differences in stock prices as factors.
- **Statistical factor models** apply statistical methods on historical returns of a group of securities to extract factors that explain observed returns.

MACROECONOMIC FACTOR MODELS

Macroeconomic factor models assume that return on each asset is correlated with **surprises** in certain factors related to the broader economy.

- A **surprise** refers to the difference between the actual value and expected value of a variable.
- A factor's surprise refers to the component of the factor's return that was unexpected, and factor surprises serve as explanatory or independent variables in the model.

Assuming that a stock's returns can be explained by (1) surprises in inflation rates and (2) surprises in GDP growth rates, the equation for a macroeconomic factor model would be expressed as:

$$R_i = a_i + b_{i1}F_{INFL} + b_{i2}F_{GDP} + \varepsilon_i$$

R_i = the return to stock i
a_i = the expected return to stock i
F_{INFL} = the surprise in inflation rates
F_{GDP} = the surprise in GDP growth
b_{i1} = the sensitivity of the return on stock i to surprises in inflation
b_{i2} = the sensitivity of the return on stock i to surprises in GDP growth
ε_i = an error term with a zero mean that represents the portion of the return to stock i that is not explained by the factor model

Assumptions

- The two factors in the model, the surprise in inflation rates and the surprise in GDP growth are uncorrelated.
- Inflation rates and GDP growth rates are both priced risks.

The **intercept term** (a_i) reflects the effects of the predicted values of inflation and GDP growth on the expected return on stock i.

The **slope coefficients in the model** (b_{i1} and b_{i2}) are known as **factor sensitivities, factor betas**, or **factor loadings**. A factor sensitivity measures the change in the dependent variable to a one-unit change in the factor, holding all other factors constant.

The error term reflects the portion of the return on stock i that is unexplained by the systematic factors included in the model. If the model incorporates all systematic factors (i.e., all sources of common risk), then ε_i represents **stock- or company-specific risk**.

FUNDAMENTAL FACTOR MODELS

Assuming that a stock's returns can be explained by its (1) dividend yield and (2) P-E ratio, the equation for a fundamental factor model would be expressed as:

$$R_i = a_i + b_{i1}F_{DY} + b_{i2}F_{PE} + \varepsilon_i$$

R_i = the return to stock i
a_i = intercept
F_{DY} = return associated with the dividend yield factor
F_{PE} = return associated with the P-E factor
b_{i1} = the sensitivity of the return on stock i to the dividend yield factor
b_{i2} = the sensitivity of the return on stock i to the P-E factor
ε_i = an error term

In fundamental factor models:

- The factors (F_{DY} and F_{PE}) are stated as **returns** rather than return surprises in relation to predicted values (as is the case with macroeconomic factor models). Therefore, the factors do not usually have an expected value of zero.
- The factor sensitivities can be attributes of the security (dividend yield and P-E ratio in our example) or of the issuing company (e.g., industry membership). Further, the factor sensitivities in these models are typically standardized.
    - Sometimes however, fundamental models also incorporate factors, such as industry membership, that are represented as binary dummy variables.
- The intercept is not interpreted as expected return (as was the case in the macroeconomic factor model). The intercept has no economic interpretation when the factor sensitivities are standardized (which is typically the case). If the factor sensitivities are not standardized, the intercept term could be interpreted as the risk-free rate.
- Generally speaking, the factors used to model returns for equities can be placed into three broad groups: (1) company fundamental factors, (2) company share-related factors, and (3) macroeconomic factors.

MULTIFACTOR MODELS: SELECTED APPLICATIONS

Factor Models in Return Attribution

$$\text{Active return} = R_p - R_B$$

Active return can be broken down into:

- **The return from the portfolio manager's factor tilts:** This refers to over- or underweights relative to the benchmark factor sensitivities. The return from factor tilts is calculated as the product of the portfolio manager's active factor sensitivities (factor tilts) and the factor returns.
- **The return from individual asset selection or security selection:** This reflects the manager's skill in individual asset selection, i.e., ability to overweight securities that outperform the benchmark or underweight securities that underperform the benchmark.

$$\text{Active return} = \sum_{k=1}^{K}[(\text{Portfolio sensitivity})_k - (\text{Benchmark sensitivity})_k] \\ \times (\text{Factor return})_k + \text{Asset selection}$$

Factor Models in Risk Attribution

Active risk (also known as **tracking error, TE, or tracking risk**) is the standard deviation of active returns.

$$TE = s(R_P - R_B)$$

Active risk squared is the variance of active return.

$$\text{Active risk squared} = s^2(R_P - R_B)$$
$$\text{Active risk squared} = \text{Active factor risk} + \text{Active specific risk}$$

- **Active specific risk or asset selection risk** is the contribution to active risk squared of placing different-than-benchmark weights on individual assets after accounting for the differences in factor sensitivities between the portfolio and the benchmark.

$$\text{Active specific risk} = \sum_{i=1}^{n} w_i^a \sigma_{\varepsilon_i}^2$$

- **Active factor risk** is the contribution to active risk squared of taking different-from benchmark exposures relative to factors specified in the risk model (factor tilts).
  - ○ Active factor risk can be computed as the difference between active risk squared and active specific risk.

The Information Ratio

The **information ratio (IR)** is used to evaluate mean active return per unit of active risk.

$$IR = \frac{\bar{R}_p - \bar{R}_B}{s(R_p - R_B)}$$

The higher the information ratio, the better the risk-adjusted performance of the portfolio.

Factor Models in Portfolio Construction

- **Passive management.** If a portfolio manager wants a fund to track the performance of a particular index that consists of many securities, she may need to choose a representative sample of securities from the index for her fund. Multifactor models can be used to align the fund's factor exposures with those of the index.
- **Active management.** Multifactor models are used to predict alpha (excess risk-adjusted returns) and relative return under various active investment strategies. They are also used to establish desired risk profiles when constructing portfolios.
- **Rules-based active management (alternative indices).** These strategies routinely tilt toward factors such as size, value, quality, or momentum when constructing portfolios. Multifactor models are used in these strategies to tilt the portfolio's factor sensitivities and style biases relative to capitalization-weighted indices.

Factor Portfolios

A **factor portfolio** is constructed to have a sensitivity of 1 to a specific factor and a sensitivity of 0 to all other factors in the model. Therefore, it has exposure to only one risk factor and exactly represents the risk of that factor. Factor portfolios are of interest to managers who want to (1) hedge against a particular risk or (2) speculate on a particular outcome.

MEASURING AND MANAGING MARKET RISK
Cross-Reference to CFA Institute Assigned Reading #48

VALUE AT RISK (VAR)

Value at risk (VaR) describes a minimum loss to which a portfolio or portfolios of assets might be subject over a particular time period with a certain degree of probability.

The **parametric method** generates a VaR estimate based on return and standard deviation, typically from a normal distribution.

$$z = \frac{R - \mu}{\sigma}$$

$$E(R_P) = \sum_{i=1}^{n} w_i R_i$$

$$\sigma_P = \sqrt{w_i^2 \sigma_i^2 + w_j^2 \sigma_j^2 + 2 w_i \sigma_i w_j \sigma_j \rho_{i,j}}$$

$$\text{Unannualized } \sigma_P = \text{Annual } \sigma_P / \text{No. of days}^{0.5}$$

Note that:

- The parametric method using the normal distribution is easy to use and employs historical values that can be adjusted for reasonableness in any environment.
- However, it does not reflect the nonparametric losses that result from unexercised options in a portfolio that expire worthless.
- Further, the distribution changes as time value diminishes and the option value approaches the underlying security value at maturity.
- Finally, sensitivity to correlation changes between portfolio assets adds instability to the estimate.

The **historical simulation** method uses current portfolio weights for each asset multiplied by its percentage return for each period. All available returns representing expected reality would be used. Returns for the repriced portfolio are ranked lowest to highest, and VaR is then determined for the required confidence interval.

Note that:

- The historical simulation method can be adjusted by overweighting more current or more realistic returns while underweighting older or less realistic outcomes.
- Additionally, historical simulation can accommodate options in a portfolio because it uses outcomes that actually occurred.
- On the other hand, the historical simulation method suffers from the disadvantage of representing only historical reality rather than extreme outcomes that can occur. As a result, historical simulation is recommended only when the future appears likely to reflect past results.

Monte Carlo simulation employs user-developed assumptions to generate a distribution of random outcomes. This method overcomes the problem of potential outcomes outside past results as in a historical simulation, while avoiding complexity inherent in correlations among a wide variety of assets as in the parametric method.

- The challenge lies in the trade-off between greater reliability of many simulation runs versus the time and cost of many runs.
- Further, the distribution resulting from a Monte Carlo simulation will tend to resemble the distribution from which it is drawn.

Advantages of VaR

- Simple concept.
- Easy to communicate.
- Provides a basis for risk comparison.
- Facilitates capital allocation decisions.
- Can be used for performance evaluation.
- Reliability can be verified.
- Widely accepted by regulators.

Limitations of VaR

- Subjectivity.
- Underestimating the frequency of extreme events.
- Failure to account for liquidity.
- Sensitivity to correlation risk.
- Vulnerability to trending or volatility regimes.
- Misunderstanding the meaning of VaR.
- Oversimplification.
- Disregard of right-tail events.

Extensions of VaR

- **Conditional VaR**, also known as **expected shortfall** or **expected tail loss**, describes the average loss expected outside confidence limits.
    - Conditional VaR is not technically a VaR measure.
    - Conditional VaR will most likely be developed using historical or Monte Carlo approaches.
- **Incremental VaR (IVaR)** examines how the minimum loss will change if a position within the portfolio changes. **Marginal VaR (MVaR)** is a related concept that uses calculus to identify the change to minimum loss from some marginal change in portfolio positions.
- **Relative VaR**, also known as **ex ante tracking error**, describes the minimum loss at a given level of confidence of the manager's bets relative to a benchmark.

OTHER RISK MEASURES

Sensitivity Risk Measures

Sensitivity measures quantify how a security or portfolio will react if a single risk factor changes. Note that they do not indicate which portfolio has greater loss potential.

Beta is the most widely used equity exposure measure. It measures the sensitivity of the security's expected return to the equity risk premium. Beta is calculated as the covariance of the asset return with the market return divided by the variance of the market return.

Duration and convexity are the most widely used fixed-income exposure measures.

- **Duration** measures the change in the price of a bond in response to a change in yields.
- **Convexity** describes the sensitivity of a bond's duration to changes in interest rates. Convexity becomes more important as yield changes become larger and holding periods become longer.

$$\frac{\Delta B}{B} = -D\frac{\Delta y}{1+y} + \frac{1}{2}C\frac{(\Delta y)^2}{(1+y)^2}$$

When it comes to options, delta, gamma, and vega are used to measure risk.

Delta measures the responsiveness of the value of an option to a change in the price of the underlying.

$$Delta = \frac{\Delta c}{\Delta S}$$

Gamma measures the change in option delta in response to changes in the price of the underlying.

$$\Gamma = Gamma = \frac{\Delta Delta}{\Delta S}$$

$$c + \Delta c \approx c + \Delta_c \Delta S + \frac{1}{2}\Gamma_c(\Delta S)^2$$

Vega measures the change in the value of an option in response to changes in the volatility of the underlying.

$$Vega \approx \frac{\Delta c}{\Delta \sigma_S}$$

$$c + \Delta c \approx c + \Delta_c \Delta S + \frac{1}{2}\Gamma_c(\Delta S)^2 + Vega\, \Delta \sigma_S$$

Scenario Risk Measures

Scenario measures, including stress tests, are risk models that evaluate how a portfolio will perform under certain high-stress market conditions.

- **Historical scenarios** are scenarios that measure the portfolio return that would result from a repeat of a particular period of financial market history.

- **Hypothetical scenarios** model the impact of extreme movements and co-movements in different markets that have not previously occurred.
  - ○ **Reverse stress testing** is the process of stressing the portfolio's most significant exposures.

Advantages of Sensitivity and Scenario Risk Measures

Sensitivity and scenario risk measures can complement VaR in the following ways:

- Sensitivity measures address some of the shortcomings of position size measures.
- Sensitivity measures do not rely on history.
- Scenarios can be designed to overcome any assumption of normal distributions.
- Scenarios can be tailored to expose a portfolio's most concentrated positions to even worse movement than its other exposures, allowing liquidity to be taken into account.

Limitations

- Sensitivity measures do not generally distinguish between assets based on volatility. However, one way around this is to measure sensitivity to a one standard deviation movement in an asset's price or yield.
- History does not always repeat itself.
- Hypothetical scenarios may incorrectly specify how assets will co-move, they may get the magnitude of movements wrong, and they may inaccurately adjust for the effects of liquidity and concentration.
- Hypothetical scenarios can be very difficult to create and maintain.
- It is very difficult to know how to establish the appropriate limits on a scenario analysis or stress test.

APPLICATIONS OF RISK MEASURES

Factors That Influence the Type of Risk Measures Used by Market Participants

- The degree to which the market participant is leveraged.
- The mix of risk factors to which their business is exposed.
- The accounting or regulatory requirements that govern their reporting.

Risk Measures Used by Financial Institutions

- Banks use risk tools to assess the extent of any liquidity and asset/liability mismatch, the probability of losses in their investment portfolios, their overall leverage ratio, interest rate sensitivities, and the risk to economic capital.
- Asset managers' use of risk tools focuses primarily on volatility, probability of loss, or the probability of underperforming a benchmark.
- Pension funds use risk measures to evaluate asset/liability mismatch and surplus at risk.
- Property and casualty insurers use sensitivity and exposure measures to ensure that exposures remain within defined asset allocation ranges, economic capital and VaR measures to estimate the impairment in the event of a catastrophic loss, and scenario analysis to stress the market risks and insurance risks simultaneously.
- Life insurers use risk measures to assess the exposures of the investment portfolio and the annuity liability, the extent of any asset/liability mismatch, and the potential stress losses based on the differences between the assets in which they have invested and the liabilities resulting from the insurance contracts they have written.

PM

USING CONSTRAINTS IN MARKET RISK MANAGEMENT

- **Risk budgeting** occurs when the firm chooses a desired maximum risk and then budgets this out to business units or individual portfolios. The risk will generally be based on *ex ante* tracking error or VaR.
- **Position limits** can be formulated to avoid event risk and overconcentration, but should not be so constraining that they prevent outperforming a benchmark.
- **Scenario limits** address potential correlation changes and results from a non-normal distribution as with VaR. Scenario limits can be used to trigger asset manager actions to help protect the portfolio.
- **Stop-loss limits** require reduction in position or portfolio size, or even complete liquidation, when positions exceed their limits over a specified period.

Capital allocation aligns risk and reward by putting limits on capital assigned to each of the firm's activities. This prevents an unproven strategy from potentially siphoning away all risk capital from other potentially lucrative strategies.

ECONOMICS AND INVESTMENT MARKETS
Cross-Reference to CFA Institute Assigned Reading #49

FUNDAMENTAL PRESENT VALUE FORMULA

$$P_t^i = \sum_{s=1}^{N} \frac{E_t\left[\widetilde{CF}_{t+s}^i\right]}{\left(1 + l_{t,s} + \theta_{t,s} + \rho_{t,s}^i\right)^s}$$

Components of the Discount Rate

- Real risk-free rate ($l_{t,s}$).
- Compensation for inflation ($\theta_{t,s}$).
- Compensation for uncertainty about the asset's future cash flows ($\rho_{t,s}$).
  - The risk premium on risky assets for uncertainty increases during recessions.
  - Can also include compensation for other types of risk (e.g., liquidity risk).

Expectations and Asset Values

Current information/expectations are reflected in market prices. New information that changes expectations affects asset values and realized returns. Prices can fall (rise) despite good (bad) news if the market expected better (worse) news.

THE DISCOUNT RATE ON REAL DEFAULT-FREE BONDS

Note: Statements/assertions laid down in this section are based on the assumption that there is no default-risk and no inflation.

The decision to purchase a risk-free inflation-indexed bond is determined by the investor's willingness to substitute consumption today for consumption in the future. The **inter-temporal rate of substitution (ITRS)** is the ratio of the marginal utility of consumptions s periods in the future (MU_F) to the marginal utility from consumption today or current consumption (MU_C).

Generally speaking:

- The *greater* the amount of consumption the *lower* the marginal utility of consumption.
- The *greater* the investor's wealth, the *lower* the marginal utility of consumption.

In bad (good) economic times, the ITRS tends to be higher (lower), which leads to a higher (lower) price for a risk-free asset. Basically, the ITRS is *inversely* related to real GDP growth.

- If the price of a risk-free bond is **less** than her expected ITRS, then the investor would *purchase* more of the bond. This increase in investment leads to (1) a *decline* in current consumption, which brings about an *increase* in MU_C, and (2) an *increase* in expected future consumption which *decreases* MU_F. Consequently, the ITRS *falls* until it equals the price of the bond.
- If there are enough investors in the market who believe that the current price of the bond is lower than their expected ITRS, then there would also be an impact on the price of the bond. The higher demand for the bond will lead to an *increase* in its price and this would happen at the same time that investor's ITRSs are *falling*.

PM

- If the price of the bond is **greater** than her expected ITRS, then the investor would *sell* the bond. This decrease in investment leads to (1) an *increase* in current consumption, *decreasing* MU_C, and (2) a *decrease* in expected future consumption, *increasing* MU_F. Consequently, the ITRS *rises* until it equals the price of the bond.
- If there are enough investors in the market who believe that the current price of the bond is higher than their expected ITRS, then their selling the bond would result in a *decrease* in its price. This would happen at the same time that investor's ITRS are rising.

$$\text{Real risk-free rate}(l_{t,s}) = [1 \,/\, \text{ITRS}] - 1$$

The one-period real risk-free rate is *inversely* related to the ITRS. The *higher* the return the investor can earn, the more important current consumption becomes relative to future consumptions, and *lower* is the willingness to substitute current consumption from future consumption.

Uncertainty and Risk Premiums

- The expected marginal utility from a given expected payoff is *negatively* related to the uncertainty of the payoff. The *higher* the uncertainty of the payoff, the *lower* its marginal utility, the *greater* the required risk premium and the *higher* the required return.
- An investor's absolute risk aversion *falls* as her income/wealth increases. For a given risk, the risk premium required is *lower* for wealthier individuals. As a result, wealthier investors are willing to buy more risky assets than poorer investors, and they are only willing to buy safer investments at a lower price.

Risk Premiums on Risky Assets

The value of a risky asset can be broken down into two components:

- A **risk-neutral present value**, which is its expected future price discounted at the risk-free rate.
- The **covariance between an investor's ITRS and the expected future price of the investment** based on information available today.
  - This covariance term is the discount for risk.
  - With investors being risk-averse, for most risky assets, the covariance term is **negative**.
    - This is because when the expected future price of the asset is high, MU_F will be low (due to higher expected future consumption), resulting in a lower ITRS.
  - The negative covariance term results in a *lower* price for most risky assets, which implies a *positive* risk premium.

Takeaways:

- All other things remaining the same, the *larger* the magnitude of the (negative) covariance term, the *lower* the market price of the asset, and the *higher* the risk premium and required rate of return for the asset.
- Even the discount rate applied to a zero-coupon, risk-free, inflation-indexed bond will include a premium for risk because there is uncertainty regarding its market price before maturity.

- An asset that offers high returns in bad economic times (when MU_C is high because consumption levels are low) would be a type of hedge against recessions. Such an asset would have a *positive* covariance term, *higher* price, *lower* required return and *negative* risk premium.

Default-Free Interest Rates and Economic Growth

Real default-free interest rates are:

- Positively related to the rate of GDP growth.
- Positively related to the expected volatility of GDP growth.

THE YIELD CURVE AND THE BUSINESS CYCLE

Note: Statements/assertions laid down in this section are based on the assumption that there is no default-risk, but there is inflation.

Pricing Equation for Nominal Coupon-Paying Government Bond

$$P_t^i = \sum_{s=1}^{N} \frac{CF_{t+s}^i}{\left(1 + l_{t,s} + \theta_{t,s} + \pi_{t,s}\right)^s}$$

Short-Term Nominal Rates and the Business Cycle

Over the short term, there is minimal uncertainty over inflation so we ignore $\pi_{t,s}$

Pricing Equation for Short-Term Government Bonds

$$P_t^i = \frac{CF_{t+s}^i}{\left(1 + l_{t,s} + \theta_{t,s}\right)^s}$$

Short-term default-free nominal interest rates are:

- Positively related to short-term expected inflation ($\theta_{t,s}$).
- Influenced by the central bank's **policy rate**.
  - When inflation is above (below) the targeted level, the policy rate should be above (below) the **neutral rate**.
- Positively related with the short-term real interest rate/neutral rate ($l_{t,s}$), which in turn is positively related to (1) GDP growth rates and (2) the volatility of GDP growth.
  - Note that the neutral rate may also change if the central bank's inflation target changes.

Conventional Government Bonds

For T-Bills, since they are short-term investments, there is minimal uncertainty regarding the real value of the payoff. Therefore, these instruments are a good hedge against bad consumption outcomes, which means that the risk premium required to invest in them is close to zero.

For longer-term default-free bonds, even though the cash flow at maturity is certain, there is greater uncertainty regarding the real value of the payoff (due to the low predictability of inflation over the long run). Therefore, investors require a premium ($\pi_{t,s}$) for this uncertainty.

The **break-even inflation (BEI) rate** is the difference between the yield on a zero-coupon default-free nominal bond and the yield on a zero-coupon default-free real bond. It includes:

- Expected inflation over the investment horizon ($\theta_{t,s}$).
- A risk premium to compensate for the uncertainty about future inflation ($\pi_{t,s}$).

When there is a significant shift in the yield curve, it is useful to break down the shift into its real and inflationary components.

- A decline in the inflationary components reflects lower levels of expected future inflation.
- A decline in the real component reflects a lower level of expected future economic growth.

Level, Slope, and Curvature of the Yield Curve

- The level of the yield curve is influenced by:
  - Level of economic activity.
  - Views of future inflation.
- The slope of the yield curve is influenced by:
  - Magnitude of the risk premium.
  - Current phase of business cycle. Monetary policy has more of an impact on short-term rates than on longer-term rates.
    - The slope of the yield curve tends to increase during recessions.
- The curvature of the yield curve may increase as the economy moves out of a recession.

The Term Spread

- The **term spread** is the slope of the yield curve. It is calculated as the difference between the yield on a long-term government bond and the yield on an equivalent one-year bond.
- A steep slope (high term spread) implies that the market expects a sharp increase in interest rates.
- A steeply inverted curve (negative term spread) implies that the market expects sharply falling inflation and future interest rates.
- A recession is often preceded by a flattening, or even inversion, of the yield curve.

Risk premiums for government bonds tend to fall in times of economic uncertainty as investors place a greater value on their consumption hedging properties (higher demand → higher price → lower yield → lower risk premium). Risk premiums on these bonds tend to rise when the economy is doing well.

The slope and yield of the yield curve is influenced by the following factors:

- Expected future interest rates.
- Expected future inflation and economic growth rates.
- Maturity risk premiums.
- Supply and demand factors.
- Regulatory factors.

CREDIT PREMIUMS AND THE BUSINESS CYCLE

Note: Statements/assertions laid down in this section are based on the assumption that there is default-risk, and there is inflation.

Pricing Equation for Credit-Risky Bonds

$$P_t^i = \sum_{s=1}^{N} \frac{E_t\left[\widetilde{CF}_{t+s}^i\right]}{\left(1 + l_{t,s} + \theta_{t,s} + \pi_{t,s} + \gamma_{t,s}^i\right)^s}$$

The credit premium ($\gamma_{t,s}$) reflects the risk of uncertainty associated with the amount and timing of cash flows on a credit risky bond.

Credit Spreads and the Credit Risk Premium

The **credit spread** is the difference between the yield on the corporate bond and the yield on a default-free bond with the same currency denomination and maturity. While both risk-free and credit risky bonds are subject to interest rate risk, it is the credit risk component of the risky bond and the evolution of credit spreads over time that cause returns on government and corporate bonds to differ.

Generally speaking:

- Credit spreads on investment grade bonds are narrower than those on high-risk bonds.
- Leading up to and during recessions, credit spreads tend to widen across the board. As a result of their poor ability to hedge against bad consumption outcomes, investors demand a risk premium to invest in credit-risky bonds.
- Credit spreads tend to narrow as the economy comes out of a recession.
- When spreads are narrowing (during expansions) low-rated corporate bonds tend to outperform higher-rated bonds.
- When spreads are widening (during recessions) higher-rated bonds tend to perform better.
- During recessions:
  - Spreads for consumer cyclicals rise more than spreads for consumer non-cyclicals.
  - Recovery rates tend to be higher for secured as opposed to unsecured bonds.
  - Recovery rates tend to be lower than when the economy is expanding.

The credit spread on **sovereign bonds** issued by emerging market governments is calculated as the difference between the yields on those bonds and yields on comparable U.S. Treasuries.

Sovereign spreads tend to *rise* in an uncertain global economic environment.

EQUITIES AND THE EQUITY RISK PREMIUM

Pricing Equation for Equities

$$P_t^i = \sum_{s=1}^{\infty} \frac{E_t\left[\widetilde{CF}_{t+s}^i\right]}{\left(1 + l_{t,s} + \theta_{t,s} + \pi_{t,s} + \gamma_{t,s}^i + \kappa_{t,s}^i\right)^s}$$

$\kappa_{t,s}$ is the additional return investors demand for investing in equities over and above the return required for investing in credit-risky bonds.

The **equity risk premium (ERP)** is the return demanded on top of the return on a default-free bond denominated in the same currency.

$$ERP = \lambda_{t,s} = \gamma_{t,s} + \kappa_{t,s}$$

Generally speaking:

- Recessions have been associated with sharp falls in equity values. Because equities tend to be a poor hedge for bad consumption outcomes, the equity premium is positive.
- Corporate earnings tend to fall dramatically in a recession. However, corporate profits can also lead an economy out of a recession if companies invest aggressively in response to any resurgence in aggregate demand. This is why corporate profitability is considered a leading indicator of economic growth.
- Demand for products made by non-cyclical, defensive companies (staple or less-discretionary consumer goods) tends to remain fairly stable through the business cycle.
- Demand for products made by cyclical companies (discretionary goods) tends to fluctuate during the business cycle. A rise in earnings of cyclical companies after a period of decline is a leading indicator of wider economic growth.
- Durable goods consumption is more volatile than consumption of non-durable goods.

Factors That Can Result in a Higher P/E

- An increase in expected future real earnings growth.
- Falling interest rates.
- Falling inflation expectations.
- A decline in uncertainty regarding future inflation.
- A fall in the equity risk premium.

An alternative valuation multiple is the **real cyclically adjusted P/E (CAPE)**. It uses the real (inflation-adjusted) price of the equity market and a 10-year moving average of the market's real earnings. Periods where the market has traded at a high (low) CAPE have historically been followed by low (high) returns.

Investment Strategy

- Value stocks tend to outperform growth stocks in the period following a recession.
- Growth stocks tend to outperform value stocks when the economy is expanding.
- Small stocks tend to underperform large stocks in bad times.

COMMERCIAL REAL ESTATE

- Commercial real estate can be viewed as a part bond, part equity investment.
    - The rental income received from commercial real estate is analogous to the coupon derived from a bond. The credit quality of a portfolio of commercial real estate depends on the credit quality of the tenants. Generally speaking, the lower the credit quality of the tenants, the less likely that they will pay their rent (if at all).
    - Upon expiration of the lease of a commercial property, the investor can re-rent it, sell it or redevelop it for a future sale. This raises the possibility of a profit or loss on the capital invested, which adds an equity-like dimension to a commercial real estate investment.
- Commercial real estate investments are relatively illiquid and entail high transaction costs.

Pricing Formula for Commercial Real Estate

$$P_t^i = \sum_{s=1}^{N} \frac{E_t\left[\widetilde{CF}_{t+s}^i\right]}{\left(1 + l_{t,s} + \theta_{t,s} + \pi_{t,s} + \gamma_{t,s}^i + \kappa_{t,s}^i + \varphi_{t,s}^i\right)^s}$$

Note that:

- Expected cash flows are uncertain.
- The credit risk ($\gamma_{t,s}$) comes from the uncertainty regarding rental income receipts.
- $\kappa_{t,s}$ is the additional return required to compensate for the uncertainty regarding the value of the property at the end of the investment horizon.
- $\varphi_{t,s}$ reflects compensation for liquidity risk.

The relative sizes of the different risk premiums depend on the length of the lease, the quality of the tenant and the location of the property.

Studies have shown that historically:

- Growth in rental income on commercial real estate has been fairly stable in nominal terms.
- However, commercial property capital values have been much more sensitive to the business cycle. They tend to fall (rise) during recessions (expansions).
- This pro-cyclical nature of commercial property prices leads to investors demanding a high risk premium (it is a poor hedge against bad consumption outcomes). The risk premium on commercial real estate is closer to the premium demanded on equities than to the premium on risk-free government bonds.

PM

ANALYSIS OF ACTIVE PORTFOLIO MANAGEMENT
Cross-Reference to CFA Institute Assigned Reading #50

Value Added

$$\text{Value added or active return} = R_A = R_P - R_B$$

$$R_A = \sum_{i=1}^{N} \Delta w_i R_i$$

$$R_A = \sum_{i=1}^{N} \Delta w_i R_{Ai}$$

Decomposition of Value Added

- **Value added from asset allocation.** This refers to the value added by changing the weights of various asset classes in the managed portfolio relative to the benchmark.
- **Value added from security selection.** This refers to the value added by changing the composition of various individual securities within an asset class relative to the benchmark.

$$R_A = \text{Value added from security selection} + \text{Value added from active allocation}$$
$$= (w_{P,Stocks} R_{A,Stocks} + w_{P,Bonds} R_{A,Bonds}) + (\Delta w_{Stocks} R_{B,Stocks} + + \Delta w_{Bonds} R_{B,Bonds})$$

For more than two asset classes:

$$\text{Value added} = R_A + \sum_{j=1}^{M} w_{P,j} R_{A,j} + \sum_{j=1}^{M} \Delta w_j R_{B,j} \text{ where } M = \text{Number of asset classes}$$

COMPARING RISK AND RETURN

The Sharpe Ratio

The Sharpe ratio measures a portfolio's excess return per unit of risk, where risk is measured by the standard deviation of the portfolio return (also known as **total risk** or **volatility**).

$$SR_P = \frac{R_P - R_F}{[(STD(R)]_p)}$$

- When comparing two funds based on historical Sharpe ratios, we must ensure that they are computed from the same measurement period.
- The Sharpe ratio is unaffected by the addition of cash or leverage to a portfolio.
- The two fund separation theorem asserts that all investors would hold some combination of the risk-free asset and the risky asset portfolio with the highest Sharpe ratio. If the investor wants to increase her portfolio's expected return she could add leverage to her portfolio, and if she wants to reduce her expected risk she would hold more cash and less of the risky asset portfolio.

The Information Ratio

The information ratio measures the **active return** from a portfolio relative to a benchmark per unit of **active risk** (which is the **volatility of the active return**, and also known as **benchmark tracking risk**). The information ratio is used to evaluate the consistency of active return.

$$\text{Information ratio(IR)} = \frac{\text{Active return}}{\text{Active risk}} = \frac{R_A}{\sigma(R_A)} = \frac{R_P - R_B}{\sigma(R_P - R_B)}$$

- Since active management is a zero-sum game, the realized information ratio across all funds with the same benchmark should be close to zero.
- If an investor does not expect a positive *ex ante* information ratio, she should just invest in the benchmark.
- Rankings based on active risk (standard deviation of active return) can be different from rankings based on total risk (standard deviation of returns).
- Unlike the Sharpe ratio, the information ratio **is affected** by the addition of cash or leverage to a portfolio. If cash is added to a portfolio, the information ratio of the combined portfolio will fall.
- The information ratio is **not affected** by the magnitude of active weights.
  - Note that an outside investor cannot change the active risk of a managed portfolio by changing its individual asset active weights. However, she can effectively change her active risk exposure by taking appropriate positions on the benchmark.

CONSTRUCTING THE OPTIMAL PORTFOLIO

$$SR_P^2 = SR_B^2 + IR^2$$

All other things remaining the same, an investor should choose the investment manager with the highest level of skill (as measured by her information ratio) because investing with her will produce the highest Sharpe ratio for her own portfolio.

Determining the Optimal Amount of Active Risk

The **optimal level of active risk** is the level of active risk that yields the highest Sharpe ratio for the investor.

For **unconstrained portfolios**, the optimal level of active risk (also known as the **optimal amount of aggressiveness**) is computed as:

$$\sigma^*(R_A) = \frac{IR}{SR_B}\sigma(R_B)$$

PM

THE FUNDAMENTAL LAW OF ACTIVE MANAGEMENT

The Correlation Triangle

The Correlation Triangle

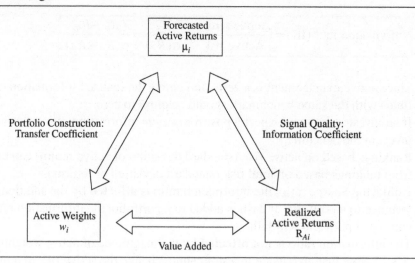

- The correlation between active weights and realized active returns (the base of the triangle) reflects realized value added through active portfolio management.
- The correlation between forecasted active returns and realized active returns (right vertical leg of the triangle) represents **signal quality**, which is commonly referred to as the **information coefficient (IC)**.
- The correlation between forecasted active returns and active weights (left vertical leg of the triangle) represents the extent to which the investor's forecasts are translated into active weights in her portfolio. It is commonly referred to as the **transfer coefficient (TC)**.

Assuming that active returns on individual securities are uncorrelated, the mean-variance-optimal active security weights, subject to a limit on active portfolio risk are given by:

$$\Delta W_i^* = \frac{\mu_i}{\sigma_i^2} \frac{\sigma_A}{IC\sqrt{BR}} \text{ where } \mu_i = IC * \sigma_i * S_i$$

- The **information coefficient (IC)** is the *ex ante*, or anticipated correlation between active return forecasts and realized active returns.
- **Breadth (BR)** represents the number of independent active decisions made by the investor per year in constructing the portfolio.

Remember that:

- The larger the forecasted active return for a security (μ_i), the larger its desired active weight (ΔW_i^*).
- The greater the forecasted volatility of active return for a security (σ_i), the lower its desired active weight (ΔW_i^*).
- The greater the desired active portfolio risk (σ_A), the larger the individual active weights (ΔW_i^*).

The Basic Fundamental Law

$$E(R_A)^* = IC\sqrt{BR}\sigma_A$$

$$\frac{E(R_A)}{\sigma(R_A)} = \text{Information ratio}(IR^*) = IC\sqrt{BR}$$

The Full Fundamental Law

$$E(RA) = TC\ IC\sqrt{BR}\sigma A$$

Note that there is no * with the expected active return here because the portfolio is constructed with constrained active security weights.

$$\frac{E(R_A)}{\sigma(R_A)} = \text{Information ratio}(IR) = TC * IC * \sqrt{BR}$$

Optimal Amount of Active Risk for a Constrained Portfolio

$$\sigma(RA) = TC\frac{IR^*}{SR_B}\sigma(RB)$$

Maximum Value of the Constrained Portfolio's Sharpe Ratio

$$SP2P = SR2B + (TC)^2(IR^*)^2$$

Ex Post Performance Measurement

The **realized information coefficient (IC$_R$)**, which reflects how actual active returns correlate with realized active returns, allows us to determine what realized return to expect given the transfer coefficient.

Expected value added conditional on the realized information coefficient, IC$_R$, is calculated as:

$$E(RA|ICR) = (TC)(ICR)\sqrt{BR}\ \sigma A$$

The realized value added from an actively managed portfolio can be broken down into two parts:

- The expected value added given the realized skill of the investor for the period, $E(R_A \mid IC_R)$.
- Any noise that results from constraints that prevent the portfolio constructed from being optimal.

$$RA = E(RA|ICR) + \text{Noise}$$

Ex post or realized active return variance can also be broken down into two parts:

- Variation due to the realized information coefficient.
  - Studies have shown that the proportion of realized variance that can be attributed to this part equals TC^2.
- Variation due to noise induced by constraints on the portfolio.
  - Studies have shown that the proportion of realized variance that can be attributed to this part equals $1 - TC^2$.
- This implies that if an investor's TC is low, there is a high probability that when his forecasts are accurate, his actual performance is poor, and when his forecasts are inaccurate, his performance is actually good.

APPLICATIONS OF THE FUNDAMENTAL LAW

- Given the number of individual assets being considered (N), if the correlations between different assets does not equals zero, the value of breadth will be different from the number of assets.
- The more ambitious the forecasts, the greater the value of the information coefficient (IC) in the fundamental law.
  - For example, consider Assets X and Y, whose active returns are believed to be positively correlated. If an investment manager forecasts that the active returns on these two assets will actually go in different directions (a relatively ambitious forecast), the IC used in fundamental law accounting will increase.
- If constraints are placed in portfolio construction, there will be reduction in the transfer of active return forecasts into active weights (i.e., the transfer coefficient, TC will be lower). This reduction in the TC will lead to a decrease in the expected active return and in the information ratio.
- For an unconstrained portfolio, an increase in allowed active risk leads to a proportionate increase in active return, leaving the information ration unchanged. However, for a constrained portfolio, the information ratio decreases with the level of aggressiveness of the strategy. Specifically, it decreases at an increasing rate due to an increasingly lower transfer coefficient.

PRACTICAL LIMITATIONS

Ex Ante Measurement of Skill

Studies have shown that realized active portfolio risk is a function of (1) benchmark tracking risk predicted by the risk model **and** (2) the uncertainty of the information coefficient.

$$E(R_A) = \frac{IC}{\sigma_{IC}} \sigma_A$$

The greater the uncertainty regarding forecasting ability, the lower the expected value added.

Independence of Investment Decisions

BR does not equal N when (1) the active returns between individual assets are correlated, or (2) forecasts are not independent from period to period. BR can then be estimated as:

$$BR = \frac{N}{1+(N-1)\rho}$$

- For hedging strategies that make use of derivatives and other form of arbitrage, BR will be much higher than the number of securities.
- For arbitrage strategies, the information ratio will be quite high even for relatively modest values of IC.

In the fixed-income arena, almost all bonds are, at least to a certain extent, driven by interest rate risk and credit risk, resulting in some correlation between returns.

When it comes to market-timing active management strategies:

- More frequent rebalancing can increase the information ratio, but only to the extent that forecasts are independent form one period to the next.
- Generally speaking, there are such few opportunities to make active decisions that in order to achieve a high expected active return or a high information ratio, the portfolio manager must have a higher information coefficient.

Other practical limitations of the fundamental law include:

- Transaction costs and taxes are ignored.
- The limitations of mean-variance optimization also apply here.
- The problems associated with estimation and use of risk models (e.g., identifying the right set of risk factors, non-linearities, and non-stationary returns).

ALGORITHMIC TRADING AND HIGH-FREQUENCY TRADING
Cross-Reference to CFA Institute Assigned Reading #51

Algorithmic trading uses a computer to find opportunities, place orders, and manage their execution in a series of programmed steps called an algorithm.

EXECUTION ALGORITHMS VERSUS HIGH-FREQUENCY TRADING ALGORITHMS

Execution algorithms automate decisions on *how* to place trades into markets. They attempt to minimize trading impacts of large trades by breaking them down into smaller trades that can be introduced into the market over time. This reduces visibility of the trading strategy to other traders and algorithms, and better matches supply with demand for the asset. Approaches to breaking up the large order include volume-weighted average price (VWAP), market participation, and implementation shortfall.

High-frequency trading (HFT) algorithms focus on *when* to trade or *what* to trade. They aim to find and execute opportunistic trades, often small in size but designed to be profitable on volume.

- **Event-driven algorithms** systematically analyze whether events confirm or could potentially change asset values. Types of HFT-relevant events include quote events, trade events, and news events.
- **Statistical arbitrage algorithms** monitor instruments that are known to be statistically correlated with the goal of detecting breaks in the correlation that indicate trading opportunities. Examples include:
  - Pairs trading: Correlation changes between assets (e.g., options and the underlying).
  - Index arbitrage: Correlation changes between individual instruments and an index.
  - Basket trading: Correlation changes within a basket of securities included in an index (includes aspects of pairs trading and index arbitrage).
  - Spread trading: Spread changes between two instruments, particularly popular in commodities markets and usually involving a long position and a short position. Some examples include:
    - *Intramarket spread*—Spread changes for instruments representing the same commodity but different delivery dates (e.g., between July and March wheat).
    - *Intermarket spread*—Spread changes for instruments representing different commodities of the same delivery date (e.g., July gold and silver).
    - *Interexchange spread*—Spread between the same commodity in different exchanges (e.g., corn in Kansas City vs. Chicago market).
    - *Crack spread*—Spread between crude oil and petroleum products.
    - *Spark spread*—Spread between input costs (including operating) and output price for units of electricity (i.e., operating margin).
    - *Crush spread*—Spread between commodity and output prices (e.g., soybeans and soybean oil).
  - Mean reversion: Purchasing oversold or selling overbought instruments to capture profit when the asset returns to its average price.
  - Delta neutrality: Neutralizing option delta to profit from volatility or time decay without regard to price moves of the underlying.

PM

Low latency is very important in HFT strategies. **Latency** refers to the amount of time taken for market data to be received, a pattern to be identified, a decision to be made, and trades to be placed. A low latency value chain has the following components:

- Quick access to market data
- Complex event processing (CEP) technologies
- Quick order execution
- Physical connection to market data
- Co-location with trading venues

High-frequency algorithmic techniques are also used in:

- Liquidity aggregation and smart order routing
- Real-time pricing of instruments
- Trading on news
- Genetic tuning, which allows survival of the fittest algorithm while dropping less profitable algorithms

The life cycle of an algorithm includes:

- Alpha discovery to find new patterns
- Algorithm implementation
- Back-testing
- Production
- Tuning

Approaches to Developing Algorithms

- A **black-box approach** denies users access to knowledge of the programmed steps and may allow limited or no flexibility in setting up or operating the algorithm. Black-box algorithms often provide the least costly option, but make earning a profit more difficult because other traders compete for profits from the same strategy.
- A **white-box approach** provides additional flexibility over black-box applications by allowing users to integrate with market feeds, control entry and exit points, combine with other algorithms, and view the strategy's progress. White-box strategies cost more, but provide the benefits of some customization and less competition if the user specifies unique parameters.
- **Bespoke algorithms** (i.e., **custom algorithms**) are very expensive but offer the best profit opportunities because the firm has few competitors in exploiting a strategy.

Key Drivers to the Evolution of Algorithmic Trading and HFT

- **Market fragmentation** (i.e., the same instrument traded in multiple markets) has increased as new markets develop in response to competitive opportunities and new technology. In response to increased fragmentation, traders developed liquidity aggregation that creates a "super book" of quote and depth across many markets. Companies use methods such as smart order routing to introduce orders in markets that offer the best prices and most favorable market impact.
- **New asset classes**: Although equity and futures markets were initial targets of algorithmic trading, bond markets, foreign exchange, and even energy trading have become algo-friendly markets.
- **Cross-asset trading**: Arbitrageurs have begun trading across correlated asset classes.

PM

- **Cross-border trading:** Differences in trading platforms and venues have also opened opportunities for cross-border arbitrage in which firms buy low in one country's market and sell higher in another country's market.
- **New geographic areas:** Although available initially only in the United States and United Kingdom, algorithmic trading has spread across the world's larger markets, most recently in Brazil.

KEY TECHNOLOGIES INTEGRAL TO ALGORITHMIC TRADING

- **Execution management systems (EMS):** Front-end trading systems that allow access to broker algorithms as well as custom algorithms integrated with the EMS.
- **Tick database:** Records all transactions across all markets for use with the appropriate algorithms. It may also be used for back-testing strategies.
- **Complex event processing (CEP):** Uses instantaneous information to adjust existing algorithms or develop new ones with little human involvement.

USES OF ALGORITHMIC TECHNIQUES AS A SAFETY NET

Risk Management Uses of Trading Algorithms

- Real-time pre-trade risk firewall: **Real-time pre-trade risk assessment can block trades from going to market if they violate previously established risk guidelines.**
- Back-testing and market simulation: **Traders can model trades using actual historical situations and even potential but highly unlikely events to assess risk before placing a trade, although this typically increases latency.**

Regulatory Oversight: Real-Time Market Monitoring and Surveillance

Regulators can use modern technologies (e.g., tick databases, CEP) for enhanced surveillance and detection across markets and exchanges, or even prevent abuses before they occur. Examples of potential abuses detectable via regulatory algorithms include fictitious trades, front running, wash trading, painting the tape, and collusion.

IMPACT OF ALGORITHMIC TRADING AND HFT ON THE SECURITIES MARKETS

Advantages

- Minimized market impact of large trades
- Lower costs of execution
- Improved efficiency in certain markets
- More open and competitive trading markets
- Improved and more efficient trading venues

Issues and Concerns

- Fear of an unfair advantage
- Acceleration and accentuation of market movements
- Gaming the market
- Increased risk profile
- Algorithms going wild
- Potential for market "denial of service" style attacks
- Additional load on trading volumes
- Increased difficulty in policing the market